Whillans's Tax Tables

CW01524648

Finance Act Edition 2014

Edited by

Claire Hayes CTA

Kevin Walton MA

Consultant Editor

Rebecca Benneyworth BSC, FCA, MBE

Tolley®

Members of the LexisNexis Group worldwide

United Kingdom	LexisNexis, a Division of Reed Elsevier (UK) Ltd, 30 Farringdon Street, London EC4A 4HH, and London House, 20–22 East London Street, Edinburgh EH7 4BQ
Australia	LexisNexis Butterworths, Chatswood, New South Wales
Austria	LexisNexis Verlag ARD Orac GmbH & Co KG, Vienna
Benelux	LexisNexis Benelux, Amsterdam
Canada	LexisNexis Canada, Markham, Ontario
China	LexisNexis China, Beijing and Shanghai
France	LexisNexis SA, Paris
Germany	LexisNexis Deutschland GmbH, Munster
Hong Kong	LexisNexis Hong Kong, Hong Kong
India	LexisNexis India, New Delhi
Italy	Giuffrè Editore, Milan
Japan	LexisNexis Japan, Tokyo
Malaysia	Malayan Law Journal Sdn Bhd, Kuala Lumpur
New Zealand	LexisNexis NZ Ltd, Wellington
Poland	Wydawnictwo Prawnicze LexisNexis Sp, Warsaw
Singapore	LexisNexis Singapore, Singapore
South Africa	LexisNexis Butterworths, Durban
USA	LexisNexis, Dayton, Ohio

First published in 1948

Published by LexisNexis
This is a Tolley title

A CIP Catalogue record for this book is available from the British Library.

ISBN for this volume: 9781405788403

Printed and bound by CPI Group (UK) Ltd, Croydon, CR0 4YY

Visit LexisNexis at www.lexisnexis.co.uk

Preface

Welcome to the 2014 Finance Act Edition of Whillans's Tax Tables. Once again, all of the tax data that you will need is presented here in a clear and useable format, with each topic presented on a separate page to make locating the information you need as easy as possible. It has become a tradition for the Chancellor to announce changes in rates and allowances for income and corporation tax for several tax years together in his Budget and Autumn statement announcements, so we hope that this Edition will help you by separating out a range of information into the relevant tax years. As in previous years, we have also rationalised the information on penalties so that checking which penalty rules apply to a case is now much easier. We have also included information about the new Social Investment Tax Relief, introduced in the Finance Act 2014, and arrangements for accounting for foreign VAT under the Mini One Stop Shop scheme (MOSS) which commences in January 2015.

Rebecca Benneyworth

Administration

Bank base rates

Period	*Rate*
from 5 March 2009	**0.50%**
5 February 2009–4 March 2009	1.00%
8 January 2009–4 February 2009	1.50%
4 December 2008–7 January 2009	2.00%
6 November 2008–3 December 2008	3.00%
8 October 2008–5 November 2008	4.50%
10 April 2008–7 October 2008	5.00%
7 February 2008–9 April 2008	5.25%
6 December 2007–6 February 2008	5.50%
5 July 2007–5 December 2007	5.75%
10 May 2007–4 July 2007	5.50%
11 January 2007–9 May 2007	5.25%
9 November 2006–10 January 2007	5.00%
3 August 2006–8 November 2006	4.75%
4 August 2005–2 August 2006	4.50%
5 August 2004–3 August 2005	4.75%
10 June 2004–4 August 2004	4.50%
6 May 2004–9 June 2004	4.25%
5 February 2004–5 May 2004	4.00%
6 November 2003–4 February 2004	3.75%
10 July 2003–5 November 2003	3.50%
6 February 2003–9 July 2003	3.75%
8 November 2001–5 February 2003	4.00%
4 October 2001–7 November 2001	4.50%
18 September 2001–3 October 2001	4.75%
2 August 2001–17 September 2001	5.00%
10 May 2001–1 August 2001	5.25%
5 April 2001–9 May 2001	5.50%
8 February 2001–4 April 2001	5.75%
10 February 2000–7 February 2001	6.00%
13 January 2000–9 February 2000	5.75%
4 November 1999–12 January 2000	5.50%
8 September 1999–3 November 1999	5.25%
10 June 1999–7 September 1999	5.00%
8 April 1999–9 June 1999	5.25%
4 February 1999–7 April 1999	5.50%
7 January 1999–3 February 1999	6.00%
10 December 1998–6 January 1999	6.25%
5 November 1998–9 December 1998	6.75%
8 October 1998–4 November 1998	7.25%
4 June 1998–7 October 1998	7.50%
6 November 1997–3 June 1998	7.25%
7 August 1997–5 November 1997	7.00%
10 July 1997–6 August 1997	6.75%

Due dates for tax

Capital gains tax

Normally 31 January following end of year of assessment. (TMA 1970 s 59B)

(See also *Extended due dates* under **Income tax**, below.)

Corporation tax

Must be paid electronically for tax due on or after 1 April 2011.

Generally (TMA 1970 s 59D)

9 months and 1 day after end of accounting period.

Instalments for larger companies (TMA 1970 s 59E, SI 1998/3175)

A 'large company' is any company responsible for paying the bank levy, and one whose augmented profits (see p 63) exceed £1.5m a year, divided by 1 plus the number of any active associated companies. A company is not a large company in respect of an accounting period if its total liability for that period is not more than £10,000, or if its profits for an accounting period are £10m or less and it was not a large company in the 12 months preceding that accounting period. For most large companies (those with no ring fence profits) the amount of each instalment for a 12 month accounting period will be one quarter of its total liability. The amount of each instalment for any accounting period longer than 3 months but shorter than 12 months is calculated using the formula 3 x CTI/n where CTI is the amount of a company's total liability for that accounting period, and n is the number of months in the accounting period. The due dates of instalments are as follows:

1st instalment: 6 months and 13 days from start of accounting period (or date of final instalment if earlier);
2nd instalment: 3 months after 1st instalment, if length of accounting period allows;
3rd instalment: 3 months after 2nd instalment, if length of accounting period allows;
Final instalment: 3 months and 14 days from end of accounting period.

Close companies: tax on loans or benefits to participators

9 months and 1 day after the end of the accounting period. To be included in instalment payments for large companies (see above) (TMA 1970 s 59E(11)).

Income tax

Payments on account (TMA 1970 s 59A, SI 1996/1654)

A payment on account is required where a taxpayer was assessed to income tax in the immediately preceding year to an amount exceeding the amount of tax deducted at source in respect of that year (subject to a de minimis limit, see below).

The payment on account (which includes Class 4 NIC) is made in 2 equal instalments due on:

(a) 31 January during the year of assessment, and
(b) 31 July in the following year of assessment.

No payments on account are required where either:

(a) the aggregate of the liability (including Class 4 NIC) for the preceding year (net of tax deducted at source) is less than £1,000 (£500 for 2008–09 and previous years (SI 2008/838)); or
(b) more than 80% of the taxpayer's income tax and Class 4 NIC liability for the preceding year was met by tax deducted at source (including PAYE).

Final payment (TMA 1970 s 59B, Sch 3ZA)

Balance of income tax due for a year of assessment (after deducting payments on account, tax deducted at source and credits in respect of dividends, etc) is due on:

31 January following end of year of assessment (TMA 1970 s 59B(4)).

Extended due dates:

(a) If a taxpayer has given notice of liability within 6 months of the end of the year of assessment , but a notice to make a return is not given until after 31 October following the end of the year of assessment, the due date is 3 months after the notice is given (TMA 1970 s 59B(3)).
(b) If tax is payable as a result of a taxpayer's notice of amendment, an HMRC notice of correction or an HMRC notice of closure following enquiry, in each case given less than 30 days before the due date (or the extended due date at (a) above), the due date is on or before the day following the end of a 30-day period beginning on the day on which the notice is given (TMA 1970 s 59B(5), Sch 3ZA).
(c) If an assessment other than a self-assessment is made, tax payable under the assessment is due on the day following the end of a 30-day period beginning on the day on which notice of the assessment is given (TMA 1970 s 59B(6)).

The extensions under (b) and (c) do *not* alter the due date for *interest purposes* (see p 4).

Harmonised interest regime see p 4.
Interest on overdue tax see p 4.
Interest on overpaid tax see p 6.
Penalties see p 12.

Remission of tax see p 9.

Inheritance tax

(IHTA 1984 s 226)

Chargeable transfers other than on death, made between:

6 April and 30 September	–	30 April in next year.
1 October and 5 April	–	6 months after end of month in which chargeable transfer is made.

Chargeable events following conditional exemption for heritage etc property and charge on disposal of trees or underwood before the second death:

– 6 months after end of month in which chargeable event occurs.

Transfers on death:

Earlier of	(*a*)	6 months after end of month in which death occurs, and
	(*b*)	delivery of account by personal representatives.

Tax or extra tax becoming payable on death:

Chargeable transfers and potentially exempt transfers within 7 years of death.

– 6 months after end of month in which death occurs.

PAYE and national insurance

(SSCBA 1992 s 15, SI 2001/1004, SI 2003/2682)

Employer's tax and Class 1 national insurance payable under PAYE.	In-year payments – 14 days after end of tax month or quarter to which it relates (extended to 17 days where payments are made by electronic means). Final payment for tax year – 19 April following deduction year (extended to 22 April where payments are made by electronic means).
Class 1A national insurance.	19 July following year in which contributions due (extended to 22 July where payments are made by electronic means).
PAYE settlement agreement and Class 1B national insurance.	19 October following year to which agreement relates (extended to 22 October where payments are made by electronic means).
Class 2 national insurance.	From April 2011 due in 2 instalments on 31 January and 31 July. From April 2014 HMRC may collect outstanding Class 2 by an adjustment to PAYE codes[1].
Class 4 national insurance.	See under income tax on p 2.

1 Proposed to be collected via self-assessment alongside income tax and Class 4 NICs from April 2016.

Paying HMRC

HMRC have a number of bank accounts. The respective accounts to which payments should be made from UK bank accounts for the main taxes are as follows:

Tax	Account name	Sort code	Account number
Self-assessment/ capital gains tax	HMRC Shipley	08 32 10	12001020
Self-assessment/ capital gains tax	HMRC Cumbernauld	08 32 10	12001039
Corporation tax	HMRC Shipley	08 32 10	12001020
Corporation tax	HMRC Cumbernauld	08 32 10	12001039
PAYE/ Class 1 NIC	HMRC Cumbernauld	08 32 10	12001039
Class 1A NIC	HMRC Shipley	08 32 10	12001020
Class 1A NIC	HMRC Cumbernauld	08 32 10	12001039
Class 2 NIC	HMRC NICO	08 32 20	12001004

Where both Shipley and Cumbernauld can apply and a taxpayer does not know which accounts office he normally pays, generally he should send payment to Cumbernauld. For details of other taxes see the A–Z list of taxes at www.hmrc.gov.uk/bankaccounts/index.htm.

Harmonised interest regime

(FA 2009 ss 101–104, Schs 53–54A; SI 2011/701; SI 2011/2391; SI 2013/280; SI 2013/2472; SI 2014/992)

A harmonised interest regime is being phased in for all taxes and duties and currently applies to:

- income and capital gains tax self-assessment amounts including penalties from 31 October 2011,
- CIS late return penalties from 6 October 2011,
- tax agent dishonest conduct penalties from 1 April 2013 (see p 20),
- annual tax on enveloped dwellings and penalties from 1 October 2013 (see p 65),
- PAYE and CIS in-year amounts for 2014–15 onwards from 6 April 2014 (although from 6 October 2014 for in-year late filing penalties and 6 April 2015 for in-year late payment penalties).

For amounts outstanding immediately prior to 31 October 2011, the previous legislation for income and capital gains tax self-assessment (TMA 1970 s 86, TA 1988 s 824 and TCGA 1992 s 283) had effect up to and including 30 October 2011 (see below and p 6), and the new legislation applies thereafter.

For annual PAYE payments such as Classes 1A and 1B national insurance contributions HMRC will continue to charge interest on any amount which remains unpaid after the due date.

Planned implementation dates for other taxes and duties covered in this publication have not yet been announced.

The measure provides for differential interest charged and paid by HMRC to be based around the Bank of England base rate. The current rates are:

- 3.0% for late payment interest,
- 0.5% for repayment interest,

ie those already applying from 29 September 2009 for interest on overdue and overpaid tax outlined in the tables below.

Late payment interest runs from the start date to the date of payment. The start date is generally the date on which the amount becomes due and payable, but special rules apply as follows:

Where an amount is due as a result of—

(a) an amendment or correction to an assessment or self-assessment; or
(b) an HMRC assessment in place of, or in addition to, an assessment made by the taxpayer; or
(c) an HMRC assessment in place of an assessment which ought to have been made by the taxpayer,

the start date is the date it would have been if the original assessment or self-assessment had been complete and accurate and made on the date (if any) by which it was required to be made, and the tax had been due and payable as a result of the original assessment or self-assessment.

Repayment interest runs from the start date until the date the payment or repayment is made. The start date in the case of an amount paid to HMRC is the later of—

(i) the date the amount was paid to HMRC; and
(ii) the date on which the amount became due and payable to HMRC (in a case where the amount has been paid in connection with a liability to make a payment to HMRC, and it is to be repaid by them).

The start date, in the case of an amount which has not been paid to HMRC and which is payable by virtue of a return or a claim having been submitted, is the later of—

(1) the date (if any) on which the return or claim was required to be submitted; and
(2) the date on which the return or claim was submitted.

The start date in the case of the carry back of losses or averaging claims is 31 January following the *later* tax year in relation to the claim.

Interest on overdue tax

See above regarding the **harmonised interest regime** and the taxes to which this currently applies. The provisions on interest on overdue tax continue to apply to taxes where the harmonised interest regime does not yet apply, and applied to other taxes before the transition to the harmonised regime.

Income tax, capital gains tax, NICs Class 1, 1A, 1B, 4, stamp duty, stamp duty reserve tax and stamp duty land tax

For amounts outstanding in relation to income and capital gains tax self-assessment immediately prior to 31 October 2011 the rules under TMA 1970 s 86 have effect up to and including 30 October 2011, and the rules under FA 2009 ss 101 and 103 above have effect thereafter.

Interest runs from the due date (see p 2 for income tax and capital gains tax) to the date of payment, on the amount outstanding.

Period	*Rate*
from 29 September 2009	**3.0%**
24 March 2009–28 September 2009	2.5%
27 January 2009–23 March 2009	3.5%
6 January 2009–26 January 2009	4.5%
6 December 2008–5 January 2009	5.5%
6 November 2008–5 December 2008	6.5%
6 January 2008–5 November 2008	7.5%
6 August 2007–5 January 2008	8.5%
6 September 2006–5 August 2007	7.5%
6 September 2005–5 September 2006	6.5%

Period	Rate
6 September 2004–5 September 2005	7.5%
6 December 2003–5 September 2004	6.5%
6 August 2003–5 December 2003	5.5%

Interest is payable gross and is not tax deductible.

Corporation tax

Interest runs from the due date (see p 2) to the date of payment. For instalment payments by large companies for accounting periods ending after 30 June 1999, a special rate of interest runs from the due date to the earlier of the date of payment and nine months after the end of the accounting period (after which the normal rate applies).

Corporation tax self-assessment (accounting periods ending after 30 June 1999)

Period	*Normal rate*
from 29 September 2009	**3.0%**
24 March 2009 to 28 September 2009	2.5%
27 January 2009–23 March 2009	3.5%
6 January 2009–26 January 2009	4.5%
6 December 2008–5 January 2009	5.5%
6 November 2008–5 December 2008	6.5%
6 January 2008–5 November 2008	7.5%
6 August 2007–5 January 2008	8.5%
6 September 2006–5 August 2007	7.5%
6 September 2005–5 September 2006	6.5%
6 September 2004–5 September 2005	7.5%
6 December 2003–5 September 2004	6.5%
6 August 2003–5 December 2003	5.5%
6 November 2001–5 August 2003	6.5%

Period	*Special rate for instalment payments (except where still unpaid nine months after end of accounting period)*
from 16 March 2009	**1.50%**
16 February 2009–15 March 2009	2.00%
19 January 2009–15 February 2009	2.50%
15 December 2008–18 January 2009	3.00%
17 November 2008–14 December 2008	4.00%
20 October 2008–16 November 2008	5.50%
21 April 2008–19 October 2008	6.00%
18 February 2008–20 April 2008	6.25%
17 December 2007–17 February 2008	6.50%
16 July 2007–16 December 2007	6.75%
21 May 2007–15 July 2007	6.50%
22 January 2007–20 May 2007	6.25%
20 November 2006–21 January 2007	6.00%
14 August 2006–19 November 2006	5.75%
15 August 2005–13 August 2006	5.50%
16 August 2004–14 August 2005	5.75%
21 June 2004–15 August 2004	5.50%
17 May 2004–20 June 2004	5.25%
16 February 2004–16 May 2004	5.00%
17 November 2003–15 February 2004	4.75%
21 July 2003–16 November 2003	4.50%
17 February 2003–20 July 2003	4.75%
19 November 2001–16 February 2003	5.00%

Corporation tax pay and file (accounting periods ending after 30 September 1993)

Period	*Rate*
from 29 September 2009	**3.0%**
24 March 2009– 28 September 2009	1.75%
27 January 2009–23 March 2009	2.75%
6 January 2009–26 January 2009	3.50%
6 December 2008–5 January 2009	4.25%
6 November 2008–5 December 2008	5.00%
6 January 2008–5 November 2008	6.00%
6 August 2007–5 January 2008	6.75%

Period	Rate
6 September 2006–5 August 2007	6.00%
6 September 2005–5 September 2006	5.25%
6 September 2004–5 September 2005	6.00%
6 December 2003–5 September 2004	5.25%[1]
6 August 2003–5 December 2003	4.25%
6 November 2001–5 August 2003	5.00%

[1] This rate was corrected by HMRC (see news release HMRC 27/05 of 6 September 2005) and is higher than that previously used (5%). No attempt will be made to recover any further interest which may be due unless, exceptionally, a liability is reviewed.

Income tax on company payments (due on or after 14 October 1999)

Period	Rate
from 29 September 2009	**3.0%**
24 March 2009– 28 September 2009	2.5%
27 January 2009–23 March 2009	3.5%
6 January 2009–26 January 2009	4.5%
6 December 2008–5 January 2009	5.5%
6 November 2008–5 December 2008	6.5%
6 January 2008–5 November 2008	7.5%
6 August 2007–5 January 2008	8.5%
6 September 2006–5 August 2007	7.5%
6 September 2005–5 September 2006	6.5%
6 September 2004–5 September 2005	7.5%
6 December 2003–5 September 2004	6.5%
6 August 2003–5 December 2003	5.5%
6 November 2001–5 August 2003	6.5%

Inheritance tax

Interest runs from the due date (see p 3) to the date of payment.

Period	Rate
from 29 September 2009	**3%**
24 March 2009–28 September 2009	0%
27 January 2009–23 March 2009	1%
6 January 2009–26 January 2009	2%
6 November 2008–5 January 2009	3%
6 January 2008–5 November 2008	4%
6 August 2007–5 January 2008	5%
6 September 2006–5 August 2007	4%
6 September 2005–5 September 2006	3%
6 September 2004–5 September 2005	4%
6 December 2003–5 September 2004	3%
6 August 2003–5 December 2003	2%
6 November 2001–5 August 2003	3%

Interest on overpaid tax

See p 4 regarding the **harmonised interest regime** and the taxes to which this currently applies. The provisions on interest on overpaid tax continue to apply to taxes where the harmonised interest regime does not yet apply, and applied to other taxes before the transition to the harmonised regime.

Income tax, capital gains tax, Class 1, 1A, 1B, 4 national insurance contributions, stamp duty, stamp duty reserve tax and stamp duty land tax

For amounts in relation to income and capital gains tax self-assessment outstanding immediately prior to 31 October 2011 the rules under TA 1988 s 824 and TCGA 1992 s 283 have effect up to and including 30 October 2011, and the rules under FA 2009 ss 102 and 103 on p 4 have effect thereafter.

Calculated as simple interest on the amount of tax repaid. The supplement is tax free.

Period	Rate
from 29 September 2009	**0.50%**
27 January 2009–28 September 2009	0.00%
6 January 2009–26 January 2009	0.75%
6 December 2008–5 January 2009	1.50%

Period	Rate
6 November 2008–5 December 2008	2.25%
6 January 2008–5 November 2008	3.00%
6 August 2007–5 January 2008	4.00%
6 September 2006–5 August 2007	3.00%
6 September 2005–5 September 2006	2.25%
6 September 2004–5 September 2005	3.00%[1]
6 December 2003–5 September 2004	2.25%[1]
6 August 2003–5 December 2003	1.50%[1]
6 November 2001–5 August 2003	2.25%[1]

[1] These rates were corrected by HMRC (see HMRC 27/05, 6 September 2005) and are lower than those previously used. No attempt will be made to recover amounts overpaid by HMRC unless, exceptionally, a repayment is reviewed.

Income tax

(TA 1988 s 824; FA 1997 s 92; ITTOIA 2005 s 749, SI 2011/701)

From 1996–97 for amounts which become repayable up to and including 30 October 2011 (from 1997–98 for partnerships whose trade, profession or business commenced before 6 April 1994) repayment supplement applies to:

- (a) amounts paid on account of income tax
- (b) income tax paid by or on behalf of an individual
- (c) late payment penalties for income and capital gains tax self-assessment under FA 2009 Sch 56
- (d) penalties incurred by an individual under any provision of TMA 1970

but excluding amounts paid in excess of the maximum the taxpayer is required to pay.

Except for tax deducted at source, the repayment supplement runs *from* the date on which the tax or penalty was paid *to* the date on which the order for repayment is issued. For tax deducted at source, repayment supplement runs from 31 January after the end of the tax year for which the tax was deducted.

Capital gains tax

(TCGA 1992 s 283, SI 2011/701)

From 1996–97 for amounts which become repayable up to and including 30 October 2011 repayment supplement runs *from* the date on which the tax was paid *to* the date on which the order for repayment is issued.

Inheritance tax

(IHTA 1984 s 235)

Repayments of inheritance tax or interest paid carries interest *from* the date of payment *to* the date on which the order for repayment is issued. Before 29 September 2009, the prescribed rates for unpaid tax applied equally to repayment supplements. From 29 September 2009, the rate is 0.5%.

Companies

Corporation tax self-assessment (accounting periods ending after 30 June 1999)

Normal rates

Rates on overpaid corporation tax in respect of periods after normal due date (SI 1989/1297 reg 3BB).

Period	Rate
from 29 September 2009	**0.5%**
27 January 2009–28 September 2009	0%
6 January 2009–26 January 2009	1%
6 December 2008–5 January 2009	2%
6 November 2008–5 December 2008	3%
6 January 2008–5 November 2008	4%
6 August 2007–5 January 2008	5%
6 September 2006–5 August 2007	4%
6 September 2005–5 September 2006	3%
6 September 2004–5 September 2005	4%
6 December 2003–5 September 2004	3%
6 August 2003–5 December 2003	2%
6 November 2001–5 August 2003	3%

Special rates

For instalment payments by large companies and early payments by other companies, a special rate of interest runs from the date the excess arises (but not earlier than the due date of the first instalment) to the earlier of the date the repayment order is issued and nine months and one day after the end of the accounting period, after which the normal rate of interest (as above) applies.

Rates on overpaid instalment payments and on corporation tax paid early (but not due by instalments).

Period	*Rate*
from 21 September 2009	**0.5%**
16 March 2009–20 September 2009	0.25%
16 February 2009–15 March 2009	0.75%
19 January 2009–15 February 2009	1.25%
15 December 2008–18 January 2009	1.75%
17 November 2008–14 December 2008	2.75%
20 October 2008–16 November 2008	4.25%
21 April 2008–19 October 2008	4.75%
18 February 2008–20 April 2008	5.00%
17 December 2007–17 February 2008	5.25%
16 July 2007–16 December 2007	5.50%
21 May 2007–15 July 2007	5.25%
22 January 2007–20 May 2007	5.00%
20 November 2006–21 January 2007	4.75%
14 August 2006–19 November 2006	4.50%
15 August 2005–13 August 2006	4.25%
16 August 2004–14 August 2005	4.50%
21 June 2004–15 August 2004	4.25%
17 May 2004–20 June 2004	4.00%
16 February 2004–16 May 2004	3.75%
17 November 2003–15 February 2004	3.50%
21 July 2003–16 November 2003	3.25%
17 February 2003–20 July 2003	3.50%
19 November 2001–16 February 2003	3.75%
15 October 2001–18 November 2001	4.25%
1 October 2001–14 October 2001	4.50%
13 August 2001–30 September 2001	4.75%
21 May 2001–12 August 2001	5.00%
16 April 2001–20 May 2001	5.25%
19 February 2001–15 April 2001	5.50%
21 February 2000–18 February 2001	5.75%
24 January 2000–20 February 2000	5.50%

Corporation tax pay and file (accounting periods ending before 1 July 1999)

Period	*Rate*
from 29 September 2009	**0.50%**
27 January 2009–28 September 2009	0.00%
6 January 2009–26 January 2009	0.50%
6 December 2008–5 January 2009	1.25%
6 November 2008–5 December 2008	2.00%
6 January 2008–5 November 2008	2.75%
6 August 2007–5 January 2008	3.50%
6 September 2006–5 August 2007	2.75%
6 September 2005–5 September 2006	2.00%
6 September 2004–5 September 2005	2.75%
6 December 2003–5 September 2004	2.00%
6 August 2003–5 December 2003	1.25%
6 November 2001–5 August 2003	2.00%

Surcharge on unpaid income tax and capital gains tax before 1 April 2011 (TMA 1970 s 59C)

For tax years before 2010–11, where income tax or capital gains tax became payable and all or part of it remained unpaid the day following 28 days after the due date, the taxpayer was liable to a surcharge of 5% of the unpaid tax. A further surcharge of 5% was levied on any of the tax remaining unpaid six months and one day from the due date. Interest was payable on the surcharge from the expiry of 30 days, beginning on the day on which the surcharge was imposed until the date of payment chargeable at the above rate. Penalties for late filing of returns and late payment of tax now apply (see **penalties** p 12) and the previous rules have been repealed for tax years 2010–11 onwards.

Remission of tax

By concession, arrears of tax may be waived if they result from HMRC's failure to make proper and timely use of information supplied by the taxpayer or, where it affects the taxpayer's coding, by his or her employer. The concession also applies to information supplied by the Department for Work and Pensions affecting the taxpayer's entitlement to a retirement, disability or widow's pension (see Concession A19). The concession only applies where the taxpayer could reasonably have believed that his or her affairs were in order and (unless the circumstances are exceptional) where the taxpayer is notified of the arrears more than 12 months after the end of the tax year in which HMRC received the information indicating that more tax was due.

Special relief

(TMA 1970 Sch 1AB para 3A; FA 1998 Sch 18 para 51BA)

From 1 April 2011 a statutory 'special relief' is available which allows HMRC to give effect to a claim for repayment or discharge of an amount of tax that a person is liable to pay, but which the person believes is not due or, if it has been paid, was not due, where the usual time limits for such relief have expired. Relief is only available to taxpayers in receipt of an income tax or corporation tax self-assessment determination made by HMRC in the absence of a self-assessment return being submitted, and where the following specific conditions are met: (a) it would be unconscionable for HMRC to seek to recover the amount or to refuse to repay it if it has already been paid; (b) that the person's tax affairs are otherwise up to date, or arrangements have been put in place to HMRC's satisfaction, to bring them up to date as far as possible; and (c) the person has not previously claimed special relief, or its concessionary predecessor equitable liability, whether or not such a claim was successful. This latter condition may be waived in exceptional circumstances. There is no time limit for claiming the relief.

Certificates of tax deposit

Certificates are not available for purchase for use against corporation tax or PAYE liabilities. Certificates are available to individuals, partnerships, individual partners, trustees, personal representatives and companies for the payment of income tax, Class 4 national insurance contributions, capital gains tax (but not that payable by companies etc on disposals of high value UK residential property, see p 65), inheritance tax, petroleum revenue tax or petroleum royalty. Minimum first deposit £500; subsequent deposits not less than £250 or amount required to bring total deposits up to £500 (ie where total deposits have fallen below that amount). Interest is paid gross and is chargeable to tax. It will only be paid for the first six years of a deposit. A deposit bears interest for the first year at the rate in force at the time of the deposit and for each subsequent year at the rate in force on the anniversary of the deposit.

Date	*Amount*	*Held for (mths in yr)*	*Pay't of tax %*	*Cashed %*
11.6.04–5.8.04	Under £100,000	no limit	1.00	0.50
	£100,000 or over	under 1	1.00	0.50
		1–under 3	3.75	1.75
		3–under 6	3.50	1.75
		6–12	3.75	1.75
6.8.04–4.8.05	Under £100,000	no limit	1.25	0.50
	£100,000 or over	under 1	1.25	0.50
		1–12	3.75	1.75
5.8.05–3.8.06	Under £100,000	no limit	1.00	0.50
	£100,000 or over	under 1	1.00	0.50
		1–under 3	3.50	1.75
		3–under 6	3.25	1.50
		6–12	3.00	1.50
4.8.06–9.11.06	Under £100,000	no limit	1.75	0.75
	£100,000 or over	under 1	1.75	0.75
		1–under 3	4.25	2.00
		3–under 6	4.25	2.00
		6–12	4.00	2.00
10.11.06–11.1.07	Under £100,000	no limit	1.50	0.75
	£100,000 or over	under 1	1.50	0.75
		1–under 3	4.00	2.00
		3–under 6	4.00	2.00
		6–12	3.75	1.75
12.1.07–10.5.07	Under £100,000	no limit	1.50	0.75
	£100,000 or over	under 1	1.50	0.75
		1–under 3	4.25	2.00
		3–under 6	4.00	2.00
		6–12	4.00	2.00

Date	Amount	Held for (mths in yr)	Pay't of tax %	Cashed %
11.5.07–5.7.07	Under £100,000	no limit	2.00	1.00
	£100,000 or over	under 1	2.00	1.00
		1–under 3	4.75	2.25
		3–under 6	4.50	2.25
		6–12	4.50	2.25
6.7.07–6.12.07	Under £100,000	no limit	2.25	1.10
	£100,000 or over	under 1	2.25	1.10
		1–under 3	5.00	2.50
		3–under 6	4.75	2.25
		6–12	4.75	2.25
7.12.07–7.2.08	Under £100,000	no limit	3.00	1.50
	£100,000 or over	under 1	3.00	1.50
		1–under 3	5.50	2.75
		3–under 6	5.00	2.50
		6–under 9	4.75	2.25
		9–12	4.50	2.25
8.2.08–10.4.08	Under £100,000	no limit	2.00	1.00
	£100,000 or over	under 1	2.00	1.00
		1–under 3	4.50	2.25
		3–under 6	4.25	2.00
		6–under 9	4.00	2.00
		9–12	3.75	1.50
11.4.08–8.10.08	Under £100,000	no limit	2.00	1.00
	£100,000 or over	Under 1	2.00	1.00
		1–under 3	4.75	2.25
		3–under 6	4.50	2.25
		6–under 9	4.25	2.00
		9–12	4.25	2.00
9.10.08–6.11.08	Under £100,000	No limit	2.50	1.25
	£100,000 or over	under 1	2.50	1.25
		1–under 3	5.25	2.50
		3–under 6	5.00	2.50
		6–under 9	5.00	2.50
		9–12	4.75	2.25
7.11.08–4.12.08	Under £100,000	No limit	1.75	0.75
	£100,000 or over	under 1	1.75	0.75
		1–under 3	4.50	2.25
		3–under 6	4.25	2.00
		6–under 9	4.25	2.00
		9–12	4.00	2.00
5.12.08–8.1.09	Under £100,000	No limit	0.00	0.00
	£100,000 or over	under 1	0.00	0.00
		1–under 3	2.50	1.25
		3–under 6	2.50	1.25
		6–under 9	2.50	1.25
		9–12	2.25	1.00
9.1.09–5.2.09	Under £100,000	No limit	0.00	0.00
	£100,000 or over	under 1	0.00	0.00
		1–under 3	1.50	0.75
		3–under 6	1.25	0.50
		6–under 9	1.25	0.50
		9–12	1.25	0.50
6.2.09–5.3.09	Under £100,000	No limit	0.00	0.00
	£100,000 or over	under 1	0.00	0.00
		1–under 3	1.00	0.50
		3–under 6	1.00	0.50
		6–under 9	1.00	0.50
		9–12	0.75	0.25
6.3.09–	Under £100,000	No limit	0.00	0.00
	£100,000 or over	under 1	0.00	0.00
		1–under 3	0.75	0.25
		3–under 6	0.75	0.25
		6–under 9	0.75	0.25
		9–12	0.75	0.25

Student loan deductions

	Percentage of income above the threshold	Threshold
2014–15	**9%**	**£16,910 per year** **£1,409.16 per month** **£325.19 per week**
2013–14	9%	£16,365 per year £1,363.75 per month £314.71 per week
2012–13	9%	£15,795 per year £1,316.25 per month £303.75 per week
2005–06 to 2011–12	9%	£15,000 per year £1,250 per month £288.46 per week

Filing dates

Corporation tax

(FA 1998 Sch 18 paras 14, 15; SI 2003/282 reg 3(2A))

The return must be filed on the latest of the following dates—

(a) 12 months from the end of the period for which the return is made;

(b) where the company makes up its accounts for a period not exceeding 18 months, 12 months from the end of that period;

(c) where the company makes up its accounts for a period exceeding 18 months, 30 months from the start of that period;

(d) 3 months from the date of issue of the notice requiring the return.

From 1 April 2011 all company returns for accounting periods ending after 31 March 2010 must be filed online. Computations and, in most cases, accounts must be submitted in iXBRL format.

Income tax and capital gains tax

(TMA 1970 ss 8, 8A, 12AA; SI 2003/2682 reg 186)

Basic position for paper returns.	On or before 31 October following end of tax year.
Basic position for electronic returns.	On or before 31 January following end of tax year.
Paper return and notice to file return issued after 31 July but on or before 31 October following end of tax year.	Within 3 months of date of notice.
Electronic return and notice to file return issued after 31 July but on or before 31 October following end of tax year.	On or before 31 January following end of tax year.
Paper or electronic return and notice to file return issued after 31 October following end of tax year.	Within 3 months of date of notice.
Paper return and taxpayer wishes tax underpayment of less than £3,000[1] to be coded out.	On or before 31 October following end of tax year.
Electronic return and taxpayer wishes tax underpayment of less than £3,000[1] to be coded out.	Before 31 December following end of tax year.

[1] Applies to self-assessment underpayments of less than £2,000 before 2011–12.

Withdrawal of self-assessment notice

(FA 2013 Sch 51)

HMRC may withdraw a notice to file a self-assessment tax return in certain circumstances. The statutory power has effect for returns for 2012–13 onwards. Penalties for failure to make a return may be cancelled.

Penalties

Penalties — modernised penalty regime

A modernised penalty regime is being rolled out to all taxes and duties with the exception of tax credits. The penalty regime in force in respect of various defaults is set out below. Planned implementation dates for other taxes and duties have not yet been announced.

Inaccuracy in return or other document

(FA 2007 Sch 24)

Applies to	Commencement date	Penalty details
IT, CGT, CT, VAT, CIS, NIC Classes 1 and 4[1]	Return periods starting 1 April 2008 where the return is due to be filed on or after 1 April 2009	Penalty based on potential lost revenue Careless inaccuracy — 30% Deliberate but not concealed — 70% Deliberate and concealed — 100% *Reductions for disclosure* Unprompted disclosure minimum penalties nil, 20% and 30% Prompted disclosure minimum penalties 15%, 35% and 50%
IHT, SDLT, SDRT, other taxes, levies and duties (except tax credits)	Return periods starting 1 April 2009 where the return is due to be filed on or after 1 April 2010, or where the liability arises on or after 1 April 2010; for IHT in respect of deaths from 1 April 2009	
Class 1A NIC	2010–11 returns	
Corporation tax credit, return by registered pension scheme	Return periods starting 1 April 2009 where the return is due to be filed on or after 1 April 2010	
Annual tax on enveloped dwellings	2013–14 returns	
IT, CGT but offshore matter	6 April 2011	Penalties above are increased by either 0%, 50% or 100% depending on the territory concerned (see table on pp 15–16 for a list of territories in each category)

1 From 2013–14 for RTI purposes an inaccuracy in any full payment submission can attract a penalty. HMRC may issue one penalty notice for multiple inaccuracy penalties in a year.

Inaccuracy in return or other document as a result of third party providing incorrect (or withholding) information

(FA 2007 Sch 24)

Applies to	Commencement date	Penalty details
IT, CGT, CT, VAT, IHT, CIS, NIC Classes 1 and 4, SDLT, SDRT, other taxes, levies and duties (except tax credits)	1 April 2009 where the return is due to be filed on or after 1 April 2010	100% of potential lost revenue Subject to reduction for disclosure as for inaccuracies above.
Class 1A NIC	2010–11 returns	
Annual tax on enveloped dwellings	2013–14 returns	

Failure to notify HMRC of an error in an assessment (within 30 days)

(FA 2007 Sch 24)

Applies to	Commencement date	Penalty details
IT, CGT, CT, VAT, CIS, NIC Classes 1 and 4	1 April 2008 where the return is due to be filed on or after 1 April 2009	30% of potential lost revenue *Reductions for disclosure* Unprompted disclosure minimum penalty nil Prompted disclosure minimum penalty 15%
IHT, SDLT, SDRT, other taxes, levies and duties (except tax credits)	1 April 2009 where the return is due to be filed on or after 1 April 2010	
Class 1A NIC	2010–11 returns	
Annual tax on enveloped dwellings	2013–14 returns	

Failure to notify chargeability (includes failure to register for VAT)

(FA 2008 Sch 41)

Applies to	Commencement date	Penalty details
IT, CGT, NIC Class 4 (Class 2 similar provisions but in separate legislation)	2009–10	Penalty based on potential lost revenue Failure to notify — 30% Deliberate but not concealed — 70% Deliberate and concealed — 100%
CT	Accounting periods ending on or after 31 March 2010	*Reductions for disclosure* Unprompted disclosure minimum penalties nil (within 12 months late), 10% (more than 12 months late), 20% and 30% Prompted disclosure minimum penalties 15%, 35%, 50%
Other taxes, levies and duties (not IHT, SDLT, SDRT)	Obligations arising on or after 1 April 2010	
IT, CGT but offshore matter	6 April 2011	Penalties above are increased by either 0%, 20% or 100% depending on the territory concerned (see table on pp 15–16 for a list of territories in each category)

Failure to make returns on time

(FA 2009 Sch 55; FA 2010 Sch 1)

<table>
<tr><th>Applies to</th><th>Commencement date</th><th>Penalty details</th></tr>
<tr><td>Bank Payroll Tax</td><td>31 August 2010</td><td rowspan="4">Initial penalty £100
Failure continues for more than three months — with notice — £10 per day for up to 90 days
Six months late — greater of 5% of the tax due and £300
12 months late — same penalty as for 6 months late unless deliberately withholding the return
Deliberate withholding of the return more than 12 months — 70% of tax due (minimum £300)
Deliberate and concealed withholding of the return more than 12 months — 100% of tax due (minimum £300)
Reductions for disclosure
Unprompted disclosure minimum penalty 20% and 30%
Prompted disclosure minimum penalties 35% and 50%</td></tr>
<tr><td>IT, CGT, NIC Class 4</td><td>6 April 2011</td></tr>
<tr><td>Return by Registered Pension scheme</td><td>1 April 2011</td></tr>
<tr><td>Annual tax on enveloped dwellings</td><td>2013–14 returns due 1 October 2013</td></tr>
<tr><td>CIS returns</td><td>6 October 2011</td><td>Initial penalty £100
After two months — £200
Six months late — greater of 5% of the tax due and £300
12 months late — same penalty as for 6 months late unless deliberately withholding the return
Deliberate withholding of the return more than 12 months — 70% of tax due (minimum £1,500)
Deliberate and concealed withholding of the return more than 12 months — 100% of tax due (minimum £3,000)
Reductions for disclosure
Unprompted disclosure minimum penalty 20% and 30%
Prompted disclosure minimum penalties 35% and 50%
Special rules apply to the first returns made on registration for CIS so that the maximum total penalty that can apply for the initial and second fixed penalties for all such returns is £3,000. Subsequent tax-geared penalties may still be incurred.
Where a CIS return only relates to persons registered for 'gross payment' a tax-geared penalty after 6 months or 12 months cannot apply. In these cases the person is liable to the fixed amount penalty.</td></tr>
<tr><td>IT, CGT but offshore matter</td><td>6 April 2011</td><td>Penalties above for a return later than 12 months which has been withheld are increased by either 0%, 50% or 100% depending on the territory concerned (see table on pp 15–16 for a list of territories in each category)</td></tr>
<tr><td>PAYE Real Time Information. Failure during a tax month to make a return on or before the filing date (normally the date employee is paid)</td><td>6 October 2014 in relation to 2014–15 onwards[1]</td><td>First failure in a tax year — nil
Second and subsequent failure in tax year — an amount calculated in accordance with regulations yet to be finalised[2]
Failure continues for more than three months — with notice — 5% of tax due
New employers only: A failure in the 'initial period'[3] — nil</td></tr>
</table>

1 For 2013–14 the rules in the PAYE table on p 17 under 'failure to submit year-end PAYE returns' apply. It had been intended to charge automatic in-year late filing penalties for RTI from 6 April 2014 but HMRC have delayed the start of these penalties until 6 October 2014.

2 Calculation proposed to be a fixed amount based on the number of employees — monthly penalty of £100 for 1–9 employees, £200 for 10–49 employees, £300 for 50–249 employees, £400 for 250 or more employees.

3 A penalty will not be issued to a new employer if their first FPS is received within 30 days of making the first payment to their employee(s) (known as the 'initial period' and 30-day duration is as outlined in draft regulations). After that, normal penalties rules will apply if there is a failure to file on time.

Failure to pay tax on time

(FA 2009 Sch 56; FA 2010 Sch 1)

Applies to	Commencement date	Penalty details
PAYE[1], NIC Class 1, CIS[2], student loan deductions.	2010–11 liabilities (on a risk assessed basis at present)	Penalty based on number of late payments in a year applied to the amounts paid late 1 late payment — nil 2, 3, 4 late payments — 1% 5, 6, 7 late payments — 2% 8, 9, 10 late payments — 3% 11, 12 late payments — 4% Any amount paid 6 months late — 5% Any amount paid 12 months late — 5%
NIC Class 1A and 1B (SI 2001/1004 reg 67B)	2010–11	31 days late — 5% 6 months late — 5% 12 months late — 5%
Bank Payroll Tax	31 August 2010	5% 5 months late — 5% 11 months late — 5%
Tax due by Registered Pension schemes	Payments due 30 September 2010	31 days late — 5% 6 months late — 5% 12 months late — 5%
IT, CGT payable under self-assessment	6 April 2011 for self-assessment for 2010–11 onwards	31 days late — 5% 6 months late — 5% 12 months late — 5%
Annual tax on enveloped dwellings	2013–14 payments due 31 October 2013	31 days late — 5% 6 months late — 5% 12 months late — 5%

1 These existing rules apply for RTI for 2013–14 and 2014–15. It had been intended to charge automatic in-year late payment penalties for RTI from 6 April 2014 but HMRC have delayed the start of these penalties until 6 April 2015. From 2014–15 a 'tolerance' of £100 has been introduced for PAYE in-year late payment penalties. Where the difference between the total of all the amounts that the employer is due to pay to HMRC for a tax period and the amount paid over for that period is no more than £100 the employer will not be liable to a late payment penalty.

2 From 2014–15 a 'tolerance' of £100 has been introduced for CIS in-year late payment penalties. Where the difference between the amount that the contractor is due to pay to HMRC for a tax period and the amount paid over for that period is no more than £100 the contractor will not be liable to a late payment penalty.

Offshore penalties — territory categories

Category 1

Anguilla	Estonia	Japan	Poland
Aruba	Finland	Korea, South	Portugal[4]
Australia	France[2]	Latvia	Romania
Belgium	Germany	Liechtenstein (from 24 July 2013)[7]	Slovakia
Bulgaria	Greece	Lithuania	Slovenia
Canada	Guernsey[3]	Malta	Spain[5]
Cayman Islands	Hungary	Montserrat	Sweden
Cyprus	Ireland	Netherlands (not including Bonaire, Sint Eustatius and Saba)	Switzerland (from 24 July 2013)[7]
Czech Republic	Isle of Man	New Zealand (not including Tokelau)	USA (not including overseas territories and possessions)[6]
Denmark (not including Faroe Islands or Greenland)[1]	Italy	Norway	

1 Faroe Islands and Greenland are in Category 2.

2 Includes overseas Departments of France; the overseas collectivities of France are in Category 2.
3 Includes Alderney and Sark.
4 Includes Madeira and the Azores.
5 Includes the Canary Islands and other overseas territories of Spain.
6 The overseas territories and possessions of the USA are in Category 2.
7 SI 2013/1618 changed the level of penalties which may be charged for 14 specified countries from 24 July 2013. This is to reflect the entry into force of tax information exchange and enhanced tax cooperation agreements with those countries. Liechtenstein and Switzerland were previously in Category 2.

Category 2

Territories not listed in Categories 1 or 3 (other than the UK) will be in Category 2. Crown Dependencies and Overseas Territories of the UK are, unless listed, in Category 2.

Category 3

Albania	Costa Rica	Kyrgyzstan	(Before 24 July 2013) *Saint Lucia*[2]
Algeria	Curaçao	Lebanon	(Before 24 July 2013) *Saint Vincent and the Grenadines*[2]
Andorra	Cuba	Macau[1]	(Before 24 July 2013) *San Marino*[2]
(Before 24 July 2013) *Antigua and Barbuda*[2]	Democratic People's Republic of Korea	Marshall Islands	Seychelles
(Before 24 July 2013) *Armenia*[2]	(Before 24 July 2013) *Dominica*[2]	(Before 24 July 2013) *Mauritius*[2]	Sint Maarten
(Before 24 July 2013) *Bahrain*[2]	Dominican Republic	Micronesia, Federated States of	Suriname
(Before 24 July 2013) *Barbados*[2]	Ecuador	Monaco	Syria
(Before 24 July 2013) *Belize*[2]	El Salvador	Nauru	Tokelau
Bonaire, Sint Eustatius and Saba	Gabon	Nicaragua	Tonga
Brazil	(Before 24 July 2013) *Grenada*[2]	Niue	Trinidad and Tobago
Cameroon	Guatemala	Palau	United Arab Emirates
Cape Verde	Honduras	Panama	Uruguay
Colombia	Iran	Paraguay	
Congo, Republic of the	Iraq	Peru	
Cook Islands	Jamaica	(Before 24 July 2013) *Saint Kitts and Nevis*[2]	

1 China and Hong Kong are in Category 2.
2 SI 2013/1618 changed the level of penalties which may be charged for 14 specified countries from 24 July 2013. This is to reflect the entry into force of tax information exchange and enhanced tax cooperation agreements with those countries. 12 of the countries highlighted in this table are in Category 2 from 24 July 2013.

Personal tax and corporation tax

Offence	*Penalty*
Failure to render return for corporation tax (FA 1998 Sch 18 paras 17, 18).	(*a*) £100 if up to three months late (£500 if previous two returns also late); (*b*) £200 if over three months late (£1,000 if previous two returns also late); (*c*) if failure continues, on final day for delivery of return or, if later, 18 months after return period, 10% of tax unpaid 18 months after return period (20% of tax unpaid at that date if return not made within two years of return period).
Failure to maintain records supporting personal and trustees' returns of partnership returns (TMA 1970 s 12B).	Up to £3,000.
Fraudulently or negligently making an incorrect statement in connection with a claim to reduce payments on account (TMA 1970 s 59A(6)).	Up to the amount (or additional amount) payable on account if a correct statement had been made.

Offence	Penalty
Deliberately or recklessly failing to pay corporation tax due in respect of total liability of company for accounting period, or fraudulently or negligently making claim for repayment (TMA 1970 s 59E(4); SI 1998/3175 reg 13).	Penalty not exceeding twice amount of interest charged under SI 1998/3175 reg 7.
Repealed provisions	
Failure to notify chargeability to income or capital gains tax within six months of tax year or to corporation tax within one year of accounting period (TMA 1970 s 7; FA 1998 Sch 18).	*Up to tax liability still unpaid after 31 January following tax year (IT or CGT) or one year after end of accounting period (CT).* ***Repealed for failures on or after 1 April 2010 and replaced by penalties under FA 2008 Sch 41.***
Failure to render return for income tax or capital gains tax (TMA 1970 ss 93, 93A).	(*a*) *Initial penalty of £100 (or tax due if less);* (*b*) *upon direction by Commissioners, further penalty up to £60 for each day failure continues;* (*c*) *if failure continues after six months from filing date, and no penalty imposed under (b), a further penalty of £100 (or tax due if less);* (*d*) *if failure continues after one year from filing date, a further penalty up to amount of tax due.* ***Repealed and replaced by penalty under FA 2009 Sch 55 above for 2010–11 onwards.***
Fraudulently or negligently delivering incorrect return or accounts or making an incorrect claim for an allowance, deduction or relief (TMA 1970 ss 95, 95A; FA 1998 Sch 18 para 89).	*Up to amount of tax underpaid by reason of incorrectness for (IT and CGT) the tax year (or following tax year and any preceding tax year) in which the return or claim is delivered, (CT) the accounting period(s) to which the return or claim relates.* ***Repealed for returns or claims for periods to which penalty under FA 2007 Sch 24 applies (see p 12).***
Failure to notify within charge to corporation tax within three months after the beginning of the first accounting period and any subsequent accounting period not following on immediately from the end of a previous accounting period. With effect for accounting periods beginning on or after 22 July 2004 (FA 2004 s 55).	(*a*) *Initial penalty up to £300; and* (*b*) *a continuing penalty up to £60 for each day on which the failure continues.* ***Repealed for accounting periods ending after 31 March 2010 and replaced by penalties under FA 2008 Sch 41.***
Failure to register as self-employed (and liable to Class 2 NIC) within three months after month in which self-employment begins (SI 2001/1004 reg 87).	*Up to £100.* ***Repealed for obligations arising after 5 April 2009 and replaced by penalties under Class 2 NIC equivalent of FA 2008 Sch 41.***

PAYE

Offence	Penalty
Failure to submit return P9D or P11D (benefits in kind) by due date (6 July following subsequent tax years) (TMA 1970 s 98(1)).	(*a*) Initial penalty up to £300; and (*b*) continuing penalty up to £60 for each day on which the failure continues.
Failure to submit year-end PAYE returns currently final FPS, or EPS, or EYU as applicable, formerly P14 (individual end of year summary), P35 (annual return), P38 or P38A (supplementary returns for employees not on P35) by due date (19 May following tax year) (TMA 1970 s 98A)[1].	(*a*) First 12 months: penalty of £100 for each 50 employees (or part thereof) for each month the failure continues; (*b*) failures exceeding 12 months: penalty up to amount of PAYE or NIC due and unpaid after 19 April following tax year.
Failure to submit information in connection with mandatory e-filing from 2004–05 onwards (SI 2003/2682 as amended by 2009/2029 reg 14).	Penalty based on number of employees not exceeding £3,000 for 1,000 or more employees.
Failure to submit returns P11D(b) (Class 1A NIC returns) by due date (6 July following tax year, but by concession until 31 March 2013, 19 July applies) (SI 2001/1004 reg 81(2)).	(*a*) First 12 months: penalty of £100 for each 50 employees (or part thereof) for each month the failure continues (but total penalty not to exceed total Class 1A NIC due); (*b*) failures exceeding 12 months: a penalty not exceeding the amount of Class 1A NIC due and unpaid after 19 July following tax year.
Repealed provisions	
Fraudulently or negligently submitting incorrect forms P14, P35, P38 or P38A (TMA 1970 s 98A).	*Penalty up to the amount of tax due.* ***Repealed from 1 April 2008 in relation to documents for tax periods commencing on or after that date.***
Fraudulently or negligently submitting incorrect return P9D or P11D (TMA 1970 s 98(2)).	*Penalty up to £3,000.* ***Does not apply from 1 April 2009 when penalty for careless or deliberate error under FA 2007 Sch 24 applies.***
Fraudulently or negligently submitting incorrect form P11D(b) (2001/1004 reg 81(1) before substitution by SI 2010/721).	*Up to the difference between the amount paid and the amount which should have been paid if the return had been correct.* ***Does not apply from 2010–11 when FA 2007 Sch 24 applies.***

[1] See p 14 for penalties for failure to make returns on time under PAYE Real Time Information from 6 October

2014 for 2014–15 onwards.

Inheritance tax returns and information

Offence	*Penalty*
Failure to deliver an account within 12 months of death (unless tax is less than £100 or there is a reasonable excuse) (IHTA 1984 s 245).	(*a*) Initial penalty of £100 (or the amount of tax payable if less); (*b*) further penalty up to £60 (where penalty determined by court or tribunal) for each day on which the failure continues; (*c*) if failure continues after six months after the date on which account is due, and proceedings not commenced, a further penalty of £100 (or amount of tax payable if less); and (*d*) if failure continues one year after end of the period in which account is due, and IHT is payable, a penalty not exceeding £3,000.
Failure to submit account or notify HMRC under IHTA 1984 s 218A if a disposition on a death is varied within six months of the variation and additional tax is payable (IHTA 1984 s 245A(1A), (1B)).	(*a*) Initial penalty up to £100; (*b*) further penalty up to £60 (if determined by court or tribunal) for each day on which the failure continues; (*c*) up to £3,000 if failure continues after 12 months from date notification is due.
Failure to provide information etc under IHTA 1984 s 218 concerning a settlement by a UK-domiciled settlor with non-resident trustees (IHTA 1984 s 245A(1)).	(*a*) Initial penalty up to £300; and (*b*) further penalty up to £60 (where penalty determined by court or tribunal) for each day on which the failure continues.
Person other than the taxpayer fraudulently or negligently delivering, furnishing or producing incorrect accounts, information or documents (IHTA 1984 s 247(3); FA 2004 s 295(4), (9)).	Up to £3,000.
Repealed provisions	
Failure to provide documents etc under IHTA 1984 s 219A(1) or (4) (IHTA 1984 s 245A(3)).	(*a*) *Initial penalty up to £50; and* (*b*) *further penalty up to £30 (where penalty determined by court or tribunal) for each day on which the failure continues.* ***Repealed with effect from 1 April 2010 and replaced by penalties under FA 2008 Sch 36 (see p 20).***
Taxpayer fraudulently or negligently delivering, furnishing or producing incorrect accounts, information or documents (IHTA 1984 s 247(1); FA 2004 s 295(4), (9)).	*Penalty up to the amount of tax payable.* ***Repealed for accounts etc to which penalty under FA 2007 Sch 24 applies (see p 12).***
Incorrect return etc: Assisting in or inducing the delivery, furnishing or production of any account, information or document knowing it to be incorrect (IHTA 1984 s 247(4)).	*Up to £3,000.* ***Repealed with effect from 1 April 2013. See now tax agent dishonest conduct penalties under FA 2012 Sch 38 (see p 20).***

Special returns of information

Offence	*Penalty*
Failure to comply with a notice to deliver a return or other document, furnish particulars or make anything available for inspection under any of the provisions listed in column 1 of the table in TMA 1970 s 98.	(*a*) Initial penalty up to £300; (*b*) further penalty up to £60 for each day on which the failure continues.
Failure to furnish information, give certificates or produce documents or records under any of the provisions listed in column 2 of the table in TMA 1970 s 98.	(*a*) Initial penalty up to £300; and (*b*) further penalty up to £60 for each day on which the failure continues.
Failure to deduct income tax at source from payments of interest or royalties under ITA 2007 Part 15 where the exemption does not apply and the company did not believe or could not reasonably have believed that it would apply (TMA 1970 s 98(4A)–(4E)).	(*a*) Initial penalty up to £3,000; and (*b*) further penalty up to £600 for each day on which the failure continues.
Failure of an employment intermediary to furnish information or produce documents or records (TMA 1970 s 98(4F)).	(*a*) Initial penalty up to £3,000; and (*b*) further penalty up to £600 for each day on which the failure continues.
Advance pricing agreements: Fraudulently or negligently making a false or misleading statement in the preparation of, or application to enter into, any advance pricing agreement (TIOPA 2010 s 227).	Penalty up to £10,000.
Declaration of non-UK residence: Fraudulently or negligently making a false or misleading declaration of non-UK residence to a deposit-taker or building society under ITA 2007 ss 858-861 (TMA 1970 s 99B).	Penalty up to £3,000.

Offence	*Penalty*
Repealed provisions	
Fraudulently or negligently delivering any incorrect document, information etc required under the above provisions (TMA 1970 s 99; SI 2013/279).	*Penalty up to £3,000.* ***Repealed with effect from 1 April 2013. See now tax agent dishonest conduct penalties under FA 2012 Sch 38 (see p 20).***

Other offences by taxpayers, agents etc

Offence	*Penalty*
Falsification of documents. Intentionally falsifying, concealing or destroying documents required under TMA 1970 ss 20A (repealed with effect from 1 April 2013) or 20BA (TMA 1970 s 20BB).	On summary conviction, a fine up to the statutory maximum (£5,000); on conviction on indictment, imprisonment for a term not exceeding two years or a fine or both.
European Economic Interest Groupings– Offences in connection with the supply of information:	
(i) failure to supply information	Initial penalty up to £300 per member of the Grouping at the time of failure and after direction by the tribunal: continuing penalty up to £60 per member of the Grouping at the end of the day for each day on which the failure continues.
(ii) fraudulent or negligent delivery of an incorrect return, accounts or statement	Up to £3,000 for each member of the Grouping at the time of delivery.
(TMA 1970 s 98B).	
Certificates of non-liability to income tax: Fraudulently or negligently giving such a certificate for the purposes of receiving interest gross on a bank or building society account, or failing to comply with an undertaking given in such a certificate (TMA 1970 s 99A).	Penalty up to £3,000.
Refusal to allow a deduction of income tax at source (TMA 1970 s 106).	£50.
Construction Industry Scheme: (post 31 March 2007 scheme) Making false statements etc for the purpose of obtaining a gross payment certificate (FA 2004 s 72).	Up to £3,000.
Fraudulent evasion of income tax (TMA 1970 s 106A).	On summary conviction, imprisonment for up to six months or a fine up to the statutory maximum (£5,000) or both; on conviction on indictment, imprisonment for up to seven years or a fine or both.
Enterprise investment scheme relief: Issue by a company of a certificate of approval for such relief fraudulently or negligently or without the authority of HMRC (ITA 2007 s 207).	Not exceeding £3,000.
Failure of a company to maintain records (other than those only required for claims, etc, or dividend vouchers and certificates of income tax deducted where other evidence is available) (FA 1998 Sch 18 para 23).	Penalty not exceeding £3,000.
Failure to notify notifiable proposals or notifiable arrangements, or failure to notify the client of the relevant scheme reference number under the provisions of FA 2004 ss 306–319 (TMA 1970 s 98C; SI 2007/3104; SI 2008/1935; SI 2010/3019; FA 2013 s 223).	(*a*) Up to 31 December 2010 an initial penalty not exceeding £5,000; (i) From 1 January 2011 in the case of provisions under FA 2004 ss 308(1) and (3), 309(1) and 310 up to £600 per day in 'initial period' (but a tribunal can determine a higher penalty up to £1 million); (ii) From 1 January 2011 in the case of provisions in FA 2004 ss 312(2), 312A(2), 313ZA, 313A, 313B, 313C, and from 17 July 2013 in the case of provisions in ss 312B and 313ZB, an initial penalty up to £5,000. Where a disclosure order is made the amount in (i) above is increased up to £5,000 per day that failure continues from ten days after the order is made. (*b*) a continuing penalty not exceeding £600 for each day on which the failure continues after imposition of initial penalty. Where a disclosure order is made the amount is increased up to £5,000 per day that failure continues from ten days after the order is made.
Failure to notify scheme reference number etc under FA 2004 s 313(1);	Penalty of £100 in respect of each scheme to which the failure relates;
for second failure, occurring within three years from the date on which the first failure began;	penalty of £500 in respect of each scheme to which the failure relates;
for subsequent failures, occurring within three years from the date on which the previous failure began.	penalty of £1,000 in respect of each scheme to which the failure relates.
(TMA 1970 s 98C; FA 2004 s 315(1)).	
Failure to comply with HMRC investigatory powers under FA 2008 Sch 36.	(*a*) an initial penalty of £300;

Offence	*Penalty*
Failure to comply with an information notice within FA 2008 Sch 36 Pt 1 or deliberately obstructing an HMRC officer in the course of an inspection of business premises under FA 2008 Sch 36 Pt 2 which has been approved by the First-tier Tribunal. Applies to IT (including PAYE and CIS), CT, CGT, VAT and certain foreign taxes with effect from 1 April 2009. Extended to IHT, SDLT and other taxes from 1 April 2010, to Bank Payroll Tax (BPT) from 31 August 2010, to ATED from 17 July 2013 and to pension scheme registration applications from 17 July 2014.	(*b*) if failure/obstruction continues, a further penalty up to £60 per day; (*c*) if failure/obstruction continues after penalty under (*a*) imposed, a tax-related amount determined by the Upper Tribunal.
Carelessly or deliberately providing inaccurate information or an inaccurate document in response to an information notice.	Up to £3,000 per inaccuracy.
Failure of a senior accounting officer to ensure a company maintains appropriate tax accounting arrangements (FA 2009 Sch 46).	£5,000.
Failure of a senior accounting officer to provide a certificate stating whether the company had appropriate tax accounting arrangements (FA 2009 Sch 46).	£5,000.
Failure to notify Commissioners of name of senior accounting officer (FA 2009 Sch 46).	£5,000.
Failure of a third party to notify the contact details of a debtor (FA 2009 Sch 49).	£300.
Tax agent failure to comply with file access notice (FA 2012 Sch 38).	(*a*) an initial penalty of £300. (*b*) if failure continues, a further penalty up to £60 per day.
Tax agent engaging in dishonest conduct (FA 2012 Sch 38).	£5,000 minimum to £50,0000 maximum subject to the quality of disclosure and compliance with any access notice, with possible special reduction of £5,000 penalty to nil at HMRC's discretion.
Failure to keep records for the purposes of the annual tax on enveloped dwellings (FA 2013 Sch 33).	Up to £3,000
Corrective action not taken in response to follower notice (FA 2014 s 208).	50% of value of the denied advantage (20% for relevant partners). May be reduced for co-operation.
Failure to pay accelerated payment (FA 2014 s 226).	(*a*) Initial penalty of 5% of any amount unpaid at end of payment period (or where the accelerated payment relates to an instalment of IHT, 5% of any amount unpaid by the later due date of that instalment if applicable). (*b*) Further penalty of 5% of any amount unpaid after 5 months. (*c*) Further penalty of 5% of any amount unpaid after 11 months.
Failure of monitored promoter of a tax avoidance scheme, or their intermediary, to comply with various duties to notify clients, provide information or produce documents (FA 2014 Sch 35 para 2).	(*a*) Initial maximum penalty of £5,000, £7,500, £10,000, or £1,000,000 depending on failure. (*b*) Further daily penalty for each day on which failure continues of up to £10,000 where the maximum penalty could have been £1,000,000, or otherwise, £600.
Provision of inaccurate information or document by a monitored promoter of a tax avoidance scheme when complying with an information duty (FA 2014 Sch 35 para 4).	Maximum penalty of £5,000, £10,000, or £1,000,000 depending on duty being complied with.
Concealing, destroying etc documents required to be produced in connection with a monitored promoter of a tax avoidance scheme (FA 2014 s 280).	On summary conviction, a fine; on conviction on indictment, imprisonment for up to two years or a fine or both.
Failure of a company to provide a return in respect of a SIP, SAYE option, CSOP, EMI or other employee share scheme (ITEPA 2003 Sch 2 para 81C; Sch 3 para 40C; Sch 4 para 28C; Sch 5 para 57B; s 421JC).	(*a*) Initial penalty of £100. (*b*) Further penalty of £300 if failure continues for 3 months. (*c*) Further penalty of £300 if failure continues for 6 months. (*d*) Further penalty of £10 for each day that failure continues beyond 9 months (with notice).
Inaccurate return provided by a company, or return not filed electronically as required in respect of a SIP, SAYE option, CSOP, EMI or other employee share scheme (ITEPA 2003 Sch 2 para 81E; Sch 3 para 40E; Sch 4 para 28E; Sch 5 para 57C; s 421JD).	Up to £5,000.
Failure of a company to comply with the rules in respect of a SIP, SAYE option, or CSOP scheme (ITEPA 2003 Sch 2 para 81H–81I; Sch 3 para 40H–41I; Sch 4 para 28H–28I).	If scheme does not comply at all, penalty not exceeding twice the tax and NIC HMRC estimate has been 'saved'. Otherwise, up to £5,000.

Offence	Penalty
Failure of a company to provide to HMRC a declaration under ITEPA 2003 Sch 5 para 44(6) by individual to whom an EMI option is granted (ITEPA 2003 Sch 5 para 57A).	£500.
A social enterprise fraudulently or negligently issuing a compliance certificate or statement (ITA 2007 s 257PD).	Up to £3,000.
Repealed provisions	
Assisting in the delivery of incorrect returns, accounts or information (TMA 1970 s 99; SI 2013/279).	*Penalty up to £3,000.* ***Repealed with effect from 1 April 2013. See now tax agent dishonest conduct penalties under FA 2012 Sch 38 on p 20.***
Obstruction of officer in inspection of property to ascertain its market value (TMA 1970 s 111).	*Up to £50.* ***Repealed with effect from 1 April 2010 and replaced by penalties under FA 2008 Sch 36.***
Construction Industry Scheme: (pre 1 April 2007 scheme) Failure by contractor to check validity of registration card (TA 1988 s 566(2B)–(2E)).	*Up to £3,000.* ***Repealed for payments after 5 April 2007 and replaced by penalties under FA 2004 s 72.***
(pre 1 April 2007 scheme) Fraudulent attempt by sub-contractor to obtain or misuse a sub-contractor's certificate (TA 1988 s 561(10), (11)).	*Up to £3,000.* ***Repealed for payments after 5 April 2007 and replaced by penalties under FA 2004 s 72.***
Treasury consent: Creation or transfer of shares or debentures in a non-resident subsidiary company without the consent of HM Treasury (TA 1988 s 766).	*On conviction on indictment—* (*a*) *imprisonment for not more than two years or a fine, or both; or* (*b*) *in the case of a UK company, a fine not exceeding the greater of £10,000, or three times the tax payable by the company attributable to income and gains arising in the previous 36 months.* ***Repealed with effect from 1 July 2009 and replaced by penalties under TMA 1970 s 98.***
Failure to produce documents etc for the purposes of an enquiry under TMA 1970 s 19A or under FA 1998 Sch 18 para 27 (TMA 1970 s 97AA; FA 1998 Sch 18 para 29).	(*a*) *Initial penalty of £50; and* (*b*) *further penalty up to £30 (if determined by HMRC) or £150 (if determined by tribunal) for each day on which failure continues.* ***Repealed on or after 1 April 2009 and replaced by penalties under FA 2008 Sch 36.***

Mitigation of penalties

HMRC have discretion to mitigate or entirely remit any penalty or to stay or compound any penalty proceedings (TMA 1970 s 102).

Interest on penalties

Penalties under TMA 1970 Parts II (ss 7–12B), IV (ss 28A–43B), VA (ss 59A–59D) and X (ss 93–107), and FA 1998 Sch 18 carry interest at the prescribed rate (see p 4): TMA 1970 s 103A. This applies to penalties in relation to promoters of tax avoidance schemes from 17 July 2014. For interest which applies to penalties under the **harmonised interest regime** see p 4. For tax years before 2010–11, surcharges on unpaid income tax and capital gains tax carried interest under TMA 1970 s 59C. Surcharges have been replaced by a modernised penalty regime (see p 12).

Publishing details of deliberate tax defaulters

From 1 April 2010 HMRC have the power to publish the names and details of taxpayers who are penalised for deliberate defaults leading to a loss of tax of more than £25,000 (FA 2009 s 94).

Tax agent dishonest conduct

From 1 April 2013, in addition to the penalties listed above, HMRC have the power to publish names and details of tax agents who incur penalties for dishonest conduct over £5,000 (FA 2012 Sch 38; SI 2013/279).

Failure to provide security

A person who fails to comply with a requirement imposed under the PAYE regulations to give security or further security is liable on summary conviction to a fine not exceeding level 5 on the standard scale (£5,000) (ITEPA 2003 s 684(4A)).

Time limits for claims and elections

Whenever possible, a claim or election must be made on the tax return or by an amendment to the return (TMA 1970 s 42 and FA 1998 Sch 18 paras 9, 10, 67 and 79). Exceptions to this general rule are dealt with in TMA 1970 Sch 1A. Except where another period is expressly prescribed, a claim for relief in respect of income tax and capital gains tax must be made within four years after the end of the tax year (for claims made before 1 April 2010 such claims had to be made within five years from the 31 January following the year of assessment to which they related). (TMA 1970 s 43(1); FA 2008 Sch 39 para 12.) The time limit for claims by companies is four years from the end of the accounting period to which it relates (six years for claims made before 1 April 2010)

(FA 1998 Sch 18 para 55; FA 2008 Sch 39 para 45). The tables below set out some of the main exceptions to the general limits.

Income tax

Claim	*Time limit*
Trading losses: Loss sustained in a trade, profession or vocation to be set against other income of the year or the last preceding year. Extended to certain pre-trading expenditure by ITTOIA 2005 s 57 (ITA 2007 s 64).	One year after 31 January next following tax year in which loss arose.
Unrelieved trading losses to be set against capital gains (TCGA 1992 ss 261B, 261C).	One year after 31 January next following tax year in which loss arose.
Losses of new trade etc: Loss sustained in the first four years of a new trade, profession or vocation to be offset against other income arising in the three years immediately preceding the year of loss. Extended to certain pre-trading expenditure by ITTOIA 2005 s 57 (ITA 2007 s 72).	One year after 31 January next following tax year in which loss arose.
Property business losses: Claim for relief against total income (ITA 2007 s 124).	One year after 31 January next following tax year specified in claim.
Loss on disposal of unlisted shares: Loss on disposal of shares in an EIS company or a qualifying trading company to be offset against other income of the year of loss or the last preceding year (ITA 2007 s 132).	One year after 31 January next following tax year in which loss arose.
Gift aid: Election to treat donations to charity under gift aid made after 5 April 2003 as made in the previous tax year (ITA 2007 s 426).	On or before date on which donor delivers tax return for the previous tax year and not later than 31 January after that year.

Capital gains

Claim	*Time limit*
Assets of negligible value: Loss to be allowed where the value of an asset has become negligible (TCGA 1992 s 24(2)).	Two years after end of chargeable period of deemed sale (and reacquisition).
Assets held on 31 March 1982: Events occurring prior to 31 March 1982 to be ignored in computing gains arising after 5 April 1988 (TCGA 1992 s 35(5), (6) as amended).	Two years after end of accounting period in which first relevant disposal made after 31.3.88; or such further time as HMRC may allow (corporation tax). *One year after 31 January next following tax year in which first relevant disposal made after 5.4.88* (***capital gains tax for tax years before 2008–09 only***).
Main residence: Determination of main residence for principal private residence exemption (TCGA 1992 s 222(5)(*a*)).	Two years after acquisition of second residence.
Relief for loans to traders: Losses on certain loans to traders to be allowed as capital losses at the time of claim or 'earlier time' (TCGA 1992 s 253(3A)).	Two years after the end of the tax year or accounting period of loss.
Relief for loans to traders (payments by guarantor): Losses arising from payments by guarantor of certain irrecoverable loans to traders to be allowed as capital losses at time of claim or 'earlier time' (TCGA 1992 s 253(4), (4A)).	Four years after the end of the tax year or accounting period in which payment made (for claims before 1 April 2010, five years after 31 January following tax year in which payment made (capital gains tax); six years after end of accounting period in which payment made (corporation tax)).
Election for valuation at 6 April 1965: Gain on a disposal of an asset held at 6 April 1965 to be computed as if the asset had been acquired on that date. An election once made is irrevocable (TCGA 1992 Sch 2 para 17).	Two years after end of accounting period in which disposal made; or such further time as HMRC may allow (corporation tax). *One year after 31 January following tax year in which disposal made* (***capital gains tax for tax years before 2008–09 only***).

Corporation tax

Claim	*Time limit*
Trading losses: Loss sustained by a company in a trade in an accounting period to be offset against profits of that accounting period and profits of the preceding year. Extended to certain pre-trading expenditure by CTA 2009 s 61 (CTA 2010 s 37(7)).	Two years after end of loss-making period; or such further period as HMRC may allow.
Group relief: Group relief to be given for accounting periods ending after 30 June 1999. The surrendering company must consent to the claim (FA 1998 Sch 18 paras 66–77).	The last of: (*a*) one year from filing date of claimant company's return for accounting period for which claim is made; (*b*) 30 days after end of an enquiry into return; (*c*) if HMRC amend return after an enquiry, 30 days after issue of notice of amendment; (*d*) if an appeal is made against amendment, 30 days after determination of appeal; (or such later time as HMRC may allow).
Non-trading deficit on loan relationship: Claim for non-trading deficits on loan relationships (including non-trading debits on derivative contracts) in an accounting period to be:	
(*a*) offset against profits of same period or carried back (CTA 2009 s 460);	Two years after end of accounting period in which deficit arose (or such later time as HMRC may allow).
(*b*) treated as non-trading deficit of subsequent accounting period to be carried forward to succeeding accounting periods (CTA 2009 s 458).	Two years after end of that subsequent accounting period.
Intangible assets: Election to replace accounts depreciation with fixed writing-down allowance of 4% (CTA 2009 s 730).	Two years after end of the accounting period in which asset was created or acquired.
Research and development: Claim for tax relief to be made, amended or withdrawn in company tax return (or amended return) (FA 1998 Sch 18 paras 83E).	One year from the filing date for return or such later time as HMRC may allow.
UITF 40 spreading adjustment: Election to treat it as arising and charged in an accounting period rather than spreading it over three to six years (FA 2006 Sch 15 para 13).	One year from filing date for return.

Capital allowances

Claim	*Time limit*
Corporation tax claims: Claims, amended claims and withdrawals of claims in respect of corporation tax capital allowances (CAA 2001 s 3(2), (3)(*b*); FA 1998 Sch 18 para 82).	The last of: (*a*) one year after filing date of claimant company's return for accounting period for which claim is made; (*b*) 30 days after end of enquiry into return; (*c*) if HMRC amend the return after an enquiry, 30 days after issue of notice of amendment; (*d*) if appeal is made against amendment, 30 days after determination of appeal; (or such later time as HMRC may allow).
Short life assets: Plant or machinery to be treated as a short life asset (CAA 2001 s 85(2)).	One year after 31 January after tax year in which chargeable period ends (income tax); two years after end of chargeable period (corporation tax).
Connected persons: Succession to a trade between connected persons to be ignored in computing capital allowances (CAA 2001 s 266).	Two years after date of the succession.
Sales between persons under common control treated as made at the lower of open market value and tax written down value (CAA 2001 s 570(5)).	Two years after date of the disposal.

Exchanges

Recognised stock exchanges

The following is a list of countries with exchanges which have been designated as recognised stock exchanges under ITA 2007 s 1005; CTA 2010 s 1137. Unless otherwise specified, any stock exchange (or options exchange) in a country listed below is a recognised stock exchange provided it is recognised under the law of the country concerned relating to stock exchanges.

HMRC may make an order designating a market in the UK as a recognised stock exchange.

Country	*Date of recognition*
Australian Stock Exchange and its stock exchange subsidiaries	22 September 1988
National Stock Exchange of Australia	19 June 2014
Austria[3]	22 October 1970
Bahamas	
Bahamas International Securities Exchange	19 April 2010
Belgium[3]	22 October 1970
Bermuda	4 December 2007
Brazil	
Rio De Janeiro Stock Exchange	17 August 1995
São Paulo Stock Exchange	11 December 1995
Canada	
Any stock exchange prescribed for the purposes of the Canadian Income Tax Act	22 October 1970
Cayman Islands Stock Exchange	4 March 2004
Channel Islands Securities Exchange Authority	20 December 2013
China	
Hong Kong – Any stock exchange recognised under Section 2A(1) of the Hong Kong Companies Ordinance	26 February 1971
Cyprus	
Cyprus Stock Exchange	22 June 2009
Denmark	
Copenhagen Stock Exchange	22 October 1970
Estonia	
NASDAQ OMX Tallinn	5 May 2010
European Wholesale Securities Market	18 January 2013
Finland	
Helsinki Stock Exchange	22 October 1970
France[3]	22 October 1970
Germany[3]	5 August 1971
Global Board of Trade	30 July 2013
Greece	
Athens Stock Exchange	14 June 1993
Guernsey[3]	10 December 2002
GXG Main Quote	23 September 2013
GXG Official List	16 May 2013
Iceland	31 March 2006
Irish Republic[3]	22 October 1970
Italy[3]	3 May 1972
Japan[3]	22 October 1970
Korea	10 October 1994
Lithuania	
NASDAQ OMX Vilnius	12 March 2012
Luxembourg[3]	21 February 1972
Malaysia	
Kuala Lumpur Stock Exchange	10 October 1994
Malta Stock Exchange	29 December 2005
Mauritius Stock Exchange	31 January 2011
Mexico	10 October 1994
Netherlands[3]	22 October 1970
New Zealand	22 September 1988
Norway[3]	22 October 1970
Poland	
Warsaw Stock Exchange	25 February 2010
Portugal[3]	21 February 1972
Russia	
MICEX Stock Exchange	5 January 2011
Singapore	30 June 1977
South Africa	
Bond Exchange of South Africa	16 April 2008

Country	*Date of recognition*
Johannesburg Stock Exchange	22 October 1970
Spain[3]	5 August 1971
Sri Lanka	
Colombo Stock Exchange	21 February 1972
Sweden	
Stockholm Stock Exchange	16 July 1985
Swiss Stock Exchange	12 May 1997
Thailand	10 October 1994
United Kingdom	
London Stock Exchange	19 July 2007
PLUS-listed Market	19 July 2007
ICAP Securities & Derivatives Exchange Ltd	25 April 2013
LIFFE Administration and Management	26 September 2011
United States	
Any stock exchange registered with the SEC as a national securities exchange[1]	22 October 1970
Nasdaq Stock Market[2]	10 March 1992

1 'National securities exchange' does not include any local exchanges registered with Securities and Exchange Commission.
2 As maintained through the facilities of the National Association of Securities Dealers Inc and its subsidiaries.
3 i.e., a stock exchange according to the law of the country concerned relating to stock exchanges.

Recognised futures exchanges

The following is a list of exchanges which have been designated as recognised futures exchanges under TCGA 1992 s 288(6). By concession, those exchanges were recognised futures exchanges for the tax year of recognition onwards.

Recognised futures exchanges	*Date of recognition*
International Petroleum Exchange of London	6 August 1985
London Metal Exchange	6 August 1985
London Gold Market	12 December 1985
London Silver Market	12 December 1985
CME Group (formerly Chicago Mercantile Exchange and Chicago Board of Trade)	19 December 1986
New York Mercantile Exchange	19 December 1986
Philadelphia Board of Trade	19 December 1986
Mid America Commodity Exchange	29 July 1987
Montreal Exchange	29 July 1987
Hong Kong Futures Exchange	15 December 1987
Commodity Exchange (Comex)	25 August 1988
Sydney Futures Exchange	13 October 1988
Euronext (London International Financial Futures and Options Exchange)	22 March 1992
OM Stockholm	18 March 1992
OMLX (formerly OM London)	18 March 1992
New York Board of Trade	10 June 2004

Recognised investment exchanges and clearing houses

The following is a list of investment exchanges and clearing houses recognised as investment exchanges under the Financial Services and Markets Act 2000 and able to carry out investment business in the UK.

Recognised investment exchanges	*Date of recognition*
London Stock Exchange plc	22 November 2001
LIFFE Administration and Management	22 November 2001
The London Metal Exchange Ltd	22 November 2001
ICE Futures Europe	22 November 2001
ICAP Securities & Derivatives Exchange Ltd (formerly PLUS Stock Exchange plc)	19 July 2007
BATS Trading Ltd	20 May 2013
CME Europe Ltd	10 March 2014
Euronext UK markets Ltd	2 June 2014

Recognised clearing houses	*Date of recognition*
Euroclear UK & Ireland Ltd	23 November 2001
ICE Clear Europe Ltd	15 May 2008
CME Clearing Europe Ltd	15 December 2010

Note: List as at 8 July 2014 on Bank of England website. LCH.Clearnet Ltd, previously recognised as a recognised clearing house since 22 November 2001, is now a recognised central counterparty from 12 June 2014.

Recognised overseas investment exchanges and clearing houses

The following is a list of overseas investment exchanges and clearing houses recognised under the Financial Services and Markets Act 2000 and able to conduct investment business in the UK.

Recognised overseas investment exchange	*Date of recognition*
National Association of Securities Dealers Automated Quotations (NASDAQ)	23 November 2001
Australian Securities Exchange Ltd	30 January 2002
The Chicago Mercantile Exchange (CME)	23 November 2001
Chicago Board of Trade (CBOT)	23 November 2001
New York Mercantile Exchange Inc (NYMEX Inc)	23 November 2001
SIX Swiss Exchange AG	23 November 2001
EUREX (Zurich)	23 November 2001
ICE Futures US Inc	17 May 2007
NYSE LIFFE US	29 September 2009

Recognised clearing house	*Date of recognition*
SIX x-Clear	19 August 2004
The Chicago Mercantile Exchange (CME)	11 January 2008
ICE Clear US Inc	25 March 2008

Note: List as at 8 July 2014 on Bank of England website.

Alternative finance investment bonds

List of recognised stock exchanges designated solely for the purposes of ITA 2007 s 564G, TCGA 1992 s 151N, CTA 2009 s 507.

Recognised stock exchanges	*Date of recognition*
Abu Dhabi Securities Market	1 April 2007
Bahrain Stock Exchange	1 April 2007
Dubai Financial Market	1 April 2007
NASDAQ Dubai (formerly Dubai International Financial Exchange)	1 April 2007
Labuan International Financial Exchange	1 April 2007
Saudi Stock Exchange (Tadawul)	1 April 2007
Surabaya Stock Exchange	1 April 2007

Applications for clearances and approvals

Statutory clearance applications and approvals	*Address*
Demergers (CTA 2010 s 1091); Company purchase of own shares (CTA 2010 s 1044); Transactions in securities (CTA 2010 s 748; ITA 2007 s 701); Enterprise Investment Scheme – acquisition of shares by new company (ITA 2007 s 247(1)(f)); Share exchanges (TCGA 1992 s 138); Reconstruction regarding transfer of a business (TCGA 1992 s 139); Transfer of a UK trade between EU member states (TCGA 1992 ss 140B, 140D); Intangible fixed assets (CTA 2009 s 831); Loan relationships transfers/mergers (CTA 2009 ss 426, 427, 438); Derivative contracts transfers/mergers (CTA 2009 ss 677, 686); Schemes converting income to capital (TCGA 1992 ss 184G–H); Assignment of lease granted at undervalue (CTA 2009 s 237; ITTOIA 2005 s 300); Transactions in land (CTA 2010 s 831; ITA 2007 s 770); Collective investment schemes (TCGA 1992 s 103K)	HM Revenue & Customs, CA Clearance SO528, PO Box 194, Bootle, L69 9AA (Applications should be marked "market sensitive" or "non-market sensitive" as appropriate.)[1]
Employee share schemes (ITEPA 2003 Schs 2, 3, 4)	Employee Shares & Securities Unit, HM Revenue & Customs, 1st Floor, FitzRoy House, Castle Meadow Road, Nottingham NG2 1BD Questions on EMI: Small Company Enterprise Centre Admin Team, HM Revenue & Customs, Medvale House, Mote Road, Maidstone, Kent ME15 6AF Questions on share valuation: Shares and Assets Valuation, Ferrers House, PO Box 38, Castle Meadow Road, Nottingham NG2 1BB
Pensions (formerly TA 1988 ss 590, 591)	Registration of a pension scheme from 6 April 2006 must be done online, but HMRC can be contacted at Pension Schemes Services, FitzRoy House, Castle Meadow Road, Nottingham, NG2 1BD
Qualifying life assurance policies (TA 1988 Sch 15)	Darryl Wall, HM Revenue & Customs, CTISA Corporation Tax and Business Income Tax, Financial Services Team, 3rd Floor, 100 Parliament Street, London SW1A 2BQ
Transactions in shares or debentures (TA 1988 ss 765 and 765A)	The recommendation is that businesses should address the reports directly to the customer relationship manager dealing with their affairs
Transfer of long-term insurance business (TCGA 1992 s 211, TA 1988 s 444AED)	HM Revenue & Customs, CTISA Corporation Tax and Business Income Tax, Financial Services Team, 3rd Floor, 100 Parliament Street, London SW1A 2BQ
Advance pricing agreements (TIOPA 2010 Part 5)	Dominic Vines, HM Revenue & Customs, CTIS Business International, East Spur, Euston Tower, 286 Euston Road, London NW1 3UH

Non-statutory clearance applications	*Address*
Controlled foreign companies (TIOPA 2010 Part 9A; TA 1988 ss 747–756, Schs 24–26)	CTIS, Foreign Profits Team Registry (CFC clearances), 3rd floor, 100 Parliament Street, London SW1A 2BQ
Company migration (TMA 1970 s 109B–F, formerly FA 1988 s 130)	Paul Metcalfe, HM Revenue & Customs, CTIS Business International, Foreign Profits Team, 100 Parliament Street, London SW1A 2BQ
Inward investment (in Statement of Practice 02/07)	Inward Investment Support, HM Revenue & Customs, CTIAA Business International, 100 Parliament Street, London SW1A 2BQ
Creative industries (CTA 2009 Pts 15, 15A, 15B)	Creative Industries Unit (Film, Television/Animation and Video Games Tax Reliefs), Local Compliance S0717, PO Box 3900, Glasgow G70 6AA
Enterprise Investment Scheme (EIS), Seed Enterprise Investment Scheme (SEIS) and Venture Capital Trust (VCT) scheme (ITA 2007 Pts 5, 5A, 6)	Small Company Enterprise Centre (Admin Team), HM Revenue & Customs, Medvale House, Mote Road, Maidstone, Kent ME15 6AF
Business investment relief (ITA 2007 s 809VC)	HM Revenue & Customs, Business Investment Relief Team S1278, PO Box 202, Bootle L69 9AL
IHT business property relief (IHTA 1984 Pt 5 Ch 1)	HMRC, Trusts & Estates Technical Team (Clearances), Ferrers House, Castle Meadow Road, Nottingham NG2 1BB
Social investment tax relief (ITA 2007 Pt 5B)	Small Company Enterprise Centre (Admin team), Mid-size Business S0777, PO Box 3900, Glasgow G70 6AA
Other non-statutory clearances	Large businesses should contact their client relationship manager. All other businesses and their agents should send applications to HMRC Non-statutory Clearances Team, 5th Floor Alexander House, 21 Victoria Avenue, Southend-on-Sea, Essex SS99 1AA[2] or email hmrc.southendteam@hmrc.gsi.gov.uk. Regarding emails see [1]

Confirmation or pre-transaction or general advice	*Address*
General enquiries on IR35	IR35 Customer Service Unit, HM Revenue & Customs, Ground Floor, North Princess House, Cliftonville Road, Northampton, NN1 5AE Telephone 0300 200 3885
Advance thin capitalisation agreements (Statement of Practice 1/12)	The first contact for information about advance thin capitalisation agreements under the Statement of Practice should be the Customer Relationship Manager (CRM) or Customer Contact (CC) of the business concerned, and they will engage the assistance of a transfer pricing specialist. If there is no known CRM or CC, the application may be sent to the local Transfer Pricing team leader
CGT post-transaction value checks	Completed form CG34 which must be received by HMRC at least two months before the relevant filing deadline
Professional bodies (relief for subscriptions) (ITEPA 2003 s 343)	A list of approved professional bodies and learned societies is available on the HMRC website (at www.hmrc.gov.uk/list3/index.htm)
General advice on specialist technical issues	See www.hmrc.gov.uk/cap/gen-advice.htm
SDLT transactions	See www.hmrc.gov.uk/sdlt/calculate/advance-approval.htm

[1] Where clearance is sought under any one or more of the sections handled by the CA Clearance Team, clearance applications may be sent in a single letter to the above Bootle address for clearances under those sections. The letter should make clear what clearance(s) is required. HMRC acknowledge only those applications that request acknowledgement. An email acknowledgement may be requested. E-mail applications can be sent to reconstructions@hmrc.gsi.gov.uk and fax applications to 03000 589 802. Attachments to emails should be no larger than 2MB. Self-extracting zip files should not be sent as HMRC software will block them. Security of emails is not guaranteed. Information about market or price sensitive matters, or well known individuals, should not be sent by email. General enquiries can be made on 03000 589 004.

[2] Non-statutory clearances: Taxpayers may apply for a non-statutory clearance where they require clarification on guidance or legislation for other circumstances after having checked that the transaction is not covered by a more appropriate clearance or approval route. Taxpayers must provide all the necessary information requested in the relevant checklist.

Capital allowances

Rates

Agricultural buildings for periods before April 2011

	Expenditure incurred after	% Rate
Initial allowance	31 October 1992[1]	20
	31 October 1993	Nil
Writing-down allowance	31 March 1986 and before 6 April 2011 (1 April 2011 for companies)	4[2, 3]

1 Initial allowances were temporarily reintroduced for 1 year in respect of capital expenditure on agricultural buildings or works. The allowances applied to buildings or works constructed under a contract entered into between 1 November 1992 and 31 October 1993, and brought into use for the purposes of the farming trade by 31 December 1994. See CAA 1990 s 124A.

2 Agricultural buildings allowances are abolished for income tax purposes for 2011–12 onwards and for corporation tax purposes for the financial year beginning 1 April 2011 onwards. (FA 2008, s 84.)

3 As a transitional measure, writing-down allowances were stepped down over the three financial or tax years prior to abolition. For 2008–09 (for corporation tax, the financial year beginning 1 April 2008) only 75% of the allowance was given. For 2009–10 (or financial year beginning 1 April 2009) only 50% was given and for 2010–11 (or financial year beginning 1 April 2010) only 25%. Where a chargeable period fell in more than one tax or financial year, time apportionment applied to determine the amount of the allowance. (FA 2008, s 85.)

Note: For balancing events on or after 21 March 2007, no election for a balancing adjustment could be made so that the new holder of the relevant interest, in all cases, calculated writing-down allowances based on the previous owner's balance of qualifying expenditure (cost less allowances claimed).

Dredging

	Expenditure incurred after	% Rate
Writing-down allowance	**5 November 1962**	**4**

Industrial buildings and structures for periods before April 2011

		Expenditure[1] incurred after	% Rate
Initial allowance			
	Generally:	31 October 1992	20
		31 October 1993	Nil
	Exception: Enterprise zones	within 10 years of site being included in zone[2]	100
Writing-down allowance			
	Generally:	5 April 1946	2
		5 November 1962[3] and before 6 April 2011 (1 April 2011 for companies)[4, 5]	4
	Exception: Enterprise zones	within 10 years of site being included in zone[2, 4]	25

1 The amount qualifying for allowance is the price paid for the relevant interest *minus* (i) the value of the land element and (ii) any value attributable to elements over and above those which would feature in a normal commercial lease negotiated in the open market: FA 1995 s 100 confirming previous practice.

2 CAA 2001 s 306, 310. Includes expenditure on qualifying hotels. See p 34 for enterprise zones.

3 Includes expenditure on qualifying hotels (other than in an enterprise zone). Also includes expenditure on the construction of toll roads incurred for accounting periods or basis periods ending after 5 April 1991.

4 Industrial buildings allowances and allowances for buildings in enterprise zones are abolished for income tax purposes for 2011–12 onwards and for corporation tax purposes for the financial year beginning 1 April 2011 onwards. (FA 2008, ss 84, 86.)

5 As a transitional measure, writing-down allowances (other than those on enterprise zones) were stepped down over the three financial or tax years prior to abolition. For 2008–09 (for corporation tax, the financial year beginning 1 April 2008) only 75% of the allowance was given. For 2009–10 (or financial year beginning 1 April 2009) only 50% was given and for 2010–11 (or financial year beginning 1 April 2010) only 25%. Where a chargeable period fell in more than one tax or financial year, time apportionment applied to determine the amount of the allowance. (FA 2008, ss 85, 87.)

Note: For balancing events on or after 21 March 2007, no balancing adjustment arose and the new holder of the relevant interest calculated writing-down allowances based on the previous owner's balance of qualifying expenditure (cost less allowances claimed).

Flat conversions

Initial allowance	Expenditure incurred	% Rate
	10 May 2001 to 1 or 6 April 2013	**100**

Applies to expenditure incurred on renovating or converting vacant or storage space above commercial properties to provide low value flats for rent. A writing-down allowance is given at 25% (on a straight-line basis) on unrelieved expenditure. (CAA 2001 ss 393A–393W; FA 2001 s 67, Sch 19.)
This relief is withdrawn for expenditure incurred on or after 1 April 2013 (corporation tax) and on or after 6 April 2013 (income tax). The entitlement to claim writing down allowance on any outstanding residue of qualifying expenditure also ceased with effect from the same dates (FA 2012 Sch 39).

Know-how

Expenditure incurred after 31 March 1986: annual 25% writing-down allowance (reducing balance basis).

Plant and machinery

	Expenditure incurred after	Expenditure incurred before	Up to pa
Annual investment allowance[1]			
for income tax purposes	**5 April 2014**	**1 January 2016**	**£500,000**
	31 December 2012	6 April 2014	£250,000
	5 April 2012	1 January 2013	£25,000
	5 April 2010	6 April 2012	£100,000
	5 April 2008	6 April 2010	£50,000
for corporation tax purposes	**31 March 2014**	**1 January 2016**	**£500,000**
	31 December 2012	1 April 2014	£250,000
	31 March 2012	1 January 2013	£25,000
	31 March 2010	1 April 2012	£100,000
	31 March 2008	1 April 2010	£50,000
First-year allowance (FYA)[13]			
General[12]			***% Rate***
for income tax purposes	5 April 2009	6 April 2010	40
for corporation tax purposes	31 March 2009	1 April 2010	40
Small and medium-sized businesses[2]			
for income tax purposes	1 July 1998	6 April 2008	40
for corporation tax purposes	1 July 1998	1 April 2008	40
	1 July 1997	2 July 1998	50
in Northern Ireland *only*	11 May 1998	12 May 2002	100
Small businesses[3]			
for income tax purposes	5 April 2006	6 April 2008	50
	5 April 2004	6 April 2005	50
for corporation tax purposes	31 March 2006	1 April 2008	50
	31 March 2004	1 April 2005	50
ICT	31 March 2000	1 April 2004	100
Energy-saving plant or machinery[4]	**31 March 2001**		**100**
New low-emission cars and refuelling equipment[5]	**16 April 2002**	**1 April 2015**[5]	**100**
Environmentally beneficial plant or machinery[6]	**31 March 2003**		**100**
Zero-emission goods vehicles[7]			
for income tax purposes	**5 April 2010**	**6 April 2015**[7]	**100**
for corporation tax purposes	**31 March 2010**	**1 April 2015**[7]	**100**
Enterprise zones[18]	**31 March 2012**	**1 April 2020**	**100**
Writing-down allowance (WDA)[8]			
Foreign leased assets[11]	9 March 1982	1 April 2006	10
	Chargeable period beginning on or after		
Long-life assets[8, 9]			
for income tax purposes	**6 April 2012**		**8**
for corporation tax purposes	**1 April 2012**		**8**
	Chargeable period ending before		
for income tax purposes	6 April 2012		10
for corporation tax purposes	1 April 2012		10
for income tax purposes	6 April 2008		6
for corporation tax purposes	1 April 2008		6

Integral features[8, 10]	**Chargeable period beginning on or after**	
for income tax purposes	**6 April 2012**	**8**
for corporation tax purposes	**1 April 2012**	**8**
	Chargeable period ending before	
for income tax purposes	6 April 2012	10
for corporation tax purposes	1 April 2012	10
Thermal insulation[8, 15]	**Chargeable period beginning on or after**	
for income tax purposes	**6 April 2012**	**8**
for corporation tax purposes	**1 April 2012**	**8**
	Chargeable period ending before	
for income tax purposes	6 April 2012	10
for corporation tax purposes	1 April 2012	10
Certain cars[8, 14]	**Chargeable period beginning on or after**	
for income tax purposes	**6 April 2012**	**8**
for corporation tax purposes	**1 April 2012**	**8**
	Chargeable period ending before	
for income tax purposes	6 April 2012	10
for corporation tax purposes	1 April 2012	10
Solar panels[8, 17]	**Chargeable period beginning on or after**	
for income tax purposes	**6 April 2012**	**8**
for corporation tax purposes	**1 April 2012**	**8**
Cushion gas[8, 16]	**Chargeable period beginning on or after**	
for income tax purposes	**6 April 2012**	**8**
for corporation tax purposes	**1 April 2012**	**8**
	Chargeable period ending before	
for income tax purposes	6 April 2012	10
for corporation tax purposes	1 April 2012	10
Generally	**Chargeable periods beginning on or after**	
for income tax purposes	**6 April 2012**	**18**
for corporation tax purposes	**1 April 2012**	**18**
	Chargeable period ending before	
for income tax purposes	6 April 2012	20
for corporation tax purposes	1 April 2012	20
for income tax purposes	6 April 2008	25
for corporation tax purposes	1 April 2008	25
	Chargeable periods straddling	
for income tax purposes	**6 April 2012**	**Hybrid rate[8, 9]**
for corporation tax purposes	**1 April 2012**	**Hybrid rate[8, 9]**
for income tax purposes	6 April 2008	Hybrid rate[8, 9]
for corporation tax purposes	1 April 2008	Hybrid rate[8, 9]

1 **Annual investment allowance:** Applies from April 2008. The first £500,000 (£250,000 for expenditure incurred before 6 April 2014 but after 31 December 2012 (income tax) or before 1 April 2014 but after 31 December 2012 (corporation tax)) of qualifying expenditure incurred in a chargeable period qualifies for the annual investment allowance at 100%. Where a chargeable period spans the date of an increase or decrease, transitional rules apply. The limit is proportionately increased or decreased where the chargeable period is longer or shorter than a year. A group of companies (defined as for company law purposes) can only receive a single allowance. This restriction also applies to certain related businesses or companies. Expenditure on cars does not qualify. (CAA 2001 ss 38A, 38B, 51A–51N; FA 2011 s 11; FA 2013 Sch 1; FA 2014 s 10, Sch 2). **The annual investment allowance will be £25,000 from 1 January 2016**.

2 **Small and medium-sized businesses:** The allowance did not apply to certain expenditure including that on plant and machinery for leasing, motor cars, ships, railway assets or long-life assets. After the first year, allowances revert to the normal WDA. The rate of 50% applied only for expenditure incurred during the year ended 1 July 1998 when a 12% FYA applied to long-life assets. (See note 9 below.) Small and medium-sized businesses are, broadly, those satisfying any two of the following conditions: (*a*) turnover £22,800,000 or less (*b*) assets £11,400,000 or less (*c*) not more than 250 employees (CAA 1990 ss 22(3C), (6B), 22A, 44, 46–49). For accounting periods ending before 30 January 2004, the thresholds were: (*a*) turnover £11,200,000 or less (*b*) assets £5,600,000 or less.

3 **Small businesses:** See note 2 above for conditions for relief. Small businesses are, broadly, those satisfying any two of the following conditions: (*a*) turnover £5,600,000 or less (*b*) assets £2,800,000 or less (*c*) not more than 50 employees. For accounting periods ending before 30 January 2004, the thresholds were: (*a*) turnover £2,800,000 or less (*b*) assets £1,400,000 or less (FA 2004 s 142).

4 **Energy-saving plant or machinery:** The allowances are available for investment by *any* business in

designated energy-saving plant and machinery in accordance with the Government's Energy Technology Product List. 100% first-year allowances are not available for expenditure incurred on or after 1 April 2012 (corporation tax) or 6 April 2012 (income tax) on plant or machinery to generate renewable electricity or heat where tariff payments are received under either of the renewable energy schemes introduced by the Department of Energy and Climate Change. The restriction applies from April 2014 for combined heat and power equipment (CAA 2001 ss 45A–45C, 46; FA 2001 s 65, Sch 17; SI 2001/2541; SI 2005/1114). The product lists are available at www.eca.gov.uk.

5 **Low-emission cars:** The allowance is given on (*a*) new cars which are either electrically propelled or emit not more than 95g/km of CO_2 (110g/km for expenditure incurred before 1 April 2013, 120g/km for expenditure incurred before 1 April 2008), registered after 16 April 2002 and (*b*) new plant and machinery to refuel vehicles in a gas refuelling station with natural gas, hydrogen fuels, or (for expenditure on or after 1 April 2008) biogas. For expenditure incurred after 31 March 2013 cars provided for leasing no longer qualify for the FYA (CAA 2001 ss 45D, 45E, 46; FA 2014 s 64). **Legislation will be introduced in Finance Bill 2015 to extend the 100% FYA to expenditure incurred before 31 March 2018. At the same time the qualifying threshold for low emission cars will be reduced to 75g/km.**

6 **Environmentally beneficial plant or machinery:** Allowances are available for expenditure by *any* business on new and unused designated technologies and products which satisfy the relevant environmental criteria in accordance with the Government's technologies or products lists (CAA 2001 ss 45H–45J, 46; FA 2003 s 167, Sch 30; SI 2003/2076). The product lists are available at www.eca.gov.uk.

7 **Zero-emission goods vehicles:** The allowance is given on new (and not second hand) vehicles which cannot under any circumstances produce CO_2 emissions when driven and which are of a design primarily suited to the conveyance of goods or burden. The expenditure must be incurred before 1 April 2015 (corporation tax) or 6 April 2015 (income tax) and is limited to expenditure of € 85 million per undertaking (as defined) over the five years. Exclusions apply (CAA 2001 ss 45DA–45DB, 212T; FA 2014 s 64, Sch 13). **Legislation will be introduced in Finance Bill 2015 to extend the 100% FYA to expenditure incurred before 1/6 April 2018. To comply with EU State aid rules the availability of the FYA will be limited to businesses that do not claim the Government's Plug-in Van Grant**.

8 **WDAs** are calculated on a reducing balance basis. For chargeable periods beginning before 6 April 2012 and ending on or after that date (income tax) or, beginning before 1 April 2012 and ending on or after that date (corporation tax) a hybrid rate of WDAs applies, calculated by time apportionment of the 20% and 18% rates, or, for the special rate expenditure, the 10% and 8% rates. For chargeable periods beginning on or after 6 April 2008 (income tax) or 1 April 2008 (corporation tax), a WDA of up to £1,000 can be claimed in respect of the main pool and/or the special rate pool where the unrelieved expenditure in the pool concerned is £1,000 or less.

9 **Long-life assets:** Applies to plant or machinery with an expected working life, when new, of 25 years or more. Applies where expenditure on long-life assets in a year is £100,000 or more (in the case of companies the de minimis limit is £100,000 divided by one plus the number of associated companies). Transitional provisions apply to maintain a 25% allowance for expenditure incurred before 1 January 2001 under a contract entered into before 26 November 1996 and to expenditure on second-hand plant or machinery if old rules applied to vendor. It does not apply to plant or machinery in a building used wholly or mainly as, or for purposes ancillary to, a dwelling-house, retail shop, showroom, hotel or office; cars; or sea-going ships and railway assets acquired before 1 January 2011. Expenditure on or after 1 April 2008 (corporation tax) or 6 April 2008 (income tax) qualifies, as special rate expenditure, for a writing down allowance of 8% (10% for periods before 1 or 6 April 2012, see note 8 above) reducing balance. The balance of the long-life asset pool at 1 or 6 April 2008 was also transferred into the special rate pool. The rate applying for chargeable periods beginning before 1 or 6 April 2008 was 6% and a hybrid rate applied for chargeable periods spanning those dates calculated by a time apportionment of the 6% and 10% rates (CAA 2001 ss 90–104, Sch 3 para 20).

10 **Integral features** of a building are electrical systems (including lighting systems); cold water systems; space or water heating systems, powered ventilation systems, air cooling or purification and any floor or ceiling comprised in such systems; lifts, escalators and moving walkways and external solar shading. Applies to expenditure incurred on or after 1 April 2008 (corporation tax) and 6 April 2008 (income tax). They all fall into the special rate pool and qualify for a 8% (10% for periods before 1 or 6 April 2012, see note 8 above) writing down allowance (CAA 2001 ss 33A, 104A).

11 **Foreign leased assets:** The relief applies only to leases finalised before 1 April 2006 (CAA 2001 s 109; FA 2006 Sch 9 para 13).

12 **First-year tax credits:** For expenditure incurred on or after 1 April 2008, a company can surrender a tax loss attributable to first-year allowances for energy-saving or environmentally beneficial equipment in exchange for a cash payment from the Government. The cash payment is equal to 19% of the loss surrendered, subject to an upper limit of the greater of £250,000 and the company's PAYE and NIC liability for the period concerned. (CAA 2001 Sch A1). Relief extended to 31 March 2018 by SI 2013/464.

13 **First year allowances**, where applicable, are available on expenditure over the annual investment allowance level or on which annual investment allowance has not been claimed, which would otherwise qualify for writing down allowance at 18% in the general plant and machinery pool.

14 **Cars:** For expenditure on and after 1 April 2009 (corporation tax), 6 April 2009 (income tax), cars with CO_2 emissions exceeding 130g/km (160g/km for expenditure incurred before 1 April 2013 (corporation tax) or 6 April 2013 (income tax)) will be allocated to the special rate pool. All other cars will go into the general pool (CAA 2001 ss 104A, 104AA).

15 **Thermal insulation**: Expenditure on thermal insulation incurred on or after 1 April 2008 (corporation tax) and 6 April 2008 (income tax) falls into the special rate pool and qualifies for a 8% (10% for periods before 1 or 6 April 2012, see note 8 above) writing down allowance (CAA 2001 ss 28, 104A).

16 **Cushion gas:** Expenditure on cushion gas incurred on or after 1 April 2010 falls into the special rate pool and qualifies for a 8% (10% for periods before 1 or 6 April 2012, see note 8 above) writing down allowance (CAA 2001 ss 70J, 104A).

17 **Solar panels**: Expenditure on solar panels incurred on or after 1 April 2012 (corporation tax) and 6 April

2012 (income tax) falls into the special rate pool and qualifies for a 8% writing down allowance (CAA 2001 s 104A).

18 **Enterprise zones:** For expenditure incurred for the purpose of a qualifying activity in the five-year period from 1 April 2012 to 31 March 2020 inclusive 100% first-year allowances will be available for companies chargeable to corporation tax which invest in unused (not second hand) plant or machinery for use primarily in designated assisted areas within certain enterprise zones. Expenditure must be incurred for the purposes of broadly a new or expanding business carried on by the company, must not be replacement expenditure and is limited to €125 million per single investment project (as defined) over the five years. Exclusions apply. A map of current enterprise zones can be found at http://enterprisezones.communities.gov.uk/enterprise-zone-map/. A pilot enterprise zone will be established in Northern Ireland. (CAA 2001 ss 45K–N, 212U; FA 2014 s 64, Sch 13).

Cars: Car hire p 80.

Mineral extraction

First-year allowance: 100% FYA is available for certain expenditure incurred after 16 April 2002 wholly for the purposes of a North Sea Oil ring-fence trade or on plant and machinery used in such a trade.

Writing-down allowance: for expenditure incurred after 31 March 1986, 10% for expenditure on the acquisition of a mineral asset and certain pre-trading expenditure, otherwise 25% (on reducing balance basis). (CAA 2001 s 418; FA 2014 ss 67, 68.)

Motor cars

Expenditure *on or after* 1 April 2009 (corporation tax) or 6 April 2009 (income tax) on cars is allocated to the special rate (currently 8%) plant and machinery pool if the car's CO_2 emissions exceed 130g/km (160g/km for expenditure incurred before 1 April 2013 (corporation tax) or 6 April 2013 (income tax)) and otherwise to the (currently 18%) main pool. Cars that have an element of non-business use are still dealt with in a single asset pool, but the rate of WDA depends on the emissions. (CAA 2001 ss 104AA, 104F, 208A, 268A-268D.)

The position for expenditure *before* 1 April 2009 (corporation tax) or 6 April 2009 (income tax) is as follows. Transitional rules apply — see note 2.

		% Rate[1, 2]
Writing-down allowance (WDA)	Chargeable period ending before 1 April 2008 for corporation tax and 5 April 2008 for income tax	25%
	Chargeable period straddling 1 April 2008 for corporation tax and 6 April 2008 for income tax	hybrid rate
	Chargeable period ending before 1 April 2012 for corporation tax or 6 April 2012 income tax	20%
	Chargeable period straddling 1 April 2012 for corporation tax and 6 April 2012 for income tax	**hybrid rate**
	Chargeable period beginning on or after 1 April 2012 for corporation tax or 6 April 2012 for income tax	**18%**

1 Restricted to £3,000 for cars costing more than £12,000 and bought outright, on hire purchase or by way of a lease with an option to purchase (CAA 2001 ss 74, 75).

2 Expenditure still in a single asset pool for cars costing more than £12,000 on the last day of the first chargeable period ending on or after 31 March 2014 (corporation tax) or 5 April 2014 (income tax) will be carried forward to the main pool (FA 2009 Sch 11 para 31).

3 See also note 5, p 32 and Car hire, p 80.

Patent rights

Writing-down allowance

Expenditure incurred after 31 March 1986: annual 25% writing-down allowance (reducing balance basis). (CAA 2001 s 472.)

Research and development (formerly scientific research)

	Expenditure incurred after	% Rate
Allowance in year 1	**5 November 1962**	**100**

Note: Land and houses are excluded from 1 April 1985.

Disadvantaged areas

Renovation of business premises

	Expenditure incurred between	% Rate
First-year allowance	**11 April 2007 and 1 or 6 April 2017**	**100**

The expenditure must be incurred on renovating or converting vacant business properties in Northern Ireland or the designated disadvantaged areas in the UK that have been vacant for at least a year, to bring the property back into business use. From April 2014 the type of qualifying expenditure has been specifically clarified. Premises refurbished by or used by businesses in the following trades are excluded from the scheme: fisheries and aquaculture, shipbuilding, the coal or steel industries, synthetic fibres, primary production of certain agricultural products and the manufacture of products which imitate or substitute for milk or milk products.) For qualifying expenditure incurred on or after 1 April 2014 (corporation tax) and on or after 6 April 2014 (income tax), allowances are not available if another form of State aid has been, or will be, received. A writing-down allowance is given at 25% (on a straight-line basis) on unrelieved expenditure. (FA 2005 s 92, Sch 6; SI 2012/868; FA 2014 s 66)

Enterprise zones

Before 1 April 2011 (corporation tax) or 6 April 2011 (income tax) an initial allowance of 100% was available for expenditure on industrial or commercial building by businesses within enterprise zones. Where the initial allowance was not or was only partially claimed a 25% writing-down allowance on cost, on a straight-line basis, applied to the unclaimed balance. There was no phasing out of the allowance between 2008 and 2011.

For 100% first-year allowances available for companies investing in plant or machinery for use primarily in designated assisted areas within certain Enterprise Zones see under **plant and machinery**.

Capital gains

Annual exemption

(TCGA 1992 s 3; FA 2014 ss 8, 9)

Individuals[a], personal representatives[b] and certain trusts[c]

a For 2008–09 onwards, an individual who claims to use the remittance basis for a tax year is not entitled to the capital gains tax annual exemption for that year. This does not apply if the individual's unremitted foreign income and gains for the year are less than £2,000 (TCGA 1992 s 3(1A); ITA 2007 s 809D).

b Year of death and following two years (maximum) (TCGA 1992 s 3(7)).

c Trusts for disabled persons as defined. Exemption divided by number of qualifying settlements created (after 9 March 1981) by one settlor, subject to a minimum of one-tenth (TCGA 1992 Sch para 1(1); FA 2005 Sch 1A).

d Exemption will be £11,100 and £5,550 in 2015–16.

Exempt amount of net gains	***2009–10***	***2010–11***	***2011–12***	***2012–13***	***2013–14***	***2014–15***
	£10,100	£10,100	£10,600	£10,600	£10,900	**£11,000**

Trusts[a] generally

Exempt amount of net gains	***2009–10***	***2010–11***	***2011–12***	***2012–13***	***2013–14***	***2014–15***
	£5,050	£5,050	£5,300	£5,300	£5,450	**£5,500**

a Exemption divided by number of qualifying settlements created (after 6 June 1978) by one settlor, subject to a minimum of one-fifth (TCGA 1992 Sch 1 para 1(4)).

Chattel exemption

(TCGA 1992 s 262)

	Disposals exemption	*Marginal relief: Maximum chargeable gain*
From 1989–90 onwards	£6,000	5/3 excess over £6,000

Rates of tax

(TCGA 1992 s 4)

2014–15	*Individuals*	• to income tax basic rate limit £31,865	**18%**
		• above income tax basic rate limit £31,865	**28%**
	Trusts and personal representatives		**28%**
2013–14	*Individuals*	• to income tax basic rate limit £32,010	18%
		• above income tax basic rate limit £32,010	28%
	Trusts and personal representatives		28%
2012–13	*Individuals*	• to income tax basic rate limit £34,370	18%
		• above income tax basic rate limit £34,370	28%
	Trusts and personal representatives		28%
2011–12	*Individuals*	• to income tax basic rate limit £35,000	18%
		• above income tax basic rate limit £35,000	28%
	Trusts and personal representatives		28%
2010–11	*Individuals*	*gains before 23 June 2010*	18%
		gains on or after 23 June 2010	
		• to income tax basic rate limit £37,400	18%
		• above income tax basic rate limit £37,400	28%
	Trusts and personal representatives		
		gains before 23 June 2010	18%
		gains on or after 23 June 2010	28%
2008–09 to 2009–10	*Individuals, trusts and personal representatives*		18%

For gains arising on or after 23 June 2010, the rate of tax for an individual is determined by treating gains as the top slice of income. Also for gains arising on or after 23 June 2010, a rate of **10% applies where entrepreneurs' relief is claimed** — see p 37. A rate of **28% applies to gains arising on disposals on or after 6 April 2013 of high value UK residential property by certain non-natural persons** — see p 65.

Trusts for vulnerable persons: From 2004–05 onwards, gains taxed at beneficiary's rates (on beneficiary if UK resident or on trustees if beneficiary not UK-resident) (FA 2005 ss 30–32).

Share identification rules

(TCGA 1992 ss 104–106A; FA 2014 Schs 12, 37)

For disposals on or after 6 April 2008 by individuals, trustees or personal representatives, shares and securities of the same class in the same company are identified with acquisitions in the following order[2]:

- acquisitions on the same day as the disposal;
- acquisitions within 30 days after the day of disposal on a first in/first out basis[1];
- shares comprised in a single pool incorporating all other shares of the same class, whenever acquired.

For the purposes of corporation tax on chargeable gains, disposals of shares etc are identified with acquisitions in the following order:

- same day acquisitions;
- acquisitions within the previous nine days on a first in/first out basis;
- the pool of shares acquired after 31 March 1982;
- any shares held at 31 March 1982;
- any shares acquired on or before 6 April 1965 on a last in/first out basis;
- (if shares disposed of still not fully matched) subsequent acquisitions.

These rules are modified for disposals of shares before 5 December 2005 if the company acquired shares of the same class within a short period and held not less than 2% of the number issued.

1 The 30-day matching rule does not apply in relation to acquisitions after 21 March 2006 where the individual making the disposal is not (or is not treated as) resident (or before 6 April 2013, ordinarily resident) in the UK at the time of the acquisition.

2 Different rules apply for SIP shares, exempt employee shareholder shares, BES shares, community investment tax relief shares, relevant EMI shares, EIS shares, VCT shares, SEIS shares, EOT exempt shares and social investment tax relief shares.

Entrepreneurs' relief

(TCGA 1992 ss 169H–169S)

Entrepreneurs' relief applies to disposals by an individual on or after 6 April 2008 of:

- all or part of a trade carried on alone or in partnership;
- assets of such a trade following cessation; or
- shares or securities in the individual's 'personal trading company' (as defined).

Where a disposal of shares or of an interest in the assets of a partnership qualifies for relief, an associated disposal of assets owned by the individual and used by the company or partnership also qualifies for relief.

Trustees can claim relief where a qualifying beneficiary has an interest in the business concerned.

Relief is extended to a disposal by an employee or officer of a trading company (or one or more companies in same trading group) of relevant EMI shares (as defined). Relief applies from 6 April 2013 where the shares were acquired on or after 6 April 2012.

The relief is available where the relevant conditions are met throughout a period of one year. For gains arising on or after 23 June 2010, the relief operates by charging qualifying net gains to CGT at 10%. Previously, it operated by reducing the amount of qualifying net gains by four-ninths (so that the gains were effectively charged to CGT at 10%). Relief is subject to a lifetime limit of gains of £10 million (£5 million for disposals before 6 April 2011; £2 million for disposals before 23 June 2010; £1 million for disposals before 6 April 2010), but disposals before 6 April 2008 do not count towards the limit. Relief given to trustees counts towards the limit of the qualifying beneficiary.

Transitional rules apply to allow relief to be claimed in certain circumstances where a gain made before 6 April 2008 is deferred and becomes chargeable on or after that date.

Leases

Depreciation table (TCGA 1992 Sch 8 para 1)

Yrs	%	*Yrs*	%	*Yrs*	%	*Yrs*	%
50 (or more)	100	37	93.497	24	79.622	11	50.038
49	99.657	36	92.761	23	78.055	10	46.695
48	99.289	35	91.981	22	76.399	9	43.154
47	98.902	34	91.156	21	74.635	8	39.399
46	98.490	33	90.280	20	72.770	7	35.414
45	98.059	32	89.354	19	70.791	6	31.195
44	97.595	31	88.371	18	68.697	5	26.722
43	97.107	30	87.330	17	66.470	4	21.983
42	96.593	29	86.226	16	64.116	3	16.959
41	96.041	28	85.053	15	61.617	2	11.629
40	95.457	27	83.816	14	58.971	1	5.983
39	94.842	26	82.496	13	56.167	0	0
38	94.189	25	81.100	12	53.191		

Formula: Fraction of expenditure disallowed—

$$\frac{AE - D}{AE}$$

Where:

AE is the percentage for duration of lease at acquisition or expenditure; and
D is the percentage for duration of lease at disposal.

Fractions of years: Add one-twelfth of the difference between the percentage for the whole year and the next higher percentage for each additional month. Odd days under 14 are not counted; 14 odd days or more count as a month.

Short leases: premiums treated as rent (TCGA 1992 Sch 8 para 5; ITTOIA 2005 ss 277–281A; CTA 2009 s 217–221A) Part of premium for grant of a short lease which is chargeable to income tax as property income:

$$P - (2\% \times (n - 1) \times P)$$

Where:

P is the amount of premium;
n is the number of complete years which lease has to run when granted.

Length of lease (complete years)	*Amount chargeable to CGT %*	*Income tax charge %*	*Length of lease (complete years)*	*Amount chargeable to CGT %*	*Income tax charge %*	*Length of lease (complete years)*	*Amount chargeable to CGT %*	*Income tax charge %*
Over 50	100	0	34	66	34	17	32	68
50	98	2	33	64	36	16	30	70
49	96	4	32	62	38	15	28	72
48	94	6	31	60	40	14	26	74
47	92	8	30	58	42	13	24	76
46	90	10	29	56	44	12	22	78
45	88	12	28	54	46	11	20	80
44	86	14	27	52	48	10	18	82
43	84	16	26	50	50	9	16	84
42	82	18	25	48	52	8	14	86
41	80	20	24	46	54	7	12	88
40	78	22	23	44	56	6	10	90
39	76	24	22	42	58	5	8	92
38	74	26	21	40	60	4	6	94
37	72	28	20	38	62	3	4	96
36	70	30	19	36	64	2	2	98
35	68	32	18	34	66	1 or less	0	100

Reliefs

The following is a summary of the other main capital gains tax reliefs and exemptions.

Charities

Gains accruing to charities which are both applicable and applied for charitable purposes are exempt. The exemption also applies from 1 April 2002 to Community Amateur Sports Clubs (CASCs).

Individuals

Companies owned by employee-ownership trusts	From 6 April 2014 relief from capital gains tax is available for disposals by a person other than a company of shares in either a trading company which is not a member of a group, or a parent company of a trading group, where the disposal is to a trust with specified characteristics. The disposal is treated as being made at no gain/no loss if the settlement is for the benefit of all eligible employees of the company or group and the settlement acquires a controlling interest in the company during the tax year in which the disposal is made. Further conditions apply.
Compensation (injury to person, profession or vocation)	Exempt.
Decorations for valour (acquired otherwise than for money or money's worth)	Gain exempt.
Employee shareholder shares (see p 97)	Gain on disposal of shares which were worth up to £50,000 on acquisition is exempt. Applies from 1 September 2013.
Enterprise Investment Scheme (see p 95)	Gain on disposal after relevant three-year period exempt to extent full relief given on shares. Deferral relief is available on gains on assets where the disposal proceeds are reinvested in EIS shares within one year before and three years after the disposal.
Entrepreneurs' relief (see p 37)	Gains on specified assets chargeable at 10% rate up to lifetime limit. (Before 23 June 2010, five ninths of qualifying gains chargeable at 18% (an effective rate of 10%) up to lifetime limit.)
Foreign currency acquired for personal expenditure	Gain exempt.
Gifts for public benefit, works of art, historic buildings etc	No chargeable gain/allowable loss.
Gifts of pre-eminent objects	Donors who gift pre-eminent objects to the nation will receive a reduction in their UK tax liability of 30% of the value of the object they are donating. The tax reduction can be against income or capital gains tax and can be spread forward across a period of up to five years starting with the tax year in which the object is offered. The legislation has effect in relation to liabilities for tax years and accounting periods beginning on or after 1 April 2012. The gift must be accepted as pre-eminent by the Arts Council under the Cultural Gifts Scheme. See p 64 for relief applying to companies.
Gilt-edged stock	No chargeable gain/allowable loss.
Hold-over relief for gifts	Restricted to: (1) gifts of business assets (including unquoted shares in trading companies and holding companies of trading groups). Relief is not available on the transfer of shares or securities to a company made after 8 November 1999 (other than transfers between 6.4.03 and 20.10.03); (2) gifts of heritage property; (3) gifts to heritage maintenance funds; (4) gifts to political parties; and (5) gifts which are chargeable transfers for inheritance tax. Where available, transferee's acquisition cost treated as reduced by held-over gain.
Married persons or civil partners living together	No chargeable gain/allowable loss on transfers between spouses or civil partners.
Motor vehicles	Gain exempt.
Principal private residence	Gain exempt if property is main residence throughout period of ownership, or throughout the period of ownership except for all or any part of the last 18 months of that period (36 months for disposals before 6 April 2014). The 36-month period continues to apply where property is disposed of by an individual who is, or whose spouse or civil partner is, a disabled person or long-term resident of a care home, provided that neither holds an interest in any other dwelling on which private residence relief can be claimed. Period of ownership does not include any period before 31 March 1982. Certain other periods of absence qualify for exemption.
If residence is partly let, exemption for the let part is limited to the smaller of–	(1) exemption on owner-occupied part; and (2) £40,000.

Qualifying corporate bonds	No chargeable gain (for loans made before 17 March 1998, allowable loss in certain cases if all or part of loss is irrecoverable).
Seed enterprise investment scheme (see p 95)	From 2012–13 reinvestment relief may be claimed where an individual realises capital gains on disposals of assets in a tax year and in the same year makes investments that qualify for, and he claims, the main seed enterprise investment scheme (SEIS) relief from income tax. For disposals of assets in 2012–13 the relief applies to the full qualifying re-invested amount. From 2013–14 the relief applies to half the qualifying re-invested amount. SEIS shares can be treated as issued in the previous tax year as a result of a SEIS income tax relief carry-back claim. SEIS re-investment relief then also has effect as if those shares had been issued on a day in the previous tax year. The maximum exemption is £100,000 of gains for 2012–13 and £50,000 thereafter. A disposal of shares on which SEIS income tax relief has been given and not withdrawn is exempt.
Social investment tax relief (see p 96)	Deferral relief is available for gains arising on assets in the period 6 April 2014 to 5 April 2019 where the disposal proceeds are reinvested in shares or debt investments which qualify for the social investment tax relief (SITR) income tax relief and investor is UK-resident. The qualifying investment must be made in the period one year before or three years after the gain arose. Limit of £1 million of gains which can be relieved in a tax year. A gain on a disposal of shares on which SITR income tax relief has been given and not withdrawn is exempt from capital gains tax where shares held for at least 3 years.
Venture capital trusts (see p 96)	Gain on disposal of shares by original investor exempt if company still a venture capital trust. Exemption applies only to shares acquired up to the permitted maximum of £200,000 per year of assessment. Deferral relief was available on gains on assets where the disposal proceeds were reinvested in VCT shares issued before 6 April 2004 and within one year before or after the disposal. This relief is withdrawn for shares issued after that date.

Businesses

Roll-over relief for replacement of business assets

(TCGA 1992 s 155; FA 2014 ss 61, 62)

Qualifying assets:
Buildings and land both occupied and used for the purposes of the trade.
Fixed plant and machinery.
Ships, aircraft and hovercraft.
Satellites, space stations and spacecraft.
Goodwill[1].
Milk and potato quotas[1].
Ewe and suckler cow premium quotas[1].
Fish quotas (from 29 March 1999)[1].
UK oil licences (from 1 July 1999).
Payment entitlement under farmers' single payment scheme (from 22 March 2005).
Payment entitlement under farmers' basic payment scheme (from 20 December 2013).

1 From 1 April 2002 onwards, subject to transitional rules, these items are removed from the list for companies only (as they fall within the intangible assets regime from that date (FA 2002 Sch 29 para 132(5)).

2 The 'replacement' assets must be acquired within 12 months before or three years after the disposal of the old asset. Both assets must be within any of the above classes. Holdover relief is available where the new asset is a depreciating asset (having a predictable useful life not exceeding 60 years).

Roll-over relief on the transfer of a business ('incorporation relief')

(TCGA 1992 s 162)

On incorporation of a business, the assets of the business are transferred to a company which then carries on the business in succession to the former proprietor. Gains realised on the transfer can be rolled over where the transfer is wholly or partly in consideration for the issue of shares. Relief is automatic (no claim is required).

See p 65 for disincorporation relief for companies. See p 39 for gifts of business assets.

Personal representatives

Allowable expenses

(SP 2/04)

Expenses allowable for the costs of establishing title in computing chargeable gains on disposal of assets in a deceased person's estate: deaths occurring after 5 April 2004. (HMRC accepts computations based either on the scale or on the actual allowable expenditure incurred.)

Gross value of estate	*Allowable expenditure*
Up to £50,000	1.8% of the probate value of the assets sold by the personal representatives.
Between £50,001 and £90,000	£900, to be divided between all the assets of the estate in proportion to the probate values and allowed in those proportions on assets sold by the personal representatives.
Between £90,001 and £400,000	1% of the probate value of the assets sold.
Between £400,001 and £500,000	£4,000, to be divided between all the assets of the estate in proportion to the probate values and allowed in those proportions on assets sold by the personal representatives.
Between £500,001 and £1,000,000	0.8% of the probate value of the assets sold.
Between £1,000,001 and £5,000,000	£8,000 to be divided between all the assets of the estate in proportion to the probate values and allowed in those proportions on assets sold by the personal representatives.
Exceeding £5,000,000	0.16% of the probate value of the assets sold subject to a maximum of £10,000.

Trustees

Allowable expenses

(SP 2/04)

Expenses allowable in computing chargeable gains of corporate trustees in the administration of trusts and estates: acquisition, disposals and deemed disposals after 5 April 2004. (HMRC accepts computations based either on the scale or on the actual allowable expenditure incurred.)

Transfers of assets to beneficiaries etc	
(*a*) Quoted stocks and shares	
(i) One beneficiary	£25 per holding.
(ii) More than one beneficiary	£25 per holding, divided equally between the beneficiaries.
(*b*) Unquoted shares	As (*a*) above, plus any exceptional expenditure.
(*c*) Other assets	As (*a*) above, plus any exceptional expenditure.
Actual disposals and acquisitions	
(*a*) Quoted stocks and shares	Investment fee as charged by the trustees (where a comprehensive annual management fee is charged, the investment fee is taken to be £0.25 per £100 of the sale or purchase moneys).
(*b*) Unquoted shares	As (*a*) above, plus actual valuation costs.
(*c*) Other assets	Investment fee (as (*a*) above), subject to a maximum of £75, plus actual valuation costs.
Deemed disposals by trustees	
(*a*) Quoted stocks and shares	£8 per holding.
(*b*) Unquoted shares	Actual valuation costs.
(*c*) Other assets	Actual valuation costs.

Indexation allowance – corporation tax on capital gains

(TCGA 1992 ss 53–57, 109)

For corporation tax purposes, an indexation allowance is given as a deduction in calculating gains on disposals from the amount realised (or deemed to be realised) on disposal. The indexation allowance is calculated by multiplying each item of allowable expenditure by:

$$\frac{RD - RI}{RI}$$

Where:

RD is the retail prices index figure for month of disposal;

RI is the retail prices index for month of expenditure (or March 1982 if later).

Indexation allowance can only be used to reduce or extinguish a gain. It cannot be used to create or increase a capital loss. It is not available to individuals, trustees and personal representatives. See p 60 for RPI values. The factors below can be used to calculate the indexation allowance for corporation tax purposes.

MONTH OF DISPOSAL

	2011	***2012***											***2013***	
1982	Dec	Jan	Feb	Mar	Apr	May	June	July	Aug	Sept	Oct	Nov	Dec	Jan	Feb
Mar	2.014	1.996	2.020	2.031	2.053	2.051	2.044	2.047	2.059	2.074	2.092	2.092	2.107	2.094	2.117
Apr	1.954	1.937	1.960	1.971	1.992	1.991	1.984	1.987	1.999	2.013	2.031	2.031	2.045	2.033	2.055
May	1.933	1.916	1.939	1.950	1.971	1.970	1.962	1.966	1.977	1.992	2.009	2.009	2.024	2.011	2.033
June	1.925	1.908	1.931	1.942	1.963	1.961	1.954	1.958	1.969	1.983	2.001	2.001	2.015	2.003	2.025
July	1.924	1.907	1.930	1.941	1.962	1.961	1.953	1.957	1.968	1.983	2.000	2.000	2.014	2.002	2.024
Aug	1.923	1.906	1.929	1.940	1.961	1.960	1.952	1.956	1.967	1.982	1.999	1.999	2.013	2.001	2.023
Sept	1.925	1.908	1.931	1.942	1.963	1.961	1.954	1.958	1.969	1.983	2.001	2.001	2.015	2.003	2.025
Oct	1.910	1.893	1.917	1.927	1.948	1.947	1.940	1.943	1.954	1.969	1.986	1.986	2.000	1.988	2.010
Nov	1.896	1.879	1.902	1.913	1.934	1.932	1.925	1.929	1.940	1.954	1.971	1.971	1.986	1.974	1.995
Dec	1.901	1.885	1.908	1.918	1.939	1.938	1.931	1.934	1.945	1.960	1.977	1.977	1.991	1.979	2.001
1983	Dec	Jan	Feb	Mar	Apr	May	June	July	Aug	Sept	Oct	Nov	Dec	Jan	Feb
Jan	1.898	1.881	1.904	1.915	1.935	1.934	1.927	1.931	1.942	1.956	1.973	1.973	1.987	1.975	1.997
Feb	1.886	1.869	1.892	1.902	1.923	1.922	1.914	1.918	1.929	1.943	1.960	1.960	1.975	1.963	1.984
Mar	1.880	1.863	1.886	1.897	1.918	1.916	1.909	1.913	1.924	1.938	1.955	1.955	1.969	1.957	1.979
Apr	1.840	1.824	1.846	1.857	1.877	1.876	1.869	1.872	1.883	1.897	1.914	1.914	1.928	1.916	1.938
May	1.828	1.812	1.834	1.845	1.865	1.864	1.857	1.860	1.871	1.885	1.902	1.902	1.916	1.904	1.925
June	1.822	1.805	1.828	1.838	1.858	1.857	1.850	1.854	1.864	1.878	1.895	1.895	1.909	1.897	1.918
July	1.807	1.790	1.812	1.823	1.843	1.842	1.835	1.838	1.849	1.863	1.879	1.879	1.893	1.882	1.903
Aug	1.794	1.778	1.800	1.811	1.830	1.829	1.822	1.826	1.836	1.850	1.867	1.867	1.881	1.869	1.890
Sept	1.782	1.766	1.788	1.798	1.818	1.817	1.810	1.813	1.824	1.838	1.854	1.854	1.868	1.856	1.877
Oct	1.772	1.756	1.778	1.788	1.808	1.807	1.800	1.803	1.814	1.828	1.844	1.844	1.858	1.846	1.867
Nov	1.762	1.746	1.768	1.778	1.798	1.797	1.790	1.793	1.804	1.818	1.834	1.834	1.848	1.836	1.857
Dec	1.755	1.739	1.761	1.771	1.791	1.790	1.783	1.786	1.796	1.810	1.826	1.826	1.840	1.829	1.849
1984	Dec	Jan	Feb	Mar	Apr	May	June	July	Aug	Sept	Oct	Nov	Dec	Jan	Feb
Jan	1.757	1.741	1.762	1.773	1.792	1.791	1.784	1.788	1.798	1.812	1.828	1.828	1.842	1.830	1.851
Feb	1.745	1.729	1.751	1.762	1.781	1.780	1.773	1.776	1.787	1.800	1.817	1.817	1.830	1.819	1.839
Mar	1.737	1.721	1.742	1.753	1.772	1.771	1.764	1.768	1.778	1.792	1.808	1.808	1.821	1.810	1.830
Apr	1.701	1.685	1.706	1.716	1.736	1.735	1.728	1.731	1.741	1.755	1.771	1.771	1.784	1.773	1.793
May	1.691	1.675	1.696	1.706	1.726	1.724	1.718	1.721	1.731	1.745	1.760	1.760	1.774	1.763	1.783
June	1.684	1.668	1.689	1.700	1.719	1.717	1.711	1.714	1.724	1.738	1.753	1.753	1.767	1.756	1.776
July	1.687	1.671	1.692	1.703	1.722	1.721	1.714	1.717	1.727	1.741	1.756	1.756	1.770	1.759	1.779
Aug	1.662	1.646	1.667	1.677	1.696	1.695	1.689	1.692	1.702	1.715	1.731	1.731	1.744	1.733	1.753
Sept	1.657	1.641	1.662	1.672	1.691	1.690	1.683	1.687	1.697	1.710	1.725	1.725	1.739	1.728	1.748
Oct	1.640	1.625	1.646	1.656	1.674	1.673	1.667	1.670	1.680	1.693	1.709	1.709	1.722	1.711	1.731
Nov	1.632	1.617	1.638	1.648	1.666	1.665	1.659	1.662	1.672	1.685	1.700	1.700	1.714	1.703	1.722
Dec	1.634	1.619	1.640	1.650	1.669	1.667	1.661	1.664	1.674	1.687	1.703	1.703	1.716	1.705	1.725
1985	Dec	Jan	Feb	Mar	Apr	May	June	July	Aug	Sept	Oct	Nov	Dec	Jan	Feb
Jan	1.625	1.610	1.630	1.640	1.659	1.658	1.651	1.654	1.664	1.678	1.693	1.693	1.706	1.695	1.715
Feb	1.604	1.589	1.609	1.619	1.638	1.637	1.630	1.633	1.643	1.656	1.671	1.671	1.684	1.674	1.693
Mar	1.580	1.565	1.585	1.595	1.613	1.612	1.606	1.609	1.619	1.631	1.647	1.647	1.659	1.649	1.668
Apr	1.526	1.511	1.531	1.541	1.559	1.558	1.551	1.554	1.564	1.577	1.591	1.591	1.604	1.593	1.612
May	1.514	1.500	1.520	1.529	1.547	1.546	1.540	1.543	1.552	1.565	1.580	1.580	1.592	1.582	1.601
June	1.509	1.494	1.514	1.524	1.542	1.541	1.534	1.537	1.547	1.559	1.574	1.574	1.587	1.576	1.595
July	1.514	1.499	1.519	1.528	1.546	1.545	1.539	1.542	1.552	1.564	1.579	1.579	1.591	1.581	1.600
Aug	1.507	1.492	1.512	1.522	1.540	1.539	1.532	1.535	1.545	1.557	1.572	1.572	1.585	1.574	1.593
Sept	1.508	1.494	1.514	1.523	1.541	1.540	1.534	1.537	1.546	1.559	1.573	1.573	1.586	1.576	1.594
Oct	1.504	1.490	1.510	1.519	1.537	1.536	1.530	1.533	1.542	1.555	1.569	1.569	1.582	1.571	1.590
Nov	1.496	1.481	1.501	1.510	1.528	1.527	1.521	1.524	1.533	1.546	1.560	1.560	1.573	1.563	1.581
Dec	1.493	1.478	1.498	1.507	1.525	1.524	1.518	1.521	1.530	1.543	1.557	1.557	1.570	1.559	1.578

MONTH OF DISPOSAL

	2013										2014			
1982	Mar	Apr	May	June	July	Aug	Sept	Oct	Nov	Dec	Jan	Feb	Mar	Apr
Mar	2.131	2.141	2.147	2.143	2.143	2.160	2.171	2.171	2.173	2.190	2.180	2.200	2.207	2.219
Apr	2.069	2.079	2.085	2.081	2.081	2.097	2.108	2.108	2.111	2.127	2.117	2.137	2.144	2.155
May	2.047	2.057	2.063	2.059	2.059	2.075	2.086	2.086	2.089	2.105	2.095	2.114	2.122	2.133
June	2.038	2.048	2.054	2.051	2.051	2.067	2.078	2.078	2.080	2.096	2.086	2.106	2.113	2.124
July	2.038	2.047	2.053	2.050	2.050	2.066	2.077	2.077	2.079	2.095	2.085	2.105	2.112	2.123
Aug	2.037	2.046	2.052	2.049	2.049	2.065	2.076	2.076	2.078	2.094	2.084	2.104	2.111	2.122
Sept	2.038	2.048	2.054	2.051	2.051	2.067	2.078	2.078	2.080	2.096	2.086	2.106	2.113	2.124
Oct	2.023	2.033	2.039	2.036	2.036	2.051	2.062	2.062	2.065	2.081	2.071	2.090	2.098	2.109
Nov	2.009	2.018	2.024	2.021	2.021	2.036	2.047	2.047	2.050	2.066	2.056	2.075	2.082	2.093
Dec	2.014	2.024	2.030	2.026	2.026	2.042	2.053	2.053	2.055	2.071	2.061	2.081	2.088	2.099
1983	Mar	Apr	May	June	July	Aug	Sept	Oct	Nov	Dec	Jan	Feb	Mar	Apr
Jan	2.010	2.020	2.026	2.023	2.023	2.038	2.049	2.049	2.052	2.067	2.058	2.077	2.084	2.095
Feb	1.998	2.007	2.013	2.010	2.010	2.025	2.036	2.036	2.039	2.054	2.045	2.064	2.071	2.082
Mar	1.992	2.002	2.008	2.004	2.004	2.020	2.031	2.031	2.033	2.049	2.039	2.058	2.066	2.076
Apr	1.951	1.960	1.966	1.963	1.963	1.978	1.989	1.989	1.991	2.007	1.997	2.016	2.023	2.034
May	1.938	1.948	1.954	1.950	1.950	1.966	1.976	1.976	1.979	1.994	1.984	2.003	2.010	2.021
June	1.931	1.941	1.947	1.943	1.943	1.958	1.969	1.969	1.971	1.987	1.977	1.996	2.003	2.014
July	1.916	1.925	1.931	1.927	1.927	1.943	1.953	1.953	1.956	1.971	1.961	1.980	1.987	1.998
Aug	1.903	1.912	1.918	1.914	1.914	1.930	1.940	1.940	1.942	1.958	1.948	1.967	1.974	1.984
Sept	1.890	1.899	1.905	1.902	1.902	1.917	1.927	1.927	1.929	1.945	1.935	1.954	1.961	1.971
Oct	1.880	1.889	1.895	1.891	1.891	1.906	1.917	1.917	1.919	1.934	1.925	1.943	1.950	1.961
Nov	1.870	1.879	1.885	1.881	1.881	1.896	1.907	1.907	1.909	1.924	1.915	1.933	1.940	1.950
Dec	1.862	1.871	1.877	1.874	1.874	1.889	1.899	1.899	1.901	1.916	1.907	1.925	1.932	1.943
1984	Mar	Apr	May	June	July	Aug	Sept	Oct	Nov	Dec	Jan	Feb	Mar	Apr
Jan	1.864	1.873	1.879	1.875	1.875	1.890	1.901	1.901	1.903	1.918	1.909	1.927	1.934	1.944
Feb	1.852	1.861	1.867	1.864	1.864	1.878	1.889	1.889	1.891	1.906	1.897	1.915	1.922	1.932
Mar	1.843	1.852	1.858	1.854	1.854	1.869	1.880	1.880	1.882	1.897	1.888	1.906	1.913	1.923
Apr	1.806	1.815	1.820	1.817	1.817	1.832	1.842	1.842	1.844	1.859	1.850	1.868	1.874	1.885
May	1.795	1.804	1.810	1.806	1.806	1.821	1.831	1.831	1.833	1.848	1.839	1.857	1.864	1.874
June	1.788	1.797	1.803	1.799	1.799	1.814	1.824	1.824	1.826	1.841	1.832	1.850	1.856	1.867
July	1.791	1.800	1.806	1.802	1.802	1.817	1.827	1.827	1.829	1.844	1.835	1.853	1.860	1.870
Aug	1.765	1.774	1.780	1.776	1.776	1.791	1.801	1.801	1.803	1.818	1.809	1.826	1.833	1.843
Sept	1.760	1.769	1.774	1.771	1.771	1.785	1.795	1.795	1.798	1.812	1.803	1.821	1.828	1.838
Oct	1.743	1.752	1.757	1.754	1.754	1.768	1.778	1.778	1.780	1.795	1.786	1.804	1.810	1.820
Nov	1.734	1.743	1.749	1.745	1.745	1.760	1.770	1.770	1.772	1.786	1.777	1.795	1.802	1.811
Dec	1.737	1.746	1.751	1.748	1.748	1.762	1.772	1.772	1.774	1.788	1.780	1.797	1.804	1.814
1985	Mar	Apr	May	June	July	Aug	Sept	Oct	Nov	Dec	Jan	Feb	Mar	Apr
Jan	1.727	1.736	1.741	1.738	1.738	1.752	1.762	1.762	1.764	1.778	1.770	1.787	1.794	1.804
Feb	1.705	1.714	1.719	1.716	1.716	1.730	1.740	1.740	1.742	1.756	1.747	1.765	1.771	1.781
Mar	1.680	1.689	1.694	1.691	1.691	1.705	1.714	1.714	1.717	1.731	1.722	1.739	1.746	1.755
Apr	1.624	1.632	1.638	1.635	1.635	1.648	1.658	1.658	1.660	1.674	1.665	1.682	1.688	1.698
May	1.612	1.621	1.626	1.623	1.623	1.636	1.646	1.646	1.648	1.662	1.653	1.670	1.676	1.686
June	1.607	1.615	1.620	1.617	1.617	1.631	1.640	1.640	1.642	1.656	1.647	1.664	1.671	1.680
July	1.611	1.620	1.625	1.622	1.622	1.636	1.645	1.645	1.647	1.661	1.652	1.669	1.676	1.685
Aug	1.605	1.613	1.618	1.615	1.615	1.629	1.638	1.638	1.640	1.654	1.645	1.662	1.668	1.678
Sept	1.606	1.614	1.620	1.616	1.616	1.630	1.639	1.639	1.642	1.655	1.647	1.664	1.670	1.679
Oct	1.602	1.610	1.615	1.612	1.612	1.626	1.635	1.635	1.637	1.651	1.643	1.659	1.666	1.675
Nov	1.593	1.601	1.606	1.603	1.603	1.617	1.626	1.626	1.628	1.642	1.633	1.650	1.656	1.666
Dec	1.589	1.598	1.603	1.600	1.600	1.613	1.623	1.623	1.625	1.638	1.630	1.647	1.653	1.662

MONTH OF DISPOSAL

	2011	**2012**											**2013**	
1986	Dec	Jan	Feb	Mar	Apr	May	June	July	Aug	Sept	Oct	Nov	Dec	Jan	Feb
Jan	1.487	1.473	1.493	1.502	1.520	1.518	1.512	1.515	1.525	1.537	1.552	1.552	1.564	1.554	1.573
Feb	1.478	1.464	1.483	1.493	1.510	1.509	1.503	1.506	1.515	1.528	1.542	1.542	1.555	1.544	1.563
Mar	1.475	1.460	1.480	1.489	1.507	1.506	1.500	1.503	1.512	1.525	1.539	1.539	1.551	1.541	1.560
Apr	1.451	1.437	1.456	1.465	1.483	1.482	1.476	1.479	1.488	1.500	1.515	1.515	1.527	1.517	1.535
May	1.447	1.432	1.452	1.461	1.478	1.477	1.471	1.474	1.484	1.496	1.510	1.510	1.522	1.512	1.531
June	1.448	1.434	1.453	1.462	1.480	1.479	1.473	1.476	1.485	1.497	1.511	1.511	1.524	1.513	1.532
July	1.455	1.441	1.460	1.469	1.487	1.486	1.480	1.483	1.492	1.504	1.519	1.519	1.531	1.521	1.539
Aug	1.447	1.433	1.452	1.462	1.479	1.478	1.472	1.475	1.484	1.496	1.511	1.511	1.523	1.513	1.531
Sept	1.435	1.421	1.440	1.450	1.467	1.466	1.460	1.463	1.472	1.484	1.498	1.498	1.511	1.500	1.519
Oct	1.432	1.417	1.437	1.446	1.463	1.462	1.456	1.459	1.468	1.480	1.495	1.495	1.507	1.497	1.515
Nov	1.411	1.397	1.416	1.425	1.442	1.441	1.435	1.438	1.447	1.459	1.474	1.474	1.486	1.476	1.494
Dec	1.403	1.389	1.408	1.417	1.434	1.433	1.427	1.430	1.439	1.451	1.465	1.465	1.477	1.467	1.485
1987	Dec	Jan	Feb	Mar	Apr	May	June	July	Aug	Sept	Oct	Nov	Dec	Jan	Feb
Jan	1.394	1.380	1.399	1.408	1.425	1.424	1.418	1.421	1.430	1.442	1.456	1.456	1.468	1.458	1.476
Feb	1.384	1.371	1.389	1.398	1.415	1.414	1.408	1.411	1.420	1.432	1.446	1.446	1.458	1.448	1.466
Mar	1.380	1.366	1.385	1.394	1.411	1.410	1.404	1.407	1.416	1.427	1.441	1.441	1.453	1.443	1.461
Apr	1.352	1.338	1.357	1.365	1.382	1.381	1.375	1.378	1.387	1.399	1.413	1.413	1.424	1.415	1.432
May	1.349	1.336	1.354	1.363	1.380	1.379	1.373	1.376	1.385	1.396	1.410	1.410	1.422	1.412	1.430
June	1.349	1.336	1.354	1.363	1.380	1.379	1.373	1.376	1.385	1.396	1.410	1.410	1.422	1.412	1.430
July	1.352	1.338	1.357	1.365	1.382	1.381	1.375	1.378	1.387	1.399	1.413	1.413	1.424	1.415	1.432
Aug	1.345	1.331	1.350	1.358	1.375	1.374	1.368	1.371	1.380	1.392	1.405	1.405	1.417	1.407	1.425
Sept	1.338	1.324	1.343	1.352	1.368	1.367	1.361	1.364	1.373	1.385	1.398	1.398	1.410	1.400	1.418
Oct	1.327	1.313	1.331	1.340	1.357	1.356	1.350	1.353	1.362	1.373	1.387	1.387	1.398	1.389	1.406
Nov	1.315	1.302	1.320	1.329	1.345	1.344	1.338	1.341	1.350	1.362	1.375	1.375	1.387	1.377	1.395
Dec	1.318	1.304	1.322	1.331	1.348	1.347	1.341	1.344	1.352	1.364	1.378	1.378	1.389	1.379	1.397
1988	Dec	Jan	Feb	Mar	Apr	May	June	July	Aug	Sept	Oct	Nov	Dec	Jan	Feb
Jan	1.318	1.304	1.322	1.331	1.348	1.347	1.341	1.344	1.352	1.364	1.378	1.378	1.389	1.379	1.397
Feb	1.309	1.295	1.313	1.322	1.338	1.338	1.332	1.335	1.343	1.355	1.368	1.368	1.380	1.370	1.388
Mar	1.300	1.286	1.305	1.313	1.329	1.329	1.323	1.326	1.334	1.346	1.359	1.359	1.371	1.361	1.378
Apr	1.263	1.250	1.267	1.276	1.292	1.291	1.285	1.288	1.297	1.308	1.321	1.321	1.333	1.323	1.340
May	1.254	1.241	1.259	1.267	1.283	1.282	1.277	1.280	1.288	1.299	1.313	1.313	1.324	1.315	1.331
June	1.246	1.233	1.250	1.259	1.275	1.274	1.268	1.271	1.280	1.291	1.304	1.304	1.315	1.306	1.323
July	1.244	1.231	1.248	1.257	1.273	1.272	1.266	1.269	1.277	1.289	1.302	1.302	1.313	1.304	1.321
Aug	1.219	1.206	1.223	1.232	1.247	1.247	1.241	1.244	1.252	1.263	1.276	1.276	1.287	1.278	1.295
Sept	1.208	1.196	1.213	1.221	1.237	1.236	1.231	1.233	1.242	1.253	1.266	1.266	1.277	1.268	1.284
Oct	1.186	1.174	1.191	1.199	1.215	1.214	1.208	1.211	1.219	1.230	1.243	1.243	1.254	1.245	1.261
Nov	1.176	1.164	1.181	1.189	1.205	1.204	1.198	1.201	1.209	1.220	1.233	1.233	1.244	1.235	1.251
Dec	1.170	1.158	1.175	1.183	1.199	1.198	1.192	1.195	1.203	1.214	1.227	1.227	1.238	1.228	1.245
1989	Dec	Jan	Feb	Mar	Apr	May	June	July	Aug	Sept	Oct	Nov	Dec	Jan	Feb
Jan	1.157	1.144	1.161	1.169	1.185	1.184	1.178	1.181	1.189	1.200	1.213	1.213	1.223	1.214	1.231
Feb	1.141	1.129	1.146	1.154	1.169	1.168	1.163	1.165	1.174	1.184	1.197	1.197	1.208	1.199	1.215
Mar	1.132	1.119	1.136	1.144	1.159	1.159	1.153	1.156	1.164	1.175	1.187	1.187	1.198	1.189	1.205
Apr	1.094	1.082	1.099	1.107	1.122	1.121	1.115	1.118	1.126	1.136	1.149	1.149	1.159	1.150	1.166
May	1.082	1.070	1.086	1.094	1.109	1.108	1.103	1.105	1.113	1.123	1.136	1.136	1.146	1.137	1.153
June	1.075	1.062	1.079	1.087	1.101	1.101	1.095	1.098	1.106	1.116	1.128	1.128	1.139	1.130	1.146
July	1.073	1.061	1.077	1.085	1.100	1.099	1.094	1.096	1.104	1.114	1.126	1.126	1.137	1.128	1.144
Aug	1.067	1.055	1.072	1.079	1.094	1.093	1.088	1.091	1.098	1.109	1.121	1.121	1.131	1.123	1.138
Sept	1.053	1.041	1.057	1.065	1.080	1.079	1.074	1.076	1.084	1.094	1.106	1.106	1.117	1.108	1.123
Oct	1.037	1.026	1.042	1.049	1.064	1.063	1.058	1.060	1.068	1.078	1.090	1.090	1.100	1.092	1.107
Nov	1.020	1.008	1.024	1.032	1.046	1.046	1.041	1.043	1.051	1.061	1.073	1.073	1.083	1.074	1.089
Dec	1.015	1.003	1.019	1.027	1.041	1.040	1.035	1.038	1.045	1.056	1.067	1.067	1.077	1.069	1.084

MONTH OF DISPOSAL

	2013										***2014***			
1986	Mar	Apr	May	June	July	Aug	Sept	Oct	Nov	Dec	Jan	Feb	Mar	Apr
Jan	1.584	1.592	1.597	1.594	1.594	1.608	1.617	1.617	1.619	1.633	1.624	1.641	1.647	1.657
Feb	1.574	1.583	1.588	1.585	1.585	1.598	1.608	1.608	1.610	1.623	1.615	1.631	1.638	1.647
Mar	1.571	1.579	1.585	1.581	1.581	1.595	1.604	1.604	1.606	1.620	1.611	1.628	1.634	1.643
Apr	1.546	1.555	1.560	1.557	1.557	1.570	1.579	1.579	1.581	1.595	1.586	1.603	1.609	1.618
May	1.542	1.550	1.555	1.552	1.552	1.565	1.574	1.574	1.577	1.590	1.582	1.598	1.604	1.613
June	1.543	1.551	1.556	1.553	1.553	1.567	1.576	1.576	1.578	1.591	1.583	1.599	1.605	1.615
July	1.550	1.559	1.564	1.561	1.561	1.574	1.583	1.583	1.585	1.599	1.590	1.607	1.613	1.622
Aug	1.542	1.551	1.556	1.553	1.553	1.566	1.575	1.575	1.577	1.590	1.582	1.599	1.605	1.614
Sept	1.530	1.538	1.543	1.540	1.540	1.553	1.563	1.563	1.565	1.578	1.570	1.586	1.592	1.601
Oct	1.526	1.534	1.539	1.536	1.536	1.549	1.559	1.559	1.561	1.574	1.566	1.582	1.588	1.597
Nov	1.505	1.513	1.518	1.515	1.515	1.528	1.537	1.537	1.539	1.552	1.544	1.560	1.566	1.575
Dec	1.496	1.505	1.510	1.507	1.507	1.520	1.529	1.529	1.531	1.544	1.536	1.552	1.558	1.567
1987	Mar	Apr	May	June	July	Aug	Sept	Oct	Nov	Dec	Jan	Feb	Mar	Apr
Jan	1.487	1.495	1.500	1.497	1.497	1.510	1.519	1.519	1.521	1.534	1.526	1.542	1.548	1.557
Feb	1.477	1.485	1.490	1.487	1.487	1.500	1.509	1.509	1.511	1.524	1.516	1.532	1.538	1.547
Mar	1.472	1.480	1.485	1.482	1.482	1.495	1.504	1.504	1.506	1.519	1.511	1.527	1.533	1.542
Apr	1.443	1.451	1.456	1.453	1.453	1.466	1.474	1.474	1.476	1.489	1.481	1.497	1.503	1.512
May	1.441	1.448	1.453	1.450	1.450	1.463	1.472	1.472	1.474	1.487	1.479	1.495	1.500	1.509
June	1.441	1.448	1.453	1.450	1.450	1.463	1.472	1.472	1.474	1.487	1.479	1.495	1.500	1.509
July	1.443	1.451	1.456	1.453	1.453	1.466	1.474	1.474	1.476	1.489	1.481	1.497	1.503	1.512
Aug	1.436	1.444	1.449	1.446	1.446	1.458	1.467	1.467	1.469	1.482	1.474	1.490	1.496	1.504
Sept	1.429	1.437	1.441	1.438	1.438	1.451	1.460	1.460	1.462	1.475	1.467	1.482	1.488	1.497
Oct	1.417	1.425	1.430	1.427	1.427	1.439	1.448	1.448	1.450	1.463	1.455	1.470	1.476	1.485
Nov	1.405	1.413	1.418	1.415	1.415	1.427	1.436	1.436	1.438	1.451	1.443	1.458	1.464	1.473
Dec	1.408	1.415	1.420	1.417	1.417	1.430	1.439	1.439	1.440	1.453	1.445	1.461	1.467	1.475
1988	Mar	Apr	May	June	July	Aug	Sept	Oct	Nov	Dec	Jan	Feb	Mar	Apr
Jan	1.408	1.415	1.420	1.417	1.417	1.430	1.439	1.439	1.440	1.453	1.445	1.461	1.467	1.475
Feb	1.398	1.406	1.411	1.408	1.408	1.420	1.429	1.429	1.431	1.444	1.436	1.451	1.457	1.466
Mar	1.389	1.397	1.402	1.399	1.399	1.411	1.420	1.420	1.422	1.434	1.427	1.442	1.448	1.456
Apr	1.351	1.358	1.363	1.360	1.360	1.372	1.381	1.381	1.383	1.395	1.388	1.403	1.408	1.417
May	1.342	1.349	1.354	1.351	1.351	1.363	1.372	1.372	1.374	1.386	1.379	1.394	1.399	1.408
June	1.333	1.341	1.345	1.342	1.342	1.355	1.363	1.363	1.365	1.377	1.370	1.385	1.390	1.399
July	1.331	1.338	1.343	1.340	1.340	1.352	1.361	1.361	1.363	1.375	1.367	1.382	1.388	1.396
Aug	1.305	1.312	1.317	1.314	1.314	1.326	1.335	1.335	1.336	1.348	1.341	1.356	1.361	1.370
Sept	1.294	1.302	1.306	1.304	1.304	1.315	1.324	1.324	1.326	1.338	1.330	1.345	1.351	1.359
Oct	1.271	1.279	1.283	1.280	1.280	1.292	1.300	1.300	1.302	1.314	1.307	1.321	1.327	1.335
Nov	1.261	1.268	1.273	1.270	1.270	1.282	1.290	1.290	1.292	1.304	1.296	1.311	1.316	1.325
Dec	1.255	1.262	1.267	1.264	1.264	1.276	1.284	1.284	1.286	1.297	1.290	1.305	1.310	1.318
1989	Mar	Apr	May	June	July	Aug	Sept	Oct	Nov	Dec	Jan	Feb	Mar	Apr
Jan	1.241	1.248	1.252	1.250	1.250	1.261	1.269	1.269	1.271	1.283	1.276	1.290	1.295	1.304
Feb	1.225	1.232	1.236	1.233	1.233	1.245	1.253	1.253	1.255	1.267	1.259	1.274	1.279	1.287
Mar	1.215	1.222	1.226	1.224	1.224	1.235	1.243	1.243	1.245	1.256	1.249	1.264	1.269	1.277
Apr	1.176	1.183	1.187	1.185	1.185	1.196	1.204	1.204	1.206	1.217	1.210	1.224	1.229	1.237
May	1.163	1.170	1.174	1.171	1.171	1.183	1.190	1.190	1.192	1.203	1.197	1.210	1.216	1.223
June	1.155	1.162	1.166	1.164	1.164	1.175	1.183	1.183	1.185	1.196	1.189	1.203	1.208	1.216
July	1.153	1.160	1.165	1.162	1.162	1.173	1.181	1.181	1.183	1.194	1.187	1.201	1.206	1.214
Aug	1.148	1.155	1.159	1.156	1.156	1.168	1.175	1.175	1.177	1.188	1.181	1.195	1.200	1.208
Sept	1.133	1.140	1.144	1.142	1.142	1.153	1.160	1.160	1.162	1.173	1.166	1.180	1.185	1.193
Oct	1.117	1.123	1.128	1.125	1.125	1.136	1.144	1.144	1.146	1.157	1.150	1.163	1.169	1.176
Nov	1.099	1.105	1.110	1.107	1.107	1.118	1.126	1.126	1.127	1.138	1.132	1.145	1.150	1.158
Dec	1.093	1.100	1.104	1.102	1.102	1.113	1.120	1.120	1.122	1.133	1.126	1.140	1.145	1.152

MONTH OF DISPOSAL

	2011	2012											2013	
1990	Dec	Jan	Feb	Mar	Apr	May	June	July	Aug	Sept	Oct	Nov	Dec	Jan	Feb
Jan	1.003	.992	1.008	1.015	1.029	1.028	1.023	1.026	1.033	1.044	1.055	1.055	1.065	1.057	1.072
Feb	.992	.980	.996	1.003	1.017	1.017	1.012	1.014	1.022	1.032	1.043	1.043	1.053	1.045	1.060
Mar	.972	.960	.976	.984	.998	.997	.992	.994	1.002	1.012	1.023	1.023	1.033	1.025	1.040
Apr	.914	.902	.918	.925	.938	.938	.933	.935	.942	.952	.963	.963	.973	.965	.979
May	.897	.886	.901	.908	.922	.921	.916	.918	.926	.935	.946	.946	.956	.948	.962
June	.890	.878	.893	.901	.914	.913	.908	.911	.918	.927	.938	.938	.948	.940	.954
July	.888	.877	.892	.899	.912	.912	.907	.909	.916	.926	.937	.937	.946	.938	.953
Aug	.869	.858	.873	.880	.893	.892	.888	.890	.897	.906	.917	.917	.927	.919	.933
Sept	.852	.841	.855	.862	.875	.875	.870	.872	.879	.889	.899	.899	.909	.901	.915
Oct	.837	.827	.841	.848	.861	.860	.856	.858	.865	.874	.885	.885	.894	.886	.900
Nov	.842	.831	.845	.852	.865	.865	.860	.862	.869	.878	.889	.889	.898	.891	.905
Dec	.843	.832	.847	.854	.867	.866	.861	.864	.871	.880	.891	.891	.900	.892	.906
1991	Dec	Jan	Feb	Mar	Apr	May	June	July	Aug	Sept	Oct	Nov	Dec	Jan	Feb
Jan	.839	.828	.843	.849	.863	.862	.857	.859	.866	.876	.886	.886	.896	.888	.902
Feb	.829	.818	.833	.840	.853	.852	.847	.850	.856	.866	.876	.876	.885	.878	.892
Mar	.822	.811	.826	.833	.846	.845	.840	.842	.849	.858	.869	.869	.878	.871	.884
Apr	.799	.788	.802	.809	.822	.821	.817	.819	.826	.835	.845	.845	.854	.847	.860
May	.793	.783	.797	.804	.816	.816	.811	.813	.820	.829	.840	.840	.849	.841	.855
June	.785	.775	.789	.796	.808	.808	.803	.805	.812	.821	.831	.831	.840	.833	.846
July	.789	.779	.793	.800	.812	.812	.807	.809	.816	.825	.836	.836	.845	.837	.851
Aug	.785	.775	.789	.796	.808	.808	.803	.805	.812	.821	.831	.831	.840	.833	.846
Sept	.779	.768	.782	.789	.802	.801	.796	.799	.805	.814	.825	.825	.834	.826	.840
Oct	.772	.762	.776	.782	.795	.794	.790	.792	.799	.808	.818	.818	.827	.819	.833
Nov	.765	.755	.769	.776	.788	.788	.783	.785	.792	.801	.811	.811	.820	.813	.826
Dec	.764	.754	.768	.775	.787	.786	.782	.784	.791	.800	.810	.810	.819	.811	.825
1992	Dec	Jan	Feb	Mar	Apr	May	June	July	Aug	Sept	Oct	Nov	Dec	Jan	Feb
Jan	.765	.755	.769	.776	.788	.788	.783	.785	.792	.801	.811	.811	.820	.813	.826
Feb	.756	.746	.760	.767	.779	.778	.774	.776	.783	.792	.802	.802	.811	.803	.817
Mar	.751	.741	.755	.762	.774	.773	.769	.771	.778	.786	.797	.797	.805	.798	.811
Apr	.725	.715	.728	.735	.747	.746	.742	.744	.751	.759	.769	.769	.778	.771	.784
May	.719	.709	.722	.729	.741	.740	.736	.738	.744	.753	.763	.763	.772	.765	.777
June	.719	.709	.722	.729	.741	.740	.736	.738	.744	.753	.763	.763	.772	.765	.777
July	.725	.715	.728	.735	.747	.746	.742	.744	.751	.759	.769	.769	.778	.771	.784
Aug	.724	.713	.727	.734	.746	.745	.741	.743	.749	.758	.768	.768	.777	.770	.783
Sept	.717	.707	.721	.727	.740	.739	.735	.737	.743	.752	.762	.762	.770	.763	.776
Oct	.711	.701	.715	.721	.733	.733	.728	.731	.737	.746	.756	.756	.764	.757	.770
Nov	.714	.704	.717	.724	.736	.735	.731	.733	.739	.748	.758	.758	.767	.759	.772
Dec	.720	.710	.723	.730	.742	.741	.737	.739	.746	.754	.764	.764	.773	.766	.779
1993	Dec	Jan	Feb	Mar	Apr	May	June	July	Aug	Sept	Oct	Nov	Dec	Jan	Feb
Jan	.736	.726	.740	.746	.759	.758	.753	.756	.762	.771	.781	.781	.790	.782	.796
Feb	.725	.715	.728	.735	.747	.746	.742	.744	.751	.759	.769	.769	.778	.771	.784
Mar	.719	.709	.722	.729	.741	.740	.736	.738	.744	.753	.763	.763	.772	.765	.777
Apr	.703	.693	.706	.713	.725	.724	.720	.722	.728	.737	.747	.747	.755	.748	.761
May	.697	.687	.700	.707	.719	.718	.714	.716	.722	.731	.741	.741	.749	.742	.755
June	.698	.688	.701	.708	.720	.719	.715	.717	.723	.732	.742	.742	.750	.743	.756
July	.701	.692	.705	.711	.724	.723	.719	.721	.727	.736	.746	.746	.754	.747	.760
Aug	.694	.684	.698	.704	.716	.715	.711	.713	.720	.728	.738	.738	.747	.740	.752
Sept	.687	.677	.691	.697	.709	.708	.704	.706	.712	.721	.731	.731	.739	.732	.745
Oct	.688	.678	.692	.698	.710	.709	.705	.707	.714	.722	.732	.732	.740	.733	.746
Nov	.691	.681	.694	.701	.713	.712	.708	.710	.716	.725	.734	.734	.743	.736	.749
Dec	.687	.677	.691	.697	.709	.708	.704	.706	.712	.721	.731	.731	.739	.732	.745

MONTH OF DISPOSAL

	2013										***2014***			
1990	Mar	Apr	May	June	July	Aug	Sept	Oct	Nov	Dec	Jan	Feb	Mar	Apr
Jan	1.081	1.088	1.092	1.090	1.090	1.100	1.108	1.108	1.110	1.121	1.114	1.127	1.132	1.140
Feb	1.069	1.076	1.080	1.077	1.077	1.088	1.096	1.096	1.097	1.108	1.101	1.115	1.120	1.127
Mar	1.049	1.055	1.059	1.057	1.057	1.068	1.075	1.075	1.077	1.087	1.081	1.094	1.099	1.106
Apr	.988	.994	.998	.996	.996	1.006	1.014	1.014	1.015	1.026	1.019	1.032	1.037	1.044
May	.971	.977	.981	.979	.979	.989	.996	.996	.998	1.008	1.002	1.014	1.019	1.026
June	.963	.969	.973	.971	.971	.981	.988	.988	.990	1.000	.994	1.006	1.011	1.018
July	.961	.968	.972	.969	.969	.979	.987	.987	.988	.998	.992	1.005	1.009	1.017
Aug	.941	.948	.952	.949	.949	.959	.966	.966	.968	.978	.972	.984	.989	.996
Sept	.923	.930	933	931	931	.941	.948	.948	.950	.960	.954	.966	.971	.978
Oct	.909	.915	.919	.916	.916	.926	.933	.933	.935	.945	.939	.951	.955	.962
Nov	.913	.919	.923	.921	.921	.931	.938	.938	.939	.949	.943	.955	.960	.967
Dec	.915	.921	.925	.922	.922	.932	.939	.939	.941	.951	.945	.957	.962	.968
1991	Mar	Apr	May	June	July	Aug	Sept	Oct	Nov	Dec	Jan	Feb	Mar	Apr
Jan	.910	.916	.920	.918	.918	.928	.935	.935	.936	.946	.940	.952	.957	.964
Feb	.900	.906	.910	.908	.908	.917	.924	.924	.926	.936	.930	.942	.947	.953
Mar	.893	.899	.903	.900	.900	.910	.917	.917	.919	.928	.922	.935	.939	.946
Apr	.869	.875	.878	.876	.876	.886	.893	.893	.894	.904	.898	.910	.914	.921
May	.863	.869	.873	.870	.870	.880	.887	.887	.888	.898	.892	.904	.909	.915
June	.855	.861	.864	.862	.862	.872	.878	.878	.880	.890	.884	.896	.900	.907
July	.859	.865	.868	.866	.866	.876	.883	.883	.884	.894	.888	.900	.904	.911
Aug	.855	.861	.864	.862	.862	.872	.878	.878	.880	.890	.884	.896	.900	.907
Sept	.848	.854	.857	.855	.855	.865	.871	.871	.873	.883	.877	.889	.893	.900
Oct	.841	.847	.850	.848	.848	.858	.865	.865	.866	.876	.870	.882	.886	.893
Nov	.834	.840	.844	.841	.841	.851	.858	.858	.859	.869	.863	.875	.879	.886
Dec	.833	.839	.842	.840	.840	.850	.856	.856	.858	.867	.861	.873	.878	.884
1992	Mar	Apr	May	June	July	Aug	Sept	Oct	Nov	Dec	Jan	Feb	Mar	Apr
Jan	.834	.840	.844	.841	.841	.851	.858	.858	.859	.869	.863	.875	.879	.886
Feb	.825	.831	.834	.832	.832	.842	.848	.848	.850	.859	.853	.865	.869	.876
Mar	.819	.825	.829	.827	.827	.836	.843	.843	.844	.854	.848	.860	.864	.871
Apr	.792	.798	.801	.799	.799	.808	.815	.815	.816	.826	.820	.831	.836	.842
May	.785	.791	.795	.793	.793	.802	.808	.808	.810	.819	.813	.825	.829	.836
June	.785	.791	.795	.793	.793	.802	.808	.808	.810	.819	.813	.825	.829	.836
July	.792	.798	.801	.799	.799	.808	.815	.815	.816	.826	.820	.831	.836	.842
Aug	.790	.796	.800	.798	.798	.807	.814	.814	.815	.824	.819	.830	.834	.841
Sept	.784	.790	.793	.791	.791	.801	.807	.807	.808	.818	.812	.824	.828	.834
Oct	.778	.783	.787	.785	.785	.794	.801	.801	.802	.811	.806	.817	.821	.828
Nov	.780	.786	.790	.787	.787	.797	.803	.803	.805	.814	.808	.820	.824	.830
Dec	.787	.792	.796	.794	.794	.803	.810	.810	.811	.820	.815	.826	.830	.837
1993	Mar	Apr	May	June	July	Aug	Sept	Oct	Nov	Dec	Jan	Feb	Mar	Apr
Jan	.803	.809	.813	.811	.811	.820	.827	.827	.828	.838	.832	.843	.848	.854
Feb	.792	.798	.801	.799	.799	.808	.815	.815	.816	.826	.820	.831	.836	.842
Mar	.785	.791	.795	.793	.793	.802	.808	.808	.810	.819	.813	.825	.829	.836
Apr	.769	.775	.778	.776	.776	.785	.792	.792	.793	.802	.797	.808	.812	.819
May	.763	.768	.772	.770	.770	.779	.785	.785	.787	.796	.790	.802	.806	.812
June	.764	.770	.773	.771	.771	.780	.787	.787	.788	.797	.791	.803	.807	.813
July	.768	.773	.777	.775	.775	.784	.790	.790	.792	.801	.795	.807	.811	.817
Aug	.760	.766	.769	.767	.767	.776	.783	.783	.784	.793	.788	.799	.803	.810
Sept	.753	.758	.762	.760	.760	.769	.775	.775	.777	.786	.780	.791	.796	.802
Oct	.754	.760	.763	.761	.761	.770	.776	.776	.778	.787	.781	.793	.797	.803
Nov	.756	.762	.766	.763	.763	.773	.779	.779	.780	.790	.784	.795	.799	.806
Dec	.753	.758	.762	.760	.760	.769	.775	.775	.777	.786	.780	.791	.796	.802

MONTH OF DISPOSAL

	2011	***2012***											***2013***	
1994	Dec	Jan	Feb	Mar	Apr	May	June	July	Aug	Sept	Oct	Nov	Dec	Jan	Feb
Jan	.694	.684	.698	.704	.716	.715	.711	.713	.720	.728	.738	.738	.747	.740	.752
Feb	.685	.675	.688	.695	.707	.706	.702	.704	.710	.719	.728	.728	.737	.730	.742
Mar	.680	.670	.684	.690	.702	.701	.697	.699	.705	.714	.724	.724	.732	.725	.738
Apr	.660	.650	.664	.670	.682	.681	.677	.679	.685	.693	.703	.703	.712	.705	.717
May	.654	.645	.658	.664	.676	.675	.671	.673	.679	.688	.697	.697	.706	.699	.711
June	.654	.645	.658	.664	.676	.675	.671	.673	.679	.688	.697	.697	.706	.699	.711
July	.663	.653	.666	.672	.684	.683	.679	.681	.688	.696	.706	.706	.714	.707	.719
Aug	.654	.645	.658	.664	.676	.675	.671	.673	.679	.688	.697	.697	.706	.699	.711
Sept	.651	.641	.654	.661	.672	.672	.668	.670	.676	.684	.694	.694	.702	.695	.708
Oct	.649	.639	.652	.658	.670	.669	.665	.667	.674	.682	.691	.691	.700	.693	.705
Nov	.648	.638	.651	.657	.669	.668	.664	.666	.672	.681	.690	.690	.699	.692	.704
Dec	.640	.630	.643	.649	.661	.660	.656	.658	.664	.673	.682	.682	.690	.684	.696
1995	Dec	Jan	Feb	Mar	Apr	May	June	July	Aug	Sept	Oct	Nov	Dec	Jan	Feb
Jan	.640	.630	.643	.649	.661	.660	.656	.658	.664	.673	.682	.682	.690	.684	.696
Feb	.630	.620	.633	.639	.651	.650	.646	.648	.654	.662	.672	.672	.680	.673	.686
Mar	.623	.614	.626	.633	.644	.643	.639	.641	.647	.656	.665	.665	.673	.666	.679
Apr	.607	.597	.610	.616	.628	.627	.623	.625	.631	.639	.648	.648	.656	.650	.662
May	.600	.591	.604	.610	.621	.620	.616	.618	.624	.632	.642	.642	.650	.643	.655
June	.598	.589	.601	.607	.619	.618	.614	.616	.622	.630	.640	.640	.648	.641	.653
July	.606	.596	.609	.615	.626	.626	.622	.624	.630	.638	.647	.647	.655	.649	.661
Aug	.597	.588	.600	.606	.618	.617	.613	.615	.621	.629	.638	.638	.646	.640	.652
Sept	.590	.580	.593	.599	.610	.610	.606	.608	.614	.622	.631	.631	.639	.632	.644
Oct	.598	.589	.601	.607	.619	.618	.614	.616	.622	.630	.640	.640	.648	.641	.653
Nov	.598	.589	.601	.607	.619	.618	.614	.616	.622	.630	.640	.640	.648	.641	.653
Dec	.589	.579	.592	.598	.609	.608	.605	.607	.612	.620	.630	.630	.638	.631	.643
1996	Dec	Jan	Feb	Mar	Apr	May	June	July	Aug	Sept	Oct	Nov	Dec	Jan	Feb
Jan	.594	.585	.597	.603	.615	.614	.610	.612	.618	.626	.635	.635	.643	.636	.648
Feb	.586	.577	.590	.596	.607	.606	.602	.604	.610	.618	.628	.628	.636	.629	.641
Mar	.580	.571	.583	.589	.601	.600	.596	.598	.604	.612	.621	.621	.629	.622	.634
Apr	.569	.560	.572	.578	.589	.588	.585	.587	.592	.600	.609	.609	.617	.611	.623
May	.566	.557	.569	.575	.586	.585	.581	.583	.589	.597	.606	.606	.614	.608	.619
June	.565	.556	.568	.574	.585	.584	.580	.582	.588	.596	.605	.605	.613	.607	.618
July	.571	.562	.574	.580	.591	.591	.587	.589	.594	.602	.612	.612	.619	.613	.625
Aug	.564	.555	.567	.573	.584	.583	.579	.581	.587	.595	.604	.604	.612	.605	.617
Sept	.557	.547	.560	.566	.577	.576	.572	.574	.580	.588	.597	.597	.605	.598	.610
Oct	.557	.547	.560	.566	.577	.576	.572	.574	.580	.588	.597	.597	.605	.598	.610
Nov	.556	.546	.559	.565	.576	.575	.571	.573	.579	.587	.596	.596	.604	.597	.609
Dec	.551	.541	.554	.560	.571	.570	.566	.568	.574	.582	.591	.591	.598	.592	.604
1997	Dec	Jan	Feb	Mar	Apr	May	June	July	Aug	Sept	Oct	Nov	Dec	Jan	Feb
Jan	.551	.541	.554	.560	.571	.570	.566	.568	.574	.582	.591	.591	.598	.592	.604
Feb	.545	.535	.548	.554	.565	.564	.560	.562	.568	.575	.585	.585	.592	.586	.597
Mar	.541	.532	.544	.550	.560	.560	.556	.558	.564	.571	.580	.580	.588	.582	.593
Apr	.532	.523	.535	.541	.552	.551	.547	.549	.555	.562	.571	.571	.579	.573	.584
May	.526	.517	.529	.535	.546	.545	.541	.543	.549	.556	.565	.565	.573	.567	.578
June	.520	.511	.523	.529	.540	.539	.535	.537	.543	.550	.559	.559	.567	.561	.572
July	.520	.511	.523	.529	.540	.539	.535	.537	.543	.550	.559	.559	.567	.561	.572
Aug	.510	.502	.514	.519	.530	.529	.526	.527	.533	.541	.550	.550	.557	.551	.562
Sept	.503	.494	.506	.512	.522	.522	.518	.520	.525	.533	.542	.542	.549	.543	.554
Oct	.501	.492	.504	.510	.520	.520	.516	.518	.524	.531	.540	.540	.547	.541	.552
Nov	.500	.491	.503	.509	.519	.519	.515	.517	.523	.530	.539	.539	.546	.540	.551
Dec	.496	.488	.499	.505	.516	.515	.511	.513	.519	.526	.535	.535	.543	.536	.548

MONTH OF DISPOSAL

	2013										**2014**			
1994	Mar	Apr	May	June	July	Aug	Sept	Oct	Nov	Dec	Jan	Feb	Mar	Apr
Jan	.760	.766	.769	.767	.767	.776	.783	.783	.784	.793	.788	.799	.803	.810
Feb	.750	.756	.759	.757	.757	.766	.773	.773	.774	.783	.778	.789	.793	.799
Mar	.745	.751	.754	.752	.752	.761	.768	.768	.769	.778	.773	.784	.788	.794
Apr	.725	.730	.734	.732	.732	.741	.747	.747	.748	.757	.752	.763	.767	.773
May	.719	.724	.728	.726	.726	.735	.741	.741	.742	.751	.746	.757	.761	.767
June	.719	.724	.728	.726	.726	.735	.741	.741	.742	.751	.746	.757	.761	.767
July	.727	.733	.736	.734	.734	.743	.749	.749	.751	.760	.754	.765	.769	.776
Aug	.719	.724	.728	.726	.726	.735	.741	.741	.742	.751	.746	.757	.761	.767
Sept	.715	.721	.724	.722	.722	.731	.737	.737	.739	.748	.742	.753	.757	.763
Oct	.713	.718	.722	.720	.720	.729	.735	.735	.736	.745	.740	.751	.755	.761
Nov	.712	.717	.721	.719	.719	.727	.734	.734	.735	.744	.738	.749	.754	.760
Dec	.703	.709	.712	.710	.710	.719	.725	.725	.727	.736	.730	.741	.745	.751
1995	Mar	Apr	May	June	July	Aug	Sept	Oct	Nov	Dec	Jan	Feb	Mar	Apr
Jan	.703	.709	.712	.710	.710	.719	.725	.725	.727	.736	.730	.741	.745	.751
Feb	.693	.698	.702	.700	.700	.709	.715	.715	.716	.725	.720	.730	.735	.741
Mar	.686	.692	.695	.693	.693	.702	.708	.708	.709	.718	.713	.723	.727	.734
Apr	.669	.674	.678	.676	.676	.685	.691	.691	.692	.701	.695	.706	.710	.716
May	.662	.668	.671	.669	.669	.678	.684	.684	.685	.694	.689	.699	.703	.709
June	.660	.666	.669	.667	.667	.676	.682	.682	.683	.692	.686	.697	.701	.707
July	.668	.673	.677	.675	.675	.683	.689	.689	.691	.700	.694	.705	.709	.715
Aug	.659	.664	.668	.666	.666	.674	.680	.680	.682	.690	.685	.696	.700	.706
Sept	.651	.657	.660	.658	.658	.667	.673	.673	.674	.683	.677	.688	.692	.698
Oct	.660	.666	.669	.667	.667	.676	.682	.682	.683	.692	.686	.697	.701	.707
Nov	.660	.666	.669	.667	.667	.676	.682	.682	.683	.692	.686	.697	.701	.707
Dec	.650	.656	.659	.657	.657	.666	.672	.672	.673	.681	.676	.687	.691	.697
1996	Mar	Apr	May	June	July	Aug	Sept	Oct	Nov	Dec	Jan	Feb	Mar	Apr
Jan	.656	.661	.664	.662	.662	.671	.677	.677	.678	.687	.682	.692	.696	.702
Feb	.648	.653	.657	.655	.655	.663	.669	.669	.671	.679	.674	.685	.689	.694
Mar	.642	.647	.650	.648	.648	.657	.663	.663	.664	.673	.667	.678	.682	.688
Apr	.630	.635	.638	.636	.636	.645	.651	.651	.652	.661	.655	.666	.670	.676
May	.627	.632	.635	.633	.633	.642	.647	.647	.649	.657	.652	.663	.666	.672
June	.625	.631	.634	.632	.632	.641	.646	.646	.648	.656	.651	.661	.665	.671
July	.632	.637	.640	.638	.638	.647	.653	.653	.654	.663	.657	.668	.672	.678
Aug	.624	.630	.633	.631	.631	.639	.645	.645	.647	.655	.650	.660	.664	.670
Sept	.617	.622	.625	.624	.624	.632	.638	.638	.639	.648	.642	.653	.657	.663
Oct	.617	.622	.625	.624	.624	.632	.638	.638	.639	.648	.642	.653	.657	.663
Nov	.616	.621	.624	.622	.622	.631	.637	.637	.638	.647	.641	.652	.656	.661
Dec	.611	.616	.619	.617	.617	.626	.631	.631	.633	.641	.636	.646	.650	.656
1997	Mar	Apr	May	June	July	Aug	Sept	Oct	Nov	Dec	Jan	Feb	Mar	Apr
Jan	.611	.616	.619	.617	.617	.626	.631	.631	.633	.641	.636	.646	.650	.656
Feb	.605	.610	.613	.611	.611	.619	.625	.625	.626	.635	.630	.640	.644	.650
Mar	.600	.606	.609	.607	.607	.615	.621	.621	.622	.631	.625	.636	.640	.645
Apr	.591	.596	.599	.598	.598	.606	.612	.612	.613	.621	.616	.626	.630	.636
May	.585	.590	.593	.591	.591	.600	.605	.605	.607	.615	.610	.620	.624	.630
June	.579	.584	.587	.585	.585	.594	.599	.599	.601	.609	.604	.614	.618	.623
July	.579	.584	.587	.585	.585	.594	.599	.599	.601	.609	.604	.614	.618	.623
Aug	.569	.574	.577	.575	.575	.584	.589	.589	.591	.599	.594	.604	.608	.613
Sept	.561	.566	.569	.567	.567	.576	.581	.581	.583	.591	.586	.596	.599	.605
Oct	.559	.564	.567	.566	.566	.574	.579	.579	.581	.589	.584	.594	.597	.603
Nov	.558	.563	.566	.565	.565	.573	.578	.578	.580	.588	.583	.593	.596	.602
Dec	.554	.559	.563	.561	.561	.569	.574	.574	.576	.584	.579	.589	.593	.598

MONTH OF DISPOSAL

	2011	**2012**												**2013**	
1998	Dec	Jan	Feb	Mar	Apr	May	June	July	Aug	Sept	Oct	Nov	Dec	Jan	Feb
Jan	.501	.492	.504	.510	.520	.520	.516	.518	.524	.531	.540	.540	.547	.541	.552
Feb	.493	.485	.497	.502	.513	.512	.508	.510	.516	.523	.532	.532	.540	.533	.545
Mar	.489	.480	.492	.498	.508	.507	.504	.506	.511	.519	.527	.527	.535	.529	.540
Apr	.472	.464	.475	.481	.491	.491	.487	.489	.494	.502	.510	.510	.518	.512	.523
May	.464	.456	.467	.473	.483	.483	.479	.481	.486	.494	.502	.502	.509	.503	.514
June	.465	.457	.468	.474	.484	.483	.480	.482	.487	.494	.503	.503	.510	.504	.515
July	.469	.460	.472	.477	.488	.487	.483	.485	.491	.498	.507	.507	.514	.508	.519
Aug	.462	.454	.465	.471	.481	.481	.477	.479	.484	.492	.500	.500	.508	.502	.513
Sept	.456	.448	.459	.465	.475	.474	.471	.473	.478	.485	.494	.494	.501	.495	.506
Oct	.455	.447	.458	.464	.474	.474	.470	.472	.477	.484	.493	.493	.500	.494	.505
Nov	.456	.448	.459	.465	.475	.474	.471	.473	.478	.485	.494	.494	.501	.495	.506
Dec	.456	.448	.459	.465	.475	.474	.471	.473	.478	.485	.494	.494	.501	.495	.506
1999	Dec	Jan	Feb	Mar	Apr	May	June	July	Aug	Sept	Oct	Nov	Dec	Jan	Feb
Jan	.465	.457	.468	.474	.484	.483	.480	.482	.487	.494	.503	.503	.510	.504	.515
Feb	.462	.454	.465	.471	.481	.481	.477	.479	.484	.492	.500	.500	.508	.502	.513
Mar	.459	.450	.462	.467	.478	.477	.473	.475	.481	.488	.497	.497	.504	.498	.509
Apr	.449	.441	.452	.458	.468	.467	.464	.465	.471	.478	.487	.487	.494	.488	.499
May	.446	.437	.449	.454	.464	.464	.460	.462	.467	.475	.483	.483	.490	.484	.495
June	.446	.437	.449	.454	.464	.464	.460	.462	.467	.475	.483	.483	.490	.484	.495
July	.450	.442	.453	.459	.469	.468	.465	.466	.472	.479	.488	.488	.495	.489	.500
Aug	.447	.438	.450	.455	.465	.465	.461	.463	.468	.476	.484	.484	.491	.485	.496
Sept	.440	.432	.443	.449	.459	.458	.455	.457	.462	.469	.478	.478	.485	.479	.490
Oct	.438	.429	.441	.446	.456	.456	.452	.454	.459	.467	.475	.475	.482	.476	.487
Nov	.436	.428	.439	.445	.455	.454	.451	.452	.458	.465	.473	.473	.481	.475	.485
Dec	.431	.423	.434	.439	.449	.449	.445	.447	.452	.460	.468	.468	.475	.469	.480
2000	Dec	Jan	Feb	Mar	Apr	May	June	July	Aug	Sept	Oct	Nov	Dec	Jan	Feb
Jan	.437	.429	.440	.445	.456	.455	.451	.453	.459	.466	.474	.474	.481	.475	.486
Feb	.429	.421	.432	.438	.448	.447	.444	.445	.451	.458	.466	.466	.473	.467	.478
Mar	.422	.413	.425	.430	.440	.439	.436	.438	.443	.450	.458	.458	.466	.460	.470
Apr	.407	.399	.410	.416	.426	.425	.422	.423	.429	.436	.444	.444	.451	.445	.456
May	.402	.394	.405	.411	.421	.420	.417	.418	.424	.431	.439	.439	.446	.440	.450
June	.399	.391	.402	.407	.417	.417	.413	.415	.420	.427	.435	.435	.442	.437	.447
July	.404	.396	.407	.412	.422	.422	.418	.420	.425	.432	.440	.440	.448	.442	.452
Aug	.404	.396	.407	.412	.422	.422	.418	.420	.425	.432	.440	.440	.448	.442	.452
Sept	.394	.386	.397	.402	.412	.412	.408	.410	.415	.422	.430	.430	.437	.432	.442
Oct	.395	.387	.398	.403	.413	.413	.409	.411	.416	.423	.431	.431	.438	.432	.443
Nov	.391	.383	.394	.399	.409	.408	.405	.407	.412	.419	.427	.427	.434	.428	.439
Dec	.390	.382	.393	.398	.408	.408	.404	.406	.411	.418	.426	.426	.433	.427	.438
2001	Dec	Jan	Feb	Mar	Apr	May	June	July	Aug	Sept	Oct	Nov	Dec	Jan	Feb
Jan	.399	.391	.402	.407	.417	.417	.413	.415	.420	.427	.435	.435	.442	.437	.447
Feb	.392	.384	.395	.400	.410	.409	.406	.408	.413	.420	.428	.428	.435	.429	.440
Mar	.390	.382	.393	.398	.408	.408	.404	.406	.411	.418	.426	.426	.433	.427	.438
Apr	.383	.375	.386	.391	.401	.400	.397	.399	.404	.411	.419	.419	.426	.420	.430
May	.374	.366	.377	.382	.392	.392	.388	.390	.395	.402	.410	.410	.417	.411	.421
June	.373	.365	.376	.381	.390	.390	.386	.388	.393	.400	.408	.408	.415	.409	.420
July	.381	.373	.384	.389	.399	.399	.395	.397	.402	.409	.417	.417	.424	.418	.429
Aug	.376	.368	.379	.384	.394	.393	.390	.391	.397	.403	.411	.411	.418	.413	.423
Sept	.371	.363	.374	.379	.389	.388	.385	.387	.392	.399	.407	.407	.414	.408	.418
Oct	.373	.365	.376	.382	.391	.391	.387	.389	.394	.401	.409	.409	.416	.410	.421
Nov	.379	.371	.382	.387	.397	.396	.393	.395	.400	.407	.415	.415	.422	.416	.426
Dec	.381	.373	.384	.389	.399	.398	.394	.396	.401	.408	.416	.416	.423	.418	.428

MONTH OF DISPOSAL

	2013										2014			
1998	Mar	Apr	May	June	July	Aug	Sept	Oct	Nov	Dec	Jan	Feb	Mar	Apr
Jan	.559	.564	.567	.566	.566	.574	.579	.579	.581	.589	.584	.594	.597	.603
Feb	.551	.556	.560	.558	.558	.566	.571	.571	.573	.581	.576	.586	.590	.595
Mar	.547	.552	.555	.553	.553	.561	.567	.567	.568	.576	.571	.581	.585	.590
Apr	.530	.534	.538	.536	.536	.544	.549	.549	.550	.558	.554	.563	.567	.573
May	.521	.526	.529	.527	.527	.535	.541	.541	.542	.550	.545	.555	.558	.564
June	.522	.527	.530	.528	.528	.536	.542	.542	.543	.551	.546	.556	.559	.565
July	.526	.531	.534	.532	.532	.540	.545	.545	.547	.555	.550	.560	.563	.569
Aug	.519	.524	.527	.525	.525	.533	.539	.539	.540	.548	.543	.553	.557	.562
Sept	.513	.518	.521	.519	.519	.527	.532	.532	.533	.541	.536	.546	.550	.555
Oct	.512	.517	.520	.518	.518	.526	.531	.531	.533	.540	.536	.545	.549	.554
Nov	.513	.518	.521	.519	.519	.527	.532	.532	.533	.541	.536	.546	.550	.555
Dec	.513	.518	.521	.519	.519	.527	.532	.532	.533	.541	.536	.546	.550	.555
1999	Mar	Apr	May	June	July	Aug	Sept	Oct	Nov	Dec	Jan	Feb	Mar	Apr
Jan	.522	.527	.530	.528	.528	.536	.542	.542	.543	.551	.546	.556	.559	.565
Feb	.519	.524	.527	.525	.525	.533	.539	.539	.540	.548	.543	.553	.557	.562
Mar	.516	.520	.523	.522	.522	.530	.535	.535	.536	.544	.539	.549	.553	.558
Apr	.505	.510	.513	.512	.512	.519	.525	.525	.526	.534	.529	.539	.542	.548
May	.502	.507	.510	.508	.508	.516	.521	.521	.522	.530	.525	.535	.539	.544
June	.502	.507	.510	.508	.508	.516	.521	.521	.522	.530	.525	.535	.539	.544
July	.506	.511	.514	.512	.512	.520	.526	.526	.527	.535	.530	.540	.543	.549
Aug	.503	.508	.511	.509	.509	.517	.522	.522	.523	.531	.526	.536	.540	.545
Sept	.496	.501	.504	.502	.502	.510	.516	.516	.517	.525	.520	.529	.533	.539
Oct	.494	.498	.502	.500	.500	.508	.513	.513	.514	.522	.517	.527	.530	.536
Nov	.492	.497	.500	.498	.498	.506	.511	.511	.512	.520	.515	.525	.528	.534
Dec	.487	.491	.494	.493	.493	.500	.506	.506	.507	.515	.510	.519	.523	.528
2000	Mar	Apr	May	June	July	Aug	Sept	Oct	Nov	Dec	Jan	Feb	Mar	Apr
Jan	.493	.498	.501	.499	.499	.507	.512	.512	.513	.521	.516	.526	.529	.535
Feb	.485	.490	.493	.491	.491	.499	.504	.504	.505	.513	.508	.518	.521	.527
Mar	.477	.482	.485	.483	.483	.490	.496	.496	.497	.505	.500	.510	.513	.518
Apr	.462	.467	.470	.468	.468	.476	.481	.481	.482	.490	.485	.494	.498	.503
May	.457	.462	.465	.463	.463	.470	.476	.476	.477	.484	.480	.489	.493	.498
June	.454	.458	.461	.459	.459	.467	.472	.472	.473	.481	.476	.486	.489	.494
July	.459	.463	.466	.465	.465	.472	.477	.477	.479	.486	.482	.491	.494	.500
Aug	.459	.463	.466	.465	.465	.472	.477	.477	.479	.486	.482	.491	.494	.500
Sept	.448	.453	.456	.454	.454	.462	.467	.467	.468	.476	.471	.480	.484	.489
Oct	.449	.454	.457	.455	.455	.463	.468	.468	.469	.477	.472	.481	.485	.490
Nov	.445	.450	.453	.451	.451	.458	.464	.464	.465	.472	.468	.477	.481	.486
Dec	.444	.449	.452	.450	.450	.458	.463	.463	.464	.472	.467	.476	.480	.485
2001	Mar	Apr	May	June	July	Aug	Sept	Oct	Nov	Dec	Jan	Feb	Mar	Apr
Jan	.454	.458	.461	.459	.459	.467	.472	.472	.473	.481	.476	.486	.489	.494
Feb	.446	.451	.453	.452	.452	.459	.465	.465	.466	.473	.469	.478	.481	.487
Mar	.444	.449	.452	.450	.450	.458	.463	.463	.464	.472	.467	.476	.480	.485
Apr	.437	.441	.444	.443	.443	.450	.455	.455	.456	.464	.459	.469	.472	.477
May	.428	.432	.435	.433	.433	.441	.446	.446	.447	.455	.450	.459	.463	.468
June	.426	.431	.433	.432	.432	.439	.444	.444	.446	.453	.448	.458	.461	.466
July	.435	.440	.443	.441	.441	.448	.454	.454	.455	.462	.458	.467	.470	.475
Aug	.429	.434	.437	.435	.435	.443	.448	.448	.449	.456	.452	.461	.464	.470
Sept	.424	.429	.432	.430	.430	.438	.443	.443	.444	.451	.447	.456	.459	.464
Oct	.427	.431	.434	.433	.433	.440	.445	.445	.446	.454	.449	.458	.462	.467
Nov	.433	.437	.440	.438	.438	.446	.451	.451	.452	.460	.455	.464	.468	.473
Dec	.434	.439	.442	.440	.440	.448	.453	.453	.454	.461	.457	.466	.469	.475

MONTH OF DISPOSAL

	2011	**2012**											**2013**	
2002	Dec	Jan	Feb	Mar	Apr	May	June	July	Aug	Sept	Oct	Nov	Dec	Jan	Feb
Jan	.381	.373	.384	.389	.399	.399	.395	.397	.402	.409	.417	.417	.424	.418	.429
Feb	.377	.369	.380	.386	.395	.395	.391	.393	.398	.405	.413	.413	.420	.414	.425
Mar	.372	.364	.375	.380	.390	.389	.386	.387	.393	.399	.407	.407	.414	.409	.419
Apr	.363	.355	.365	.371	.380	.380	.376	.378	.383	.390	.398	.398	.405	.399	.409
May	.359	.351	.362	.367	.376	.376	.372	.374	.379	.386	.394	.394	.401	.395	.405
June	.359	.351	.362	.367	.376	.376	.372	.374	.379	.386	.394	.394	.401	.395	.405
July	.361	.353	.364	.369	.379	.378	.375	.376	.381	.388	.396	.396	.403	.397	.408
Aug	.357	.349	.360	.365	.375	.374	.371	.372	.378	.384	.392	.392	.399	.393	.404
Sept	.348	.340	.351	.356	.365	.365	.361	.363	.368	.375	.383	.383	.390	.384	.394
Oct	.346	.338	.349	.354	.363	.363	.359	.361	.366	.373	.381	.381	.387	.382	.392
Nov	.343	.336	.346	.351	.361	.360	.357	.359	.364	.370	.378	.378	.385	.379	.389
Dec	.341	.333	.344	.349	.359	.358	.355	.356	.361	.368	.376	.376	.383	.377	.387
2003	Dec	Jan	Feb	Mar	Apr	May	June	July	Aug	Sept	Oct	Nov	Dec	Jan	Feb
Jan	.342	.334	.345	.350	.359	.359	.355	.357	.362	.369	.377	.377	.383	.378	.388
Feb	.335	.327	.338	.343	.352	.352	.349	.350	.355	.362	.370	.370	.376	.371	.381
Mar	.331	.323	.334	.339	.348	.347	.344	.346	.351	.357	.365	.365	.372	.366	.376
Apr	.321	.313	.324	.329	.338	.338	.334	.336	.341	.348	.355	.355	.362	.357	.366
May	.319	.311	.322	.327	.336	.336	.332	.334	.339	.345	.353	.353	.360	.354	.364
June	.320	.313	.323	.328	.338	.337	.334	.335	.340	.347	.355	.355	.361	.356	.366
July	.320	.313	.323	.328	.338	.337	.334	.335	.340	.347	.355	.355	.361	.356	.366
Aug	.318	.311	.321	.326	.335	.335	.331	.333	.338	.345	.352	.352	.359	.354	.363
Sept	.312	.304	.315	.319	.329	.328	.325	.327	.332	.338	.346	.346	.352	.347	.357
Oct	.311	.303	.314	.319	.328	.327	.324	.326	.331	.337	.345	.345	.352	.346	.356
Nov	.310	.303	.313	.318	.327	.327	.323	.325	.330	.337	.344	.344	.351	.345	.355
Dec	.305	.297	.307	.312	.322	.321	.318	.319	.324	.331	.338	.338	.345	.340	.349
2004	Dec	Jan	Feb	Mar	Apr	May	June	July	Aug	Sept	Oct	Nov	Dec	Jan	Feb
Jan	.307	.300	.310	.315	.324	.324	.321	.322	.327	.334	.341	.341	.348	.342	.352
Feb	.303	.295	.305	.310	.319	.319	.316	.317	.322	.329	.336	.336	.343	.337	.347
Mar	.297	.289	.300	.304	.314	.313	.310	.311	.316	.323	.330	.330	.337	.332	.341
Apr	.289	.282	.292	.297	.306	.305	.302	.304	.309	.315	.323	.323	.329	.324	.333
May	.284	.276	.286	.291	.300	.300	.297	.298	.303	.309	.317	.317	.323	.318	.328
June	.282	.274	.284	.289	.298	.298	.294	.296	.301	.307	.315	.315	.321	.316	.325
July	.282	.274	.284	.289	.298	.298	.294	.296	.301	.307	.315	.315	.321	.316	.325
Aug	.277	.270	.280	.285	.294	.293	.290	.292	.297	.303	.311	.311	.317	.312	.321
Sept	.273	.265	.275	.280	.289	.289	.285	.287	.292	.298	.306	.306	.312	.307	.316
Oct	.269	.262	.272	.277	.286	.285	.282	.284	.288	.295	.302	.302	.309	.303	.313
Nov	.267	.259	.269	.274	.283	.283	.279	.281	.286	.292	.299	.299	.306	.301	.310
Dec	.261	.253	.263	.268	.277	.276	.273	.275	.280	.286	.293	.293	.300	.294	.304
2005	Dec	Jan	Feb	Mar	Apr	May	June	July	Aug	Sept	Oct	Nov	Dec	Jan	Feb
Jan	.267	.260	.270	.275	.284	.283	.280	.282	.286	.293	.300	.300	.307	.301	.311
Feb	.263	.255	.265	.270	.279	.278	.275	.277	.282	.288	.295	.295	.302	.296	.306
Mar	.257	.249	.259	.264	.273	.272	.269	.271	.276	.282	.289	.289	.296	.290	.300
Apr	.249	.242	.252	.257	.266	.265	.262	.264	.268	.275	.282	.282	.288	.283	.292
May	.247	.240	.249	.254	.263	.263	.259	.261	.266	.272	.279	.279	.285	.280	.290
June	.246	.238	.248	.253	.262	.261	.258	.260	.264	.271	.278	.278	.284	.279	.288
July	.246	.238	.248	.253	.262	.261	.258	.260	.264	.271	.278	.278	.284	.279	.288
Aug	.243	.236	.246	.250	.259	.259	.255	.257	.262	.268	.275	.275	.281	.276	.286
Sept	.240	.233	.242	.247	.256	.255	.252	.254	.258	.265	.272	.272	.278	.273	.282
Oct	.238	.231	.241	.246	.255	.254	.251	.252	.257	.263	.271	.271	.277	.272	.281
Nov	.237	.229	.239	.244	.253	.252	.249	.251	.255	.261	.269	.269	.275	.270	.279
Dec	.233	.226	.236	.241	.249	.249	.246	.247	.252	.258	.265	.265	.272	.266	.276

MONTH OF DISPOSAL

	2013										***2014***			
2002	Mar	Apr	May	June	July	Aug	Sept	Oct	Nov	Dec	Jan	Feb	Mar	Apr
Jan	.435	.440	.443	.441	.441	.448	.454	.454	.455	.462	.458	.467	.470	.475
Feb	.431	.436	.438	.437	.437	.444	.449	.449	.451	.458	.453	.463	.466	.471
Mar	.425	.430	.433	.431	.431	.438	.444	.444	.445	.452	.448	.457	.460	.465
Apr	.415	.420	.423	.421	.421	.429	.434	.434	.435	.442	.438	.447	.450	.455
May	.411	.416	.419	.417	.417	.425	.430	.430	.431	.438	.434	.443	.446	.451
June	.411	.416	.419	.417	.417	.425	.430	.430	.431	.438	.434	.443	.446	.451
July	.414	.418	.421	.420	.420	.427	.432	.432	.433	.441	.436	.445	.449	.454
Aug	.410	.414	.417	.416	.416	.423	.428	.428	.429	.437	.432	.441	.444	.450
Sept	.400	.405	.408	.406	.406	.413	.418	.418	.419	.427	.422	.431	.435	.440
Oct	.398	.402	.405	.404	.404	.411	.416	.416	.417	.424	.420	.429	.432	.437
Nov	.396	.400	.403	.401	.401	.409	.414	.414	.415	.422	.418	.426	.430	.435
Dec	.393	.398	.401	.399	.399	.406	.411	.411	.412	.420	.415	.424	.427	.432
2003	Mar	Apr	May	June	July	Aug	Sept	Oct	Nov	Dec	Jan	Feb	Mar	Apr
Jan	.394	.399	.401	.400	.400	.407	.412	.412	.413	.420	.416	.425	.428	.433
Feb	.387	.392	.394	.393	.393	.400	.405	.405	.406	.413	.409	.418	.421	.426
Mar	.382	.387	.390	.388	.388	.395	.400	.400	.401	.409	.404	.413	.416	.421
Apr	.373	.377	.380	.378	.378	.385	.390	.390	.391	.398	.394	.403	.406	.411
May	.370	.375	.377	.376	.376	.383	.388	.388	.389	.396	.392	.401	.404	.409
June	.372	.376	.379	.377	.377	.384	.389	.389	.391	.398	.393	.402	.405	.410
July	.372	.376	.379	.377	.377	.384	.389	.389	.391	.398	.393	.402	.405	.410
Aug	.369	.374	.377	.375	.375	.382	.387	.387	.388	.395	.391	.400	.403	.408
Sept	.363	.367	.370	.368	.368	.375	.380	.380	.381	.388	.384	.393	.396	.401
Oct	.362	.366	.369	.367	.367	.375	.380	.380	.381	.388	.383	.392	.395	.400
Nov	.361	.366	.368	.367	.367	.374	.379	.379	.380	.387	.383	.391	.395	.400
Dec	.355	.360	.362	.361	.361	.368	.373	.373	.374	.381	.377	.385	.389	.393
2004	Mar	Apr	May	June	July	Aug	Sept	Oct	Nov	Dec	Jan	Feb	Mar	Apr
Jan	.358	.363	.365	.364	.364	.371	.376	.376	.377	.384	.380	.388	.392	.397
Feb	.353	.357	.360	.359	.359	.366	.371	.371	.372	.379	.374	.383	.386	.391
Mar	.347	.352	.354	.353	.353	.360	.365	.365	.366	.373	.368	.377	.380	.385
Apr	.339	.344	.346	.345	.345	.352	.356	.356	.358	.365	.360	.369	.372	.377
May	.334	.338	.340	.339	.339	.346	.351	.351	.352	.359	.354	.363	.366	.371
June	.331	.336	.338	.337	.337	.344	.349	.349	.350	.357	.352	.361	.364	.369
July	.331	.336	.338	.337	.337	.344	.349	.349	.350	.357	.352	.361	.364	.369
Aug	.327	.331	.334	.332	.332	.339	.344	.344	.345	.352	.348	.356	.360	.364
Sept	.322	.326	.329	.327	.327	.334	.339	.339	.340	.347	.343	.351	.355	.359
Oct	.319	.323	.326	.324	.324	.331	.336	.336	.337	.344	.339	.348	.351	.356
Nov	.316	.320	.323	.321	.321	.328	.333	.333	.334	.341	.337	.345	.348	.353
Dec	.310	.314	.316	.315	.315	.322	.326	.326	.328	.334	.330	.339	.342	.346
2005	Mar	Apr	May	June	July	Aug	Sept	Oct	Nov	Dec	Jan	Feb	Mar	Apr
Jan	.317	.321	.323	.322	.322	.329	.334	.334	.335	.341	.337	.346	.349	.354
Feb	.312	.316	.319	.317	.317	.324	.329	.329	.330	.336	.332	.341	.344	.349
Mar	.306	.310	.312	.311	.311	.318	.322	.322	.323	.330	.326	.334	.338	.342
Apr	.298	.302	.305	.303	.303	.310	.315	.315	.316	.323	.318	.327	.330	.335
May	.295	.299	.302	.301	.301	.307	.312	.312	.313	.320	.316	.324	.327	.332
June	.294	.298	.301	.299	.299	.306	.311	.311	.312	.318	.314	.323	.326	.330
July	.294	.298	.301	.299	.299	.306	.311	.311	.312	.318	.314	.323	.326	.330
Aug	.291	.295	.298	.296	.296	.303	.308	.308	.309	.316	.312	.320	.323	.328
Sept	.288	.292	.295	.293	.293	.300	.305	.305	.306	.312	.308	.316	.320	.324
Oct	.287	.291	.293	.292	.292	.298	.303	.303	.304	.311	.307	.315	.318	.323
Nov	.285	.289	.291	.290	.290	.296	.301	.301	.302	.309	.305	.313	.316	.321
Dec	.281	.285	.288	.286	.286	.293	.298	.298	.299	.306	.301	.310	.313	.317

MONTH OF DISPOSAL

	2011	2012											2013	
2006	Dec	Jan	Feb	Mar	Apr	May	June	July	Aug	Sept	Oct	Nov	Dec	Jan	Feb
Jan	.238	.231	.240	.245	.254	.253	.250	.252	.256	.263	.270	.270	.276	.271	.280
Feb	.233	.226	.235	.240	.249	.248	.245	.247	.251	.257	.265	.265	.271	.266	.275
Mar	.228	.221	.230	.235	.244	.243	.240	.242	.246	.252	.259	.259	.266	.261	.270
Apr	.218	.211	.221	.225	.234	.234	.231	.232	.237	.243	.250	.250	.256	.251	.260
May	.211	.204	.213	.218	.227	.226	.223	.225	.229	.235	.242	.242	.248	.243	.252
June	.206	.199	.209	.213	.222	.221	.218	.220	.224	.230	.237	.237	.243	.238	.247
July	.206	.199	.209	.213	.222	.221	.218	.220	.224	.230	.237	.237	.243	.238	.247
Aug	.202	.195	.204	.209	.217	.217	.214	.215	.220	.226	.233	.233	.239	.234	.243
Sept	.196	.189	.199	.203	.212	.211	.208	.210	.214	.220	.227	.227	.233	.228	.237
Oct	.195	.188	.197	.202	.210	.210	.207	.208	.213	.219	.226	.226	.232	.227	.236
Nov	.190	.183	.193	.197	.206	.205	.202	.204	.208	.214	.221	.221	.227	.222	.231
Dec	.181	.174	.184	.188	.196	.196	.193	.194	.199	.205	.212	.212	.218	.213	.222
2007	Dec	Jan	Feb	Mar	Apr	May	June	July	Aug	Sept	Oct	Nov	Dec	Jan	Feb
Jan	.188	.181	.190	.194	.203	.202	.199	.201	.205	.211	.218	.218	.224	.219	.228
Feb	.179	.172	.181	.186	.194	.194	.191	.192	.196	.202	.209	.209	.215	.210	.219
Mar	.171	.164	.174	.178	.186	.186	.183	.184	.189	.195	.202	.202	.207	.203	.211
Apr	.166	.159	.168	.172	.181	.180	.177	.179	.183	.189	.196	.196	.202	.197	.205
May	.161	.154	.163	.168	.176	.176	.173	.174	.178	.184	.191	.191	.197	.192	.201
June	.155	.148	.157	.162	.170	.169	.166	.168	.172	.178	.185	.185	.191	.186	.194
July	.162	.155	.164	.168	.177	.176	.173	.175	.179	.185	.192	.192	.197	.193	.201
Aug	.155	.148	.157	.162	.170	.169	.166	.168	.172	.178	.185	.185	.191	.186	.194
Sept	.151	.144	.153	.158	.166	.165	.163	.164	.168	.174	.181	.181	.187	.182	.190
Oct	.146	.139	.148	.153	.161	.160	.157	.159	.163	.169	.176	.176	.181	.177	.185
Nov	.142	.135	.144	.148	.156	.156	.153	.155	.159	.165	.171	.171	.177	.172	.181
Dec	.135	.128	.138	.142	.150	.149	.147	.148	.152	.158	.165	.165	.170	.165	.174
2008	Dec	Jan	Feb	Mar	Apr	May	June	July	Aug	Sept	Oct	Nov	Dec	Jan	Feb
Jan	.141	.134	.143	.148	.156	.155	.153	.154	.158	.164	.171	.171	.176	.172	.180
Feb	.132	.126	.135	.139	.147	.147	.144	.145	.149	.155	.162	.162	.167	.163	.171
Mar	.129	.122	.131	.135	.143	.143	.140	.141	.146	.151	.158	.158	.164	.159	.167
Apr	.119	.112	.121	.125	.133	.133	.130	.131	.136	.141	.148	.148	.153	.149	.157
May	.113	.106	.115	.119	.127	.127	.124	.126	.130	.135	.142	.142	.147	.143	.151
June	.104	.098	.107	.111	.119	.118	.115	.117	.121	.126	.133	.133	.138	.134	.142
July	.106	.099	.108	.112	.120	.120	.117	.118	.122	.128	.134	.134	.140	.135	.144
Aug	.102	.096	.105	.109	.116	.116	.113	.115	.119	.124	.131	.131	.136	.132	.140
Sept	.096	.090	.098	.103	.110	.110	.107	.109	.113	.118	.125	.125	.130	.125	.134
Oct	.100	.093	.102	.106	.114	.113	.111	.112	.116	.122	.128	.128	.134	.129	.137
Nov	.108	.102	.111	.115	.123	.122	.119	.121	.125	.131	.137	.137	.143	.138	.146
Dec	.124	.118	.127	.131	.139	.139	.136	.137	.141	.147	.154	.154	.159	.155	.163
2009	Dec	Jan	Feb	Mar	Apr	May	June	July	Aug	Sept	Oct	Nov	Dec	Jan	Feb
Jan	.139	.133	.142	.146	.154	.154	.151	.152	.157	.162	.169	.169	.175	.170	.178
Feb	.132	.126	.135	.139	.147	.147	.144	.145	.149	.155	.162	.162	.167	.163	.171
Mar	.133	.126	.135	.140	.148	.147	.144	.146	.150	.156	.162	.162	.168	.163	.172
Apr	.132	.125	.134	.139	.147	.146	.143	.145	.149	.155	.161	.161	.167	.162	.171
May	.125	.118	.127	.132	.140	.139	.136	.138	.142	.148	.154	.154	.160	.155	.164
June	.122	.115	.124	.128	.136	.136	.133	.134	.139	.144	.151	.151	.157	.152	.160
July	.122	.115	.124	.128	.136	.136	.133	.134	.139	.144	.151	.151	.157	.152	.160
Aug	.117	.110	.119	.123	.131	.131	.128	.129	.133	.139	.146	.146	.151	.146	.155
Sept	.112	.105	.114	.118	.126	.126	.123	.124	.129	.134	.141	.141	.146	.142	.150
Oct	.108	.102	.111	.115	.123	.122	.119	.121	.125	.131	.137	.137	.143	.138	.146
Nov	.105	.099	.108	.112	.120	.119	.116	.118	.122	.127	.134	.134	.139	.135	.143
Dec	.098	.092	.100	.105	.112	.112	.109	.111	.115	.120	.127	.127	.132	.128	.136

MONTH OF DISPOSAL

	2013										***2014***			
2006	Mar	Apr	May	June	July	Aug	Sept	Oct	Nov	Dec	Jan	Feb	Mar	Apr
Jan	.286	.290	.293	.291	.291	.298	.302	.302	.304	.310	.306	.314	.317	.322
Feb	.281	.285	.287	.286	.286	.292	.297	.297	.298	.305	.301	.309	.312	.317
Mar	.275	.279	.282	.281	.281	.287	.292	.292	.293	.299	.295	.304	.307	.311
Apr	.266	.270	.272	.271	.271	.277	.282	.282	.283	.290	.285	.294	.297	.301
May	.258	.262	.265	.263	.263	.270	.274	.274	.275	.282	.278	.286	.289	.293
June	.253	.257	.259	.258	.258	.264	.269	.269	.270	.277	.273	.281	.284	.288
July	.253	.257	.259	.258	.258	.264	.269	.269	.270	.277	.273	.281	.284	.288
Aug	.248	.253	.255	.254	.254	.260	.265	.265	.266	.272	.268	.276	.279	.284
Sept	.243	.247	.249	.248	.248	.254	.259	.259	.260	.266	.262	.270	.273	.278
Oct	.241	.245	.248	.246	.246	.252	.257	.257	.258	.264	.260	.268	.271	.276
Nov	.237	.241	.243	.242	.242	.248	.253	.253	.254	.260	.256	.264	.267	.272
Dec	.227	.231	.233	.232	.232	.238	.243	.243	.244	.250	.246	.254	.257	.261
2007	Mar	Apr	May	June	July	Aug	Sept	Oct	Nov	Dec	Jan	Feb	Mar	Apr
Jan	.234	.238	.240	.239	.239	.245	.250	.250	.250	.257	.253	.261	.264	.268
Feb	.225	.228	.231	.229	.229	.236	.240	.240	.241	.248	.244	.252	.255	.259
Mar	.217	.221	.223	.222	.222	.228	.232	.232	.233	.240	.236	.244	.247	.251
Apr	.211	.215	.217	.216	.216	.222	.226	.226	.227	.234	.230	.238	.241	.245
May	.206	.210	.212	.211	.211	.217	.222	.222	.223	.229	.225	.233	.236	.240
June	.200	.204	.206	.205	.205	.211	.215	.215	.216	.222	.219	.226	.229	.233
July	.207	.211	.213	.212	.212	.218	.222	.222	.223	.230	.226	.233	.236	.241
Aug	.200	.204	.206	.205	.205	.211	.215	.215	.216	.222	.219	.226	.229	.233
Sept	.196	.200	.202	.200	.200	.207	.211	.211	.212	.218	.214	.222	.225	.229
Oct	.191	.194	.197	.195	.195	.202	.206	.206	.207	.213	.209	.217	.220	.224
Nov	.186	.190	.192	.191	.191	.197	.201	.201	.202	.208	.205	.212	.215	.219
Dec	.179	.183	.185	.184	.184	.190	.194	.194	.195	.202	.198	.205	.208	.212
2008	Mar	Apr	May	June	July	Aug	Sept	Oct	Nov	Dec	Jan	Feb	Mar	Apr
Jan	.185	.189	.192	.190	.190	.196	.201	.201	.202	.208	.204	.212	.214	.219
Feb	.176	.180	.183	.181	.181	.187	.192	.192	.193	.199	.195	.202	.205	.210
Mar	.173	.176	.179	.177	.177	.183	.188	.188	.189	.195	.191	.198	.201	.206
Apr	.162	.166	.168	.167	.167	.173	.177	.177	.178	.184	.180	.188	.191	.195
May	.156	.160	.162	.161	.161	.167	.171	.171	.172	.178	.174	.182	.185	.189
June	.147	.151	.153	.152	.152	.158	.162	.162	.163	.169	.165	.173	.175	.179
July	.149	.152	.155	.153	.153	.159	.164	.164	.164	.170	.167	.174	.177	.181
Aug	.145	.149	.151	.150	.150	.156	.160	.160	.161	.167	.163	.170	.173	.177
Sept	.139	.142	.145	.143	.143	.149	.153	.153	.154	.160	.157	.164	.167	.171
Oct	.142	.146	.148	.147	.147	.153	.157	.157	.158	.164	.160	.168	.170	.175
Nov	.151	.155	.157	.156	.156	.162	.166	.166	.167	.173	.169	.177	.180	.184
Dec	.168	.172	.174	.173	.173	.179	.183	.183	.184	.190	.186	.194	.197	.201
2009	Mar	Apr	May	June	July	Aug	Sept	Oct	Nov	Dec	Jan	Feb	Mar	Apr
Jan	.184	.188	.190	.188	.188	.195	.199	.199	.200	.206	.202	.210	.213	.217
Feb	.176	.180	.183	.181	.181	.187	.192	.192	.193	.199	.195	.202	.205	.210
Mar	.177	.181	.183	.182	.182	.188	.192	.192	.193	.199	.195	.203	.206	.210
Apr	.176	.180	.182	.181	.181	.187	.191	.191	.192	.198	.194	.202	.205	.209
May	.169	.172	.175	.173	.173	.180	.184	.184	.185	.191	.187	.195	.197	.202
June	.165	.169	.172	.170	.170	.176	.180	.180	.181	.187	.184	.191	.194	.198
July	.165	.169	.172	.170	.170	.176	.180	.180	.181	.187	.184	.191	.194	.198
Aug	.160	.164	.166	.165	.165	.171	.175	.175	.176	.182	.178	.186	.188	.193
Sept	.155	.159	.161	.160	.160	.166	.170	.170	.171	.177	.173	.181	.183	.188
Oct	.151	.155	.157	.156	.156	.162	.166	.166	.167	.173	.169	.177	.180	.184
Nov	.148	.152	.154	.153	.153	.159	.163	.163	.164	.170	.166	.174	.176	.181
Dec	.141	.144	.147	.145	.145	.151	.156	.156	.156	.162	.159	.166	.169	.173

MONTH OF DISPOSAL

	2011	**2012**												**2013**	
2010	Dec	Jan	Feb	Mar	Apr	May	June	July	Aug	Sept	Oct	Nov	Dec	Jan	Feb
Jan	.099	.092	.101	.105	.113	.112	.110	.111	.115	.121	.127	.127	.133	.128	.136
Feb	.092	.086	.094	.099	.106	.106	.103	.104	.109	.114	.120	.120	.126	.121	.130
Mar	.085	.078	.087	.091	.099	.098	.096	.097	.101	.106	.113	.113	.118	.114	.122
Apr	.075	.068	.077	.081	.088	.088	.085	.087	.091	.096	.102	.102	.108	.103	.111
May	.071	.064	.073	.077	.085	.084	.081	.083	.087	.092	.098	.098	.104	.099	.107
June	.068	.062	.071	.075	.082	.082	.079	.080	.084	.090	.096	.096	.101	.097	.105
July	.071	.064	.073	.077	.085	.084	.081	.083	.087	.092	.098	.098	.104	.099	.107
Aug	.066	.060	.069	.073	.080	.080	.077	.078	.082	.088	.094	.094	.099	.095	.103
Sept	.063	.056	.065	.069	.076	.076	.073	.075	.079	.084	.090	.090	.095	.091	.099
Oct	.060	.054	.062	.066	.074	.074	.071	.072	.076	.081	.088	.088	.093	.089	.097
Nov	.056	.049	.058	.062	.069	.069	.066	.067	.071	.077	.083	.083	.088	.084	.092
Dec	.048	.042	.050	.054	.062	.061	.059	.060	.064	.069	.075	.075	.081	.076	.084
2011	Dec	Jan	Feb	Mar	Apr	May	June	July	Aug	Sept	Oct	Nov	Dec	Jan	Feb
Jan	.045	.039	.048	.052	.059	.059	.056	.057	.061	.066	.072	.072	.078	.073	.081
Feb	.035	.029	.037	.041	.048	.048	.045	.047	.051	.056	.062	.062	.067	.063	.070
Mar	.030	.024	.032	.036	.043	.043	.040	.041	.045	.050	.056	.056	.062	.057	.065
Apr	.021	.015	.023	.027	.035	.034	.032	.033	.037	.042	.048	.048	.053	.049	.056
May	.018	.012	.020	.024	.031	.031	.028	.029	.033	.038	.044	.044	.049	.045	.053
Jun	.018	.012	.020	.024	.031	.031	.028	.029	.033	.038	.044	.044	.049	.045	.053
July	.020	.014	.022	.026	.033	.033	.030	.032	.035	.040	.046	.046	.052	.047	.055
Aug	.014	.008	.016	.020	.027	.027	.024	.025	.029	.034	.040	.040	.045	.041	.049
Sept	.006	.000	.008	.012	.019	.019	.016	.018	.021	.026	.032	.032	.037	.033	.041
Oct	.006	.000	.008	.012	.019	.018	.016	.017	.021	.026	.032	.032	.037	.033	.040
Nov	.004	.000	.006	.010	.017	.016	.014	.015	.019	.024	.030	.030	.035	.031	.038
Dec	—	.000	.002	.006	.013	.013	.010	.011	.015	.020	.026	.026	.031	.027	.034
2012	Dec	Jan	Feb	Mar	Apr	May	June	July	Aug	Sept	Oct	Nov	Dec	Jan	Feb
Jan	—	—	.008	.012	.019	.018	.016	.017	.021	.026	.032	.032	.037	.033	.040
Feb	—	—	—	.004	.011	.010	.008	.009	.013	.018	.024	.024	.029	.025	.032
Mar	—	—	—	—	.007	.007	.004	.005	.009	.014	.020	.020	.025	.021	.028
Apr	—	—	—	—	—	.000	.000	.000	.002	.007	.013	.013	.018	.014	.021
May	—	—	—	—	—	—	.000	.000	.002	.007	.013	.013	.018	.014	.021
June	—	—	—	—	—	—	—	.001	.005	.010	.016	.016	.021	.017	.024
July	—	—	—	—	—	—	—	—	.004	.009	.014	.014	.019	.015	.023
Aug	—	—	—	—	—	—	—	—	—	.005	.011	.011	.016	.012	.019
Sept	—	—	—	—	—	—	—	—	—	—	.006	.006	.011	.007	.014
Oct	—	—	—	—	—	—	—	—	—	—	—	.000	.005	.001	.008
Nov	—	—	—	—	—	—	—	—	—	—	—	—	.005	.001	.008
Dec	—	—	—	—	—	—	—	—	—	—	—	—	—	.000	.003
2013	Dec	Jan	Feb	Mar	Apr	May	June	July	Aug	Sept	Oct	Nov	Dec	Jan	Feb
Jan	—	—	—	—	—	—	—	—	—	—	—	—	—	—	.007
Feb	—	—	—	—	—	—	—	—	—	—	—	—	—	—	—
Mar	—	—	—	—	—	—	—	—	—	—	—	—	—	—	—
Apr	—	—	—	—	—	—	—	—	—	—	—	—	—	—	—
May	—	—	—	—	—	—	—	—	—	—	—	—	—	—	—
June	—	—	—	—	—	—	—	—	—	—	—	—	—	—	—
July	—	—	—	—	—	—	—	—	—	—	—	—	—	—	—
Aug	—	—	—	—	—	—	—	—	—	—	—	—	—	—	—
Sept	—	—	—	—	—	—	—	—	—	—	—	—	—	—	—
Oct	—	—	—	—	—	—	—	—	—	—	—	—	—	—	—
Nov	—	—	—	—	—	—	—	—	—	—	—	—	—	—	—
Dec	—	—	—	—	—	—	—	—	—	—	—	—	—	—	—

MONTH OF DISPOSAL

	2013										2014			
2010	Mar	Apr	May	June	July	Aug	Sept	Oct	Nov	Dec	Jan	Feb	Mar	Apr
Jan	.141	.145	.147	.146	.146	.152	.156	.156	.157	.163	.159	.167	.169	.173
Feb	.135	.138	.141	.139	.139	.145	.149	.149	.150	.156	.152	.160	.162	.167
Mar	.127	.130	.133	.131	.131	.137	.141	.141	.142	.148	.145	.152	.155	.159
Apr	.116	.120	.122	.121	.121	.127	.131	.131	.132	.137	.134	.141	.144	.148
May	.112	.116	.118	.117	.117	.123	.127	.127	.127	.133	.130	.137	.140	.144
June	.110	.113	.116	.114	.114	.120	.124	.124	.125	.131	.127	.134	.137	.141
July	.112	.116	.118	.117	.117	.123	.127	.127	.127	.133	.130	.137	.140	.144
Aug	.108	.111	.114	.112	.112	.118	.122	.122	.123	.129	.125	.132	.135	.139
Sept	.104	.107	.110	.108	.108	.114	.118	.118	.119	.125	.121	.128	.131	.135
Oct	.101	.105	.107	.106	.106	.112	.116	.116	.116	.122	.119	.126	.128	.132
Nov	.097	.100	.102	.101	.101	.107	.111	.111	.112	.117	.114	.121	.123	.127
Dec	.089	.092	.095	.093	.093	.099	.103	.103	.104	.109	.106	.113	.116	.120
2011	Mar	Apr	May	June	July	Aug	Sept	Oct	Nov	Dec	Jan	Feb	Mar	Apr
Jan	.086	.090	.092	.090	.090	.096	.100	.100	.101	.107	.103	.110	.113	.117
Feb	.075	.079	.081	.080	.080	.085	.089	.089	.090	.096	.092	.099	.102	.105
Mar	.070	.073	.075	.074	.074	.080	.083	.083	.084	.090	.086	.093	.096	.100
Apr	.061	.064	.067	.065	.065	.071	.075	.075	.076	.081	.078	.084	.087	.091
May	.057	.061	.063	.062	.062	.067	.071	.071	.072	.077	.074	.081	.083	.087
June	.057	.061	.063	.062	.062	.067	.071	.071	.072	.077	.074	.081	.083	.087
July	.060	.063	.065	.064	.064	.069	.073	.073	.074	.080	.076	.083	.086	.089
Aug	.053	.057	.059	.058	.058	.063	.067	.067	.068	.073	.070	.077	.079	.083
Sept	.045	.049	.051	.050	.050	.055	.059	.059	.060	.065	.062	.069	.071	.075
Oct	.045	.048	.050	.049	.049	.055	.058	.058	.059	.065	.061	.068	.071	.074
Nov	.043	.046	.048	.047	.047	.052	.056	.056	.057	.062	.059	.066	.068	.072
Dec	.039	.042	.044	.043	.043	.048	.052	.052	.053	.058	.055	.062	.064	.068
2012	Mar	Apr	May	June	July	Aug	Sept	Oct	Nov	Dec	Jan	Feb	Mar	Apr
Jan	.045	.048	.050	.049	.049	.055	.058	.058	.059	.065	.061	.068	.071	.074
Feb	.037	.040	.042	.041	.041	.046	.050	.050	.051	.056	.053	.060	.062	.066
Mar	.033	.036	.038	.037	.037	.042	.046	.046	.047	.052	.049	.056	.058	.062
Apr	.026	.029	.031	.030	.030	.035	.039	.039	.040	.045	.042	.048	.051	.054
May	.026	.029	.031	.030	.030	.035	.039	.039	.040	.045	.042	.049	.051	.055
June	.029	.032	.034	.033	.033	.038	.042	.042	.043	.048	.045	.051	.054	.057
July	.027	.031	.033	.031	.031	.037	.040	.040	.041	.047	.043	.050	.052	.056
Aug	.023	.027	.029	.028	.028	.033	.037	.037	.037	.043	.040	.046	.049	.052
Sept	.018	.022	.024	.023	.023	.028	.032	.032	.032	.038	.034	.041	.043	.047
Oct	.013	.016	.018	.017	.017	.022	.026	.026	.026	.032	.029	.035	.037	.041
Nov	.013	.016	.018	.017	.017	.022	.026	.026	.026	.032	.029	.035	.037	.041
Dec	.008	.011	.013	.012	.012	.017	.021	.021	.021	.027	.024	.030	.032	.036
2013	Mar	Apr	May	June	July	Aug	Sept	Oct	Nov	Dec	Jan	Feb	Mar	Apr
Jan	.012	.015	.017	.016	.016	.021	.025	.025	.026	.031	.028	.034	.037	.040
Feb	.004	.008	.010	.008	.008	.014	.017	.017	.018	.023	.020	.027	.029	.033
Mar	—	.003	.005	.004	.004	.009	.013	.013	.014	.019	.016	.022	.025	.028
Apr	—	—	.002	.001	.001	.006	.010	.010	.010	.016	.012	.019	.021	.025
May	—	—	—	.000	.000	.004	.008	.008	.008	.014	.010	.017	.019	.023
June	—	—	—	—	.000	.005	.009	.009	.010	.015	.012	.018	.020	.024
July	—	—	—	—	—	.005	.009	.009	.010	.015	.012	.018	.020	.024
Aug	—	—	—	—	—	—	.004	.004	.004	.010	.006	.013	.015	.019
Sept	—	—	—	—	—	—	—	.000	.001	.006	.003	.009	.012	.015
Oct	—	—	—	—	—	—	—	—	.001	.006	.003	.009	.012	.015
Nov	—	—	—	—	—	—	—	—	—	.005	.002	.008	.011	.014
Dec	—	—	—	—	—	—	—	—	—	—	.000	.006	.009	.012

MONTH OF DISPOSAL

	2011	2012												2013	
2014	Dec	Jan	Feb	Mar	Apr	May	June	July	Aug	Sept	Oct	Nov	Dec	Jan	Feb
Jan	—	—	—	—	—	—	—	—	—	—	—	—	—	—	—
Feb	—	—	—	—	—	—	—	—	—	—	—	—	—	—	—
Mar	—	—	—	—	—	—	—	—	—	—	—	—	—	—	—
Apr	—	—	—	—	—	—	—	—	—	—	—	—	—	—	—

MONTH OF DISPOSAL

	2013										2014			
2014	Mar	Apr	May	June	July	Aug	Sept	Oct	Nov	Dec	Jan	Feb	Mar	Apr
Jan	—	—	—	—	—	—	—	—	—	—	—	.006	.009	.012
Feb	—	—	—	—	—	—	—	—	—	—	—	—	.002	.006
Mar	—	—	—	—	—	—	—	—	—	—	—	—	—	.004
Apr	—	—	—	—	—	—	—	—	—	—	—	—	—	—

Retail prices index

	Jan	Feb	Mar	Apr	May	Jun
1982	78.73	78.76	79.44	81.04	81.62	81.85
1983	82.61	82.97	83.12	84.28	84.64	84.84
1984	86.84	87.20	87.48	88.64	88.97	89.20
1985	91.20	91.94	92.80	94.78	95.21	95.41
1986	96.25	96.60	96.73	97.67	97.85	97.79
1987	100.00	100.40	100.60	101.80	101.90	101.90
1988	103.30	103.70	104.10	105.80	106.20	106.60
1989	111.00	111.80	112.30	114.30	115.00	115.40
1990	119.50	120.20	121.40	125.10	126.20	126.70
1991	130.20	130.90	131.40	133.10	133.50	134.10
1992	135.60	136.30	136.70	138.80	139.30	139.30
1993	137.90	138.80	139.30	140.60	141.10	141.00
1994	141.30	142.10	142.50	144.20	144.70	144.70
1995	146.00	146.90	147.50	149.00	149.60	149.80
1996	150.20	150.90	151.50	152.60	152.90	153.00
1997	154.40	155.00	155.40	156.30	156.90	157.50
1998	159.50	160.30	160.80	162.60	163.50	163.40
1999	163.40	163.70	164.10	165.20	165.60	165.60
2000	166.60	167.50	168.40	170.10	170.70	171.10
2001	171.10	172.00	172.20	173.10	174.20	174.40
2002	173.30	173.80	174.50	175.70	176.20	176.20
2003	178.40	179.30	179.90	181.20	181.50	181.30
2004	183.10	183.80	184.60	185.70	186.50	186.80
2005	188.90	189.60	190.50	191.60	192.00	192.20
2006	193.40	194.20	195.00	196.50	197.70	198.50
2007	201.60	203.10	204.40	205.40	206.20	207.30
2008	209.80	211.40	212.10	214.00	215.10	216.80
2009	210.10	211.40	211.30	211.50	212.80	213.40
2010	218.00	219.20	220.70	222.80	223.60	224.10
2011	229.00	231.30	232.50	234.40	235.20	235.20
2012	238.00	239.90	240.80	242.50	242.40	241.80
2013	245.80	247.60	248.70	249.50	250.00	249.70
2014	252.60	254.20	254.80	255.70		

Retail prices index, cont.

	Jul	Aug	Sep	Oct	Nov	Dec
1982	81.88	81.90	81.85	82.26	82.66	82.51
1983	85.30	85.68	86.06	86.36	86.67	86.89
1984	89.10	89.94	90.11	90.67	90.95	90.87
1985	95.23	95.49	95.44	95.59	95.92	96.05
1986	97.52	97.82	98.30	98.45	99.29	99.62
1987	101.80	102.10	102.40	102.90	103.40	103.30
1988	106.70	107.90	108.40	109.50	110.00	110.30
1989	115.50	115.80	116.60	117.50	118.50	118.80
1990	126.80	128.10	129.30	130.30	130.00	129.90
1991	133.80	134.10	134.60	135.10	135.60	135.70
1992	138.80	138.90	139.40	139.90	139.70	139.20
1993	140.70	141.30	141.90	141.80	141.60	141.90
1994	144.00	144.70	145.00	145.20	145.30	146.00
1995	149.10	149.90	150.60	149.80	149.80	150.70
1996	152.40	153.10	153.80	153.80	153.90	154.40
1997	157.50	158.50	159.30	159.50	159.60	160.00
1998	163.00	163.70	164.40	164.50	164.40	164.40
1999	165.10	165.50	166.20	166.50	166.70	167.30
2000	170.50	170.50	171.70	171.60	172.10	172.20
2001	173.30	174.00	174.60	174.30	173.60	173.40
2002	175.90	176.40	177.60	177.90	178.20	178.50
2003	181.30	181.60	182.50	182.60	182.70	183.50
2004	186.80	187.40	188.10	188.60	189.00	189.90
2005	192.20	192.60	193.10	193.30	193.60	194.10
2006	198.50	199.20	200.10	200.40	201.10	202.70
2007	206.10	207.30	208.00	208.90	209.70	210.90
2008	216.50	217.20	218.40	217.70	216.00	212.90
2009	213.40	214.40	215.30	216.00	216.60	218.00
2010	223.60	224.50	225.30	225.80	226.80	228.40
2011	234.70	236.10	237.90	238.00	238.50	239.40
2012	242.10	243.00	244.20	245.60	245.60	246.80
2013	249.70	251.00	251.90	251.90	252.10	253.40

Corporation tax

Rates

(CTA 2010 ss 3, 18–34; FA 2014 ss 5–7, Sch 1)

Financial year	***2009***	***2010***	***2011***	***2012***	***2013***	***2014***
Main rate	28%	28%	26%	24%	23%	**21%**
Small profits rate[2]	21%	21%	20%	20%	20%	**20%**
lower limit[1]	£300,000	£300,000	£300,000	£300,000	£300,000	**£300,000**
upper limit[1]	£1.5m	£1.5m	£1.5m	£1.5m	£1.5m	**£1.5m**
marginal relief fraction	7/400	7/400	3/200	1/100	3/400	**1/400**
effective marginal rate	29.75%	29.75%	27.5%	25%	23.75%	**21.25%**
Tax credit: from 6 April	10%	10%	10%	10%	10%	**10%**

1 Reduced proportionally for accounting periods of less than 12 months. The limits are divided by the number of associated companies and, from 1 April 2015 in the case of companies with ring fence profits, related 51% group companies (including the company in question).

2 For ring fence trades, the small profits rate is 19% for financial years 2009 to 2014 and the main rate of corporation tax is 30% for those years. The marginal relief ring fence fraction is 11/400. These rates will continue to apply to ring fence profits from financial year 2015.

3 The main rate of corporation tax will be 20% for financial year 2015 so that there will be just one rate of corporation tax for non-ring fence profits.

Marginal relief. The small profits rate applies to total taxable profits where augmented profits (see below) do not exceed the lower limit. Where a company's profits exceed the lower limit but do not exceed the upper limit, the charge to corporation tax on the company's taxable total profits is reduced by an amount calculated in accordance with a statutory formula—

$$F \times (U - A) \times \frac{N}{A}$$

where—

F is the marginal relief fraction;
U is the upper limit;
N is the amount of the taxable total profits;
A is the amount of the augmented profits—its adjusted taxable total profits plus franked investment income (other than from UK companies in the same group or owned by a consortium of which the recipient is a member). A company's adjusted taxable total profits are its profits chargeable to corporation tax as if no part of its chargeable gains and allowable losses for the period were liable to capital gains tax (ie on disposals of certain high value UK property, see p 65) instead of to corporation tax.

For financial year 2015 onwards marginal relief will only apply to companies with ring fence profits. A similar formula to that outlined above will apply with the substitution of the letter 'R' for the letter 'F', where 'R' is the marginal relief fraction. All other definitions remain unchanged.

Bank levy see p 70.

Reliefs

Corporate Venturing Scheme

(FA 2000 s 63, Schs 15, 16)

In relation to shares issued between 1 April 2000 and 31 March 2010, an investing company can obtain 20% CT relief on amounts subscribed for ordinary shares in small higher-risk unquoted trading companies which are held for at least three years. The investor must not own or be entitled to acquire more than 30% of the ordinary shares in the investee company. At least 20% must be owned by independent individuals. Chargeable gains on share disposals can be deferred by reinvestment in another shareholding. Allowable losses (net of 20% relief) can be set against income if not deducted from chargeable gains.

Research and development

(CTA 2009 ss 1039–1142; FA 2014 s 31)

Deduction scheme

An '**SME**' incurring R&D expenditure (of at least £10,000 for accounting periods ending before 1 April 2012, though this minimum expenditure requirement is now removed) in a 12-month accounting period can obtain relief for 225% (applying from 1 April 2012) of that expenditure (200% for expenditure incurred between 1 April 2011 and 1 April 2012; 175% for expenditure incurred between 1 August 2008 and 1 April 2011). **SMEs** not yet in profit or which have not yet started to trade can claim relief upfront as a cash payment (R&D tax credit).

An '**SME**' can also claim relief where it incurs expenditure on work contracted to it by a large company or by any person otherwise than in the course of carrying on a chargeable trade; or expenditure which is subsidised; or expenditure subject to the project limit (€7.5m for expenditure incurred after 31 July 2008). The relief is 130% of the expenditure. The minimum expenditure rules above applied for accounting periods ending before 1 April 2012.

An '**SME**' is a company with less than 500 employees and either annual turnover of €100m or less or annual balance sheet total of €86m or less.

Large companies incurring R&D expenditure (of at least £10,000 for accounting periods ending before 1 April 2012) can obtain relief for 130% of that expenditure.

Large companies can claim a similar relief to that for SMEs above, including tax credits, for expenditure incurred on certain vaccines research. The relief was previously also available to SMEs but was withdrawn for them from April 2012.

'Above the line' credit scheme for large companies

This scheme applies from 1 April 2013. Large companies (and certain SMEs with sub-contracted or subsidised R&D, or R&D subject to the project limit) can claim R&D relief as a taxable above the line (ATL) credit to the value of 10% of their qualifying R&D expenditure (49% for ring fence trades). The credit is fully payable, net of tax, to companies with no corporation tax liability. The scheme will initially be optional. Companies that do not elect to claim the ATL credit will be able to continue claiming R&D relief under the current large company deduction scheme (see above) until 31 March 2016. The ATL credit will become mandatory for such companies on 1 April 2016.

Real Estate Investment Trusts (REITs)

(CTA 2010 ss 518–609)

From 1 January 2007, qualifying rental income from and gains on disposals of investment properties by UK companies within the REIT scheme are exempt from corporation tax.

Gifts of pre-eminent objects

(FA 2012 Sch 14)

Companies which gift pre-eminent objects to the nation will receive a reduction in their UK tax liability of 20% of the value of the object they are donating. The legislation has effect in relation to liabilities for tax years and accounting periods beginning on or after 1 April 2012. The gift must be accepted as pre-eminent by the Arts Council under the Cultural Gifts Scheme.

Patent box

(CTA 2010 Pt 8A)

The patent box allows companies to elect to apply a 10% corporation tax rate to a proportion of profits attributable to qualifying patents, whether paid separately as royalties or embedded in the sales price of products, and to certain other qualifying intellectual property rights such as regulatory data protection (also called 'data exclusivity'), supplementary protection certificates and plant variety rights from 1 April 2013. In the first year the proportion of profits qualifying for the 10% rate is 60% and this will increase annually to 100% from April 2017. Thus, for financial year 2014 the proportion is 70%.

Disincorporation relief

(FA 2013 ss 58–61)

With effect for disincorporations between 1 April 2013 and 31 March 2018 inclusive, joint claims may be made by a company and its shareholders to allow goodwill or interests in land not held as trading stock to be transferred at a reduced value so that no corporation tax will be payable by the company on the transfer. Relief is restricted to cases where the market value of the assets allowed for disincorporation relief does not exceed £100,000. Joint claims must be made to HMRC within two years of the date of the transfer and other eligibility criteria also apply. Shareholders to whom the assets are transferred will inherit the transfer value for the purpose of capital gains tax.

Annual tax on enveloped dwellings

(FA 2013 ss 94–174, Schs 33–35; FA 2014 ss 109, 110; SI 2014/854)

From 1 April 2013 a charge is imposed on certain non-natural persons (NNPs), ie companies, partnerships with at least one company member, and collective investment schemes which hold UK residential dwellings valued at greater than £2 million on specified valuation dates. 2013–14 returns were due by 1 October 2013 and payment of tax by 31 October 2013. Returns and payment are due by 30 April[2] each year subsequently. If the payer is not chargeable for the full year, a later repayment claim can be made. Various reliefs from the charge apply. **A charge to capital gains tax**[3] at 28% also applies to the disposal of such properties, whether by UK resident or non-resident NNPs. See also p 131 regarding the 15% **stamp duty land tax** which can apply to acquisitions of such properties.

Property value[1]	**Annual tax 2013–14**	**Annual tax 2014–15**
More than £2 million[2] to £5 million	£15,000	**£15,400**
More than £5 million to £10 million	£35,000	**£35,900**
More than £10 million to £20 million	£70,000	**£71,850**
More than £20 million	£140,000	**£143,750**

1 The valuation is the market value on the last previous valuation date. The first valuation date is 1 April 2012 and then every five years thereafter. Other valuation dates can apply in certain circumstances, for example when a new property is purchased. The valuation is applied on the first day of the chargeable period if the chargeable person is within the charge on that day, otherwise the first day in the chargeable period on which they are first within the charge.

2 A new band applying to residential properties worth more than £1 million and not more than £2 million, with an annual charge of £7,000, will apply from 1 April 2015. Returns applicable to this band will not be required until 1 October 2015 with payment required by 31 October 2015. An additional band applying to residential properties worth more than £500,000 and not more than £1 million, with an annual charge of £3,500, will apply from 1 April 2016.

3 An extension to the ATED-related CGT charge will take effect from 6 April 2015 for properties worth more than £1 million and not more than £2 million. An additional extension to the ATED-related CGT charge will take effect from 6 April 2016 for properties worth more than £500,000 and not more than £1 million.

Environmental taxes and other levies

Aggregates levy

(FA 2001 ss 16–49, Schs 4–10; FA 2014 ss 94, 95; SI 2004/1959; SI 2010/2598)

Levy on commercial exploitation of aggregates including rock, gravel or sand together with any other substance incorporated or naturally occurring with it. Applies to all aggregate (not recycled) extracted in the UK or territorial waters unless exempt. Before 1 April 2014 it does not apply to quarried or mined products such as clay, shale, slate, metal and metal ores, gemstones, semi-precious gemstones and industrial minerals. From 1 April 2014, the Government has had to suspend these exemptions, exclusions and reliefs which are the subject of a State aid investigation by the European Commission. The levy was charged at 20% of the full rate for aggregate processed in Northern Ireland until 30 November 2010. From 1 December 2010 operators in Northern Ireland have to pay the full aggregate levy.

From 1 April 2009	**£2.00 per tonne**
1 April 2008 to 31 March 2009	£1.95 per tonne

Air passenger duty

(FA 1994 s 30, Sch 5A; FA 2014 ss 78–80)

APD is extended to smaller aircraft and business jets (reducing the de minimis weight limit from 10 tonnes to 5.7 tonnes) from 1.4.13 and passengers on 'luxury' business jets (20 tonnes or more and fewer than 19 seats) will pay APD at twice the standard rate. From 1.11.11 to 31.12.12 the band A rates applied to all direct long haul flights departing from Northern Ireland. The rates for all *direct* long haul flights (ie in bands B to D) departing from Northern Ireland from 1.1.13 are devolved to the Northern Ireland Assembly and set at £0.

From 1 April 2015 the destination bands will be reduced to two by merging the former bands B, C and D, and the higher rates will be set at six times the reduced rates. The band A rates will therefore be £13, £26, and £78 and the new merged band B rates will be £71, £142, and £426.

Band and distance of capital city of destination country from UK in miles	Reduced rate (lowest class of travel)			
	1.11.10–31.3.12	1.4.12–31.3.13	1.4.13–31.3.14	**From 1.4.14**
Band A (0–2,000)	£12	£13	£13	**£13**
Band B (2,001–4,000)	£60	£65	£67	**£69**
Band C (4,001–6,000)	£75	£81	£83	**£85**
Band D (over 6,000)	£85	£92	£94	**£97**

Band and distance of capital city of destination country from UK in miles	Standard rate (all classes other than lowest class)[1]			
	1.11.10–31.3.12	1.4.12–31.3.13	1.4.13–31.3.14	**From 1.4.14**
Band A (0–2,000)	£24	£26	£26	**£26**
Band B (2,001–4,000)	£120	£130	£134	**£138**
Band C (4,001–6,000)	£150	£162	£166	**£170**
Band D (over 6,000)	£170	£184	£188	**£194**

Band and distance of capital city of destination country from UK in miles	Higher rate (flights aboard aircraft of 20 tonnes and above with fewer than 19 seats)			
	1.4.11–31.3.12	1.4.12–31.3.13	1.4.13–31.3.14	**From 1.4.14**
Band A (0–2,000)	N/A	N/A	£52	**£52**
Band B (2,001–4,000)	N/A	N/A	£268	**£276**
Band C (4,001–6,000)	N/A	N/A	£332	**£340**
Band D (over 6,000)	N/A	N/A	£376	**£388**

1 From 1 November 2008, if a class of travel provides a seat pitch in excess of 1.016 metres (40 inches) the standard rate is the minimum rate that applies, even if it is the lowest or only class of travel.

The following specifies which countries come into which bands.

Band A territories — 0–2,000 miles from London		
Albania	Greenland	Morocco
Algeria	Guernsey	Netherlands
Andorra	Hungary	Norway (including Svalbard)
Austria	Iceland	Poland
Azores	Republic of Ireland	Portugal (including Madeira)
Belarus	Isle of Man	Romania
Belgium	Italy (including Sicily and Sardinia)[2]	Russian Federation (west of the Urals)
Bosnia and Herzegovina	Jersey	San Marino
Bulgaria	Republic of Kosovo	Serbia
Croatia	Latvia	Slovak Republic
Cyprus	Libya	Slovenia
Czech Republic	Liechtenstein	Spain (including the Balearic Islands and the Canary Islands)
Denmark (including the Faroe Islands)	Lithuania	Sweden
Estonia	Luxembourg	Switzerland
Finland	former Yugoslav Republic of Macedonia	Tunisia
France (including Corsica)	Malta	Turkey
Germany	Moldova	Ukraine
Gibraltar	Monaco	Western Sahara[1]
Greece	Montenegro	

1 HMRC Notice 550 Appendix 1 (updated March 2014) does not include Western Sahara.

2 HMRC Notice 550 Appendix 1 (updated March 2014) does include Vatican City even though this is not in the tables in FA 1994 Sch 5A.

Band B territories — 2,001–4,000 miles from London		
Afghanistan	Gambia	Pakistan
Armenia	Georgia	Qatar
Azerbaijan	Ghana	Russian Federation (east of the Urals)
Bahrain	Guinea	Saint Pierre and Miquelon
Benin	Guinea-Bissau	Sao Tome and Principe
Bermuda	Iran	Saudi Arabia
Burkina Faso	Iraq	Senegal
Cameroon	Israel & Occupied Palestinian Territories	Sierra Leone
Canada	Ivory Coast	South Sudan
Cape Verde	Jordan	Sudan
Central African Republic	Kazakhstan	Syria
Chad	Kuwait	Tajikistan
Democratic Republic of Congo	Kyrgyzstan	Togo
Republic of Congo	Lebanon	Turkmenistan
Djibouti	Liberia	Uganda
Egypt	Mali	United Arab Emirates
Equatorial Guinea	Mauritania	United States of America
Eritrea	Niger	Uzbekistan
Ethiopia	Nigeria	Yemen
Gabon	Oman	

Band C territories — 4,001–6,000 miles from London

Angola	Guadeloupe	Puerto Rico
Anguilla	Guatemala	Reunion
Antigua and Barbuda	Guyana	Rwanda
Aruba	Haiti	Saba
Bahamas	Honduras	Saint Barthelemy
Bangladesh	Hong Kong SAR	Saint Christopher and Nevis (St Kitts and Nevis)
Barbados	India	Saint Helena, Ascension and Tristan da Cuhna
Belize	Jamaica	Saint Lucia
Bhutan	Japan	Saint Martin
Bonaire	Kenya	Saint Vincent and the Grenadines
Botswana	North Korea	Seychelles
Brazil	South Korea	Sint Eustatius
British Indian Ocean Territory	Laos	Sint Maarten
British Virgin Islands	Lesotho	Somalia
Burma	Macao SAR	South Africa
Burundi	Madagascar	Sri Lanka
Cayman Islands	Malawi	Suriname
China	Maldives	Swaziland
Colombia	Martinique	Tanzania
Comoros	Mauritius	Thailand
Costa Rica	Mayotte	Trinidad and Tobago
Cuba	Mexico	Turks and Caicos Islands
Curaçao	Mongolia	Venezuela
Dominica	Montserrat	Vietnam
Dominican Republic	Mozambique	Virgin Islands
Ecuador	Namibia	Zambia
El Salvador	Nepal	Zimbabwe
French Guiana	Nicaragua	
Grenada	Panama	

Band D — journey ends in any other place.

Bank levy

(FA 2011 Sch 19 para 6; FA 2014 ss 119, 120)

From 1 January 2011 a bank levy is charged based on the total chargeable equity and liabilities reported in the relevant balance sheets of affected banks, banking and building society groups at the end of the chargeable period. It is payable through the existing corporation tax self assessment system. It is not charged on the first £20 billion of chargeable liabilities.

	1.1.11 – 28.2.11	1.3.11 – 30.4.11	1.5.11 – 31.12.11	1.1.12 – 31.12.12	1.1.13 – 31.12.13	**From 1.1.14**
Short-term chargeable liabilities	0.05%	0.1%	0.075%	0.088%	0.130%	**0.156%**
Long-term chargeable equity and liabilities	0.025%	0.05%	0.0375%	0.044%	0.065%	**0.078%**

Climate change levy

(FA 2000 s 30, Sch 6; FA 2014 ss 96–99, Sch 16)

Levy on supply for industrial or commercial purposes of energy, from 1.4.01, in the form of electricity, gas, petroleum and hydrocarbon gas supplied in a liquid state, coal and lignite, coke and semi-coke of coal or lignite and petroleum coke.

Taxable commodity supplied	*Rate*[1]					
	1.4.09–31.3.11	1.4.11–31.3.12	1.4.12–31.3.13	1.4.13–31.3.14	**1.4.14–31.3.15**	From 1 April 2015
Electricity	0.47p per kWh	0.485p per kWh	0.509p per kWh	0.524p per kWh	**0.541p per kWh**	0.554p per kWh
Gas supplied by a gas utility or any gas supplied in a gaseous state that is of a kind supplied by a gas utility	0.164p per kWh	0.169p per kWh	0.177p per kWh	0.182p per kWh	**0.188p per kWh**	0.193p per kWh
Gas supplied as above in Northern Ireland	Exempt	0.059p per kWh	0.062p per kWh	0.064p per kWh until 31.10.13 then main rate applies	**0.188p per kWh**	0.193p per kWh
Any petroleum gas, or other gaseous hydrocarbon supplied in a liquid state	1.05p per kg	1.083p per kg	1.137p per kg	1.172p per kg	**1.210p per kg**	1.240p per kg
Any other taxable commodity	1.281p per kg	1.321p per kg	1.387p per kg	1.429p per kg	**1.476p per kg**	1.512p per kg

1 Rate at which payable if supply is not a reduced-rate supply. The levy is charged at a reduced rate for facilities covered by a climate change agreement, generally 35% of the full rate (20% for supplies treated as taking place before 1 April 2011), but 20% from 1 April 2012 to 31 March 2014 for supplies of taxable commodities used in recycling of steel and aluminium (previously and subsequently exempt) and 10% from 1 April 2013 for electricity supplies. From 1 April 2014 supplies of taxable commodities used in metallurgical and mineralogical processes are exempt.

Carbon price support rates for climate change levy and fuel duty

The carbon price floor was introduced from 1 April 2013. Supplies of solid fossil fuels, gas and liquefied petroleum gas used in most forms of electricity generation are liable to the CPS rates of CCL, which differs from the main CCL rates (see above) levied on consumers' use of these commodities (and electricity). Oils and bioblends are not taxable commodities for CCL purposes, and are taxed under the fuel duty regime. There are, however, CPS rates of fuel duty for oils and bioblends used in the generation of electricity. Subject to state aid approval, the carbon price floor does not apply to Northern Ireland. The CPS rate is reduced by the carbon capture percentage where there is a supply of fossil fuels to an electricity generator which uses carbon capture and storage (CCS) technology.

Supplies of commodity				
	1.4.13–31.3.14	**1.4.14–31.3.15**	1.4.15–31.3.16	1.4.16–31.3.17
Gas supplied by a gas utility or any gas supplied in a gaseous state that is of a kind supplied by a gas utility	0.091p per kWh	**0.175p per kWh**	0.334p per kWh	0.331p per kWh
Any petroleum gas, or other gaseous hydrocarbon supplied in a liquid state	1.460p per kg	**2.822p per kg**	5.307p per kg	5.28p per kg
Coal and other taxable solid fossil fuels	44.264p per gross gigajoule	**81.906p per gross gigajoule**	156.86p per gross gigajoule	154.79p per gross gigajoule
Gas oil; rebated bioblend; kerosene[1]	1.365p per litre	**2.642p per litre**	4.99p per litre	4.916p per litre
Fuel oil; other heavy oil; rebated light oil	1.568p per litre	**3.011p per litre**	5.73p per litre	5.711p per litre

1 The CPS rates of fuel duty apply to duty paid kerosene used in electricity generation from 1 May 2014.

Fuel duty

(HODA 1979 s 6; SI 2011/2935)

A Rural Fuel Duty relief scheme for retailers of road fuel on the Inner and Outer Hebrides, the Northern Isles, the Islands of the Clyde and the Isles of Scilly was introduced on 1 January 2012. Retailers of road fuel within these areas are eligible to register with HMRC to claim back five pence per litre relief on unleaded petrol and diesel for retail sale within the eligible areas. The retailers will have 60 days following registration for the scheme to reduce the cost of every litre of road fuel sold by the equivalent amount of the relief claimed. (HMRC Brief 40/11)

From 1 April 2015 a reduced rate of fuel duty of 9.32p per litre will apply to methanol composed of 95% pure methanol and 5% water.

	Petrol/diesel	Biodiesel or bioethonal	LPG used as road fuel	Natural gas used as road fuel	Red diesel	Fuel oil
from 6pm 23 March 2011 to 31 August 2015	**57.95p per litre**	**57.95p per litre**	**31.61p per kg**	**24.70p per kg**	**11.14p per litre**	**10.70p per litre**
from 1 January 2011 to 6pm 23 March 2011	58.95p per litre	58.95p per litre	33.04p per kg	26.15p per kg	11.33p per litre	10.88p per litre
from 1 October 2010 to 31 December 2010	58.19p per litre	58.19p per litre	31.95p per kg	25.05p per kg	11.18p per litre	10.74p per litre
from 1 April 2010 to 30 September 2010	57.19p per litre	57.19p per litre	30.53p per kg	23.60p per kg	10.99p per litre	10.55p per litre
from 1 September 2009 to 31 March 2010	56.19p per litre	36.19p per litre	27.67p per kg	22.16p per kg	10.80p per litre	10.37p per litre
from 1 April 2009 to 31 August 2009	54.19p per litre	34.19p per litre	24.82p per kg	19.26p per kg	10.42p per litre	10.00p per litre
from 1 December 2008 to 31 March 2009	52.35p per litre	32.35 per litre	20.77p per kg	16.60p per kg	10.07p per litre	9.66p per litre
from 1 October 2007 to 30 November 2008	50.35 per litre	30.35 per litre	16.49p per kg	13.70p per kg	9.69p per litre	9.29p per litre

Insurance premium tax

(FA 1994 ss 48–74, Schs 6A, 7, 7A)

IPT is a tax on premiums received under insurance contracts other than those which are specifically exempt.

	Standard rate	*Higher rate*[1]
From 4.1.11	**6.0%**	**20.0%**
1.7.99–3.1.11	5.0%	17.5%

1 The higher rate applies to sales of motor cars, light vans and motorcycles, electrical or mechanical domestic appliances, and travel insurance.

Landfill tax

(FA 1996 ss 39–71, 197, Sch 5; SI 1996/1527; SI 1996/1528; FA 2014 s 100; Notice LFT 1 para 4.5)

Tax on disposal of waste imposed on operators of landfill sites calculated by reference to the weight and type of waste deposited. Exemption applies to mining and quarrying waste, dredging waste, pet cemeteries, disposals of NATO waste, inert waste used to fill working and old quarries and (before 1 September 2009) inert waste used to restore landfill sites. An exemption for waste from reclamation of contaminated land was abolished with effect from 30 November 2008 although some exemption certificates remained valid until 31 March 2012. Legislation introduced in Finance Act 2012 brought landfill tax legislation in Scotland into line with the rest of the UK and had retrospective effect back to 21 March 2000. The power to raise landfill tax will devolve to the Scottish Parliament from 1 April 2015.

Period	*Active waste per tonne*	*Inert waste per tonne*[2]	*Maximum credit*[1]
From 1 April 2015	£82.60	£2.60	TBA
1.4.14–31.3.15	**£80**	**£2.50**	**5.1%**
1.4.13–31.3.14	£72	£2.50	6.8%
1.4.12–31.3.13	£64	£2.50	5.6%
1.4.11–31.3.12	£56	£2.50	6.2%
1.4.10–31.3.11	£48	£2.50	5.5%
1.4.09–31.3.10	£40	£2.50	6%
1.4.08–31.3.09	£32	£2.50	6%

1 Tax credits are available to operators who make donations to environmental trusts of 90% of the donation to the maximum percentage above of the tax payable in a 12-month period.

2 For details of waste materials liable at the lower rate see SI 2011/1017 as amended by SI 2012/940 and HMRC Briefs 15/2012 and 18/2012.

Vehicle excise duty

(VERA 1994 Sch 1; FA 2014 ss 81–91, Sch 18)

Vehicle tax, or 'road tax' is charged according to CO_2 emissions, as follows:

Standard rates

Band	CO_2 (g/km)	2012–13	2013–14	2014–15
A	Up to 100	£0	£0	**£0**
B	101–110	£20	£20	**£20**
C	111–120	£30	£30	**£30**
D	121–130	£100	£105	**£110**
E	131–140	£120	£125	**£130**
F	141–150	£135	£140	**£145**
G	151–165	£170	£175	**£180**
H	166–175	£195	£200	**£205**
I	176–185	£215	£220	**£225**
J	186–200	£250	£260	**£265**
K	201–225	£270	£280	**£285**
L	226–255	£460	£475	**£485**
M	Over 255	£475	£490	**£500**

There is an alternative fuel discount of £10 for all cars from 2010–11 onwards. From 1 April 2010, a different rate of tax applies in the year of purchase of a new vehicle. In later years, the standard rate applies.

First-year rates

Band	CO_2 (g/km)	2012–13 first-year rate	2013–14 first-year rate	2014–15 first-year rate
A	Up to 100	£0	£0	**£0**
B	101–110	£0	£0	**£0**
C	111–120	£0	£0	**£0**
D	121–130	£0	£0	**£0**
E	131–140	£120	£125	**£130**
F	141–150	£135	£140	**£145**
G	151–165	£170	£175	**£180**
H	166–175	£275	£285	**£290**
I	176–185	£325	£335	**£345**
J	186–200	£460	£475	**£485**
K	201–225	£600	£620	**£635**
L	226–255	£815	£840	**£860**
M	Over 255	£1,030	£1,065	**£1,090**

Light goods vehicle rates

Tax class	2012–13	2013–14	2014–15
Light goods vehicle[1]	£215	£220	**£225**
Euro 4 & 5 LGV	£135	£140	**£140**

1 Registered on or after 1 March 2001.

Motorcycle rates

VED band	2012–13	2013–14	2014–15
Up to 150 cc	£16	£17	**£17**
151–400 cc	£36	£37	**£38**
401–600 cc	£55	£57	**£58**
Over 600 cc	£76	£78	**£80**

Income tax

Starting, basic, higher and additional rates

(ITA 2007 ss 6–21; FA 2014 ss 1–4)

Band of taxable income	*Band*	*Rate*	*Tax*	*Cumulative tax*
£	£	%	£	£
2014–15				
0–31,865	**31,865**	**20**	**6,373**	**6,373**
31,866–150,000	**118,135**	**40**	**47,254**	**53,627**
Over 150,000	**–**	**45**	**–**	**–**
2013–14				
0–32,010	32,010	20	6,402	6,402
32,011–150,000	117,990	40	47,196	53,598
Over 150,000	–	45	–	–
2012–13				
0–34,370	34,370	20	6,874	6,874
34,371–150,000	115,630	40	46,252	53,126
Over 150,000	–	50	–	–
2011–12				
0–35,000	35,000	20	7,000	7,000
35,001–150,000	115,000	40	46,000	53,000
Over 150,000	–	50	–	–
2010–11				
0–37,400	37,400	20	7,480	7,480
37,401–150,000	112,600	40	45,040	52,520
Over 150,000	–	50	–	–
2009–10				
0–37,400	37,400	20	7,480	7,480
Over 37,400	–	40	–	–

2015–16 rates The basic rate limit will be £31,785.
Child benefit income tax charge Where an individual or their partner is in receipt of child benefit a high income child benefit charge can arise from 7 January 2013. The charge is applied to the higher earner. Taxpayers with adjusted net income between £50,000 and £60,000 are subject to an income tax charge of 1% of the amount of child benefit for every £100 of income that exceeds £50,000. For taxpayers with income above £60,000, the amount of the charge will equal the amount of child benefit received. Alternatively, a taxpayer with expected income over £60,000 can elect not to receive any child benefit. The election has effect for weeks beginning after it is made. It can be revoked at any time to restore payment of child benefit, and, where the election was made in the erroneous belief that the charge would arise, it may be revoked up to two years after the end of the tax year to which it relates in order for child benefit to be paid for the period. (ITEPA 2003 ss 681B–H; Social Security Administration Act 1992, s 13A).
Taxation of savings: From 2008–09 onwards a starting rate for savings band for individuals was introduced. For 2008–09 the band is £2,320, for 2009–10 and 2010–11 it is £2,440, for 2011–12 it is £2,560, for 2012–13 it is £2,710, for 2013–14 it is £2,790, and for 2014–15 it is £2,880. Where an individual's non-savings income is less than the starting rate limit for savings, the savings income is taxable at the 10% starting rate for savings up to the limit. Where non-savings income exceeds the limit, the starting rate for savings does not apply. Savings income includes interest from banks and building societies, interest distributions from authorised unit trusts, interest on gilts and other securities including corporate bonds, purchased life annuities and discounts. From 6 April 2015, the starting rate for savings income will be reduced to 0% and the maximum amount of an individual's income that can qualify for this starting rate will increase to £5,000.
Where income does not exceed the basic rate limit, there will be no further tax to pay on savings income from which the 20% tax rate has been deducted, and any tax over-deducted is repayable. Higher rate taxpayers are liable to pay tax at 40% on that part of their savings income falling above the higher rate limit. From 2010–11 to 2012–13 additional rate taxpayers are liable to pay tax at 50% on that part of their savings income falling above the additional rate limit. From 2013–14 that rate is reduced to 45%. Savings income is generally treated as the second top slice of income behind dividends. Non-taxpayers may apply to have interest paid without deduction of tax where their total income is expected to be covered by personal allowances. Taxpayers who are entitled to a refund of tax deducted from interest can claim the refund using form R40. For HMRC advice regarding repayments see: www.hmrc.gov.uk/incometax/refund-reclaim.htm.

Taxation of dividends: UK and foreign dividends (except those foreign dividends taxed under the remittance basis) form the top slice of taxable income. Where income does not exceed the basic rate limit the rate is 10% (applied to the dividend grossed-up by a tax credit of 1/9) so that the liability is met by the tax credit. Higher rate taxpayers are liable to pay tax at 32.5% on that part of their dividend income falling above the higher rate limit. From 2010–11 to 2012–13 additional rate taxpayers are liable to pay tax at 42.5% on that part of their dividend income falling above the additional rate limit. From 2013–14 additional rate taxpayers are liable at 37.5%. See ITA 2007 s 13. A non-payable tax credit of one-ninth of the dividend was extended to individuals in receipt of dividends from non-UK resident companies where they had a holding of less than 10% and the company is not an offshore fund, by ITTOIA 2005 s 397A on or after 6 April 2008. The tax credit is extended to taxpayers with a holding of 10% or more and to distributions from offshore funds with effect on or after 22 April 2009.

Construction industry sub-contractors rate of deduction at source from 6 April 2007 (SI 2007/46)

Registered sub-contractors	**20%**	Unregistered sub-contractors	**30%**

Taxation of trusts

	Trust rate	*Dividend trust rate*
2013–14 onwards	**45%**	**37.5%**
2010–11 to 2012–13	50%	42.5%
2004–05 to 2009–10	40%	32.5%

First slice of income: For 2006–07 onwards the first £1,000 of income arising to a trust chargeable at the trust rate or the dividend trust rate is instead chargeable at the basic, savings or dividend rate.
Vulnerable beneficiaries: From 2004–05 onwards, trustees can be taxed (on election) on trust income as if it were income of the vulnerable beneficiary taking into account the beneficiary's personal allowances, starting and basic rate bands (FA 2005 ss 23–45).

Table of income tax reliefs

	2014–15	2013–14
	£	£
Personal allowance[5] born after 5.4.1948 / age under 65	**10,000**	9,440
Total income limit	**100,000**	100,000
Not beneficial if individual's		
total income exceeds	**120,000**	118,880
Age allowance[1]		
Total income limit	**27,000**	26,100
Personal allowance born after 5.4.1938 but before 6.4.1948 / age 65–74	**10,500**	10,500
Not beneficial if individual's		
total income exceeds	**28,000**	28,220
Personal allowance born before 6.4.1938 / age 75 and over	**10,660**	10,660
Not beneficial if individual's		
total income exceeds	**28,320**	28,540
Married couple's allowance[2,4]		
Elder partner 65 before 6.4.2000		
Basic allowance	**3,140**	3,040
Age allowance[3,4]		
Total income limit	**27,000**	26,100
Neither partner aged 75 or over	**N/A**	N/A
Not beneficial if relevant partner[3]		
under 65 and his total income exceeds	**N/A**	N/A
65–74 and his total income exceeds	**N/A**	N/A
Either partner aged 75 and over and born before 6 April 1935	**8,165**	7,915
Not beneficial if relevant partner[3]		
born after 5.4.1948 / under 65 and his total income exceeds	**37,050**	35,850
born after 5.4.1938 but before 6.4.1948 / 65–74 and his total income exceeds	**38,050**	37,970
born before 6.4.1938 / 75 or over and his total income exceeds	**38,370**	38,290
Blind person's allowance[6]	**2,230**	2,160

1 The higher age allowances are available if the claimant's adjusted net income does not exceed the statutory income limit.
Where the adjusted net income exceeds the statutory limit, the maximum allowance is reduced by one-half of the excess until it is reduced to the ordinary personal allowance. The allowances are frozen at the 2013–14 levels. From 2013–14 the differing levels of personal allowances apply based on specified dates of birth. For 2012–13 and earlier years they applied to those under age 65, those age 65–74 and those age over 75.

2 The universal married couple's allowance was withdrawn for 2000–01 onwards but continues to be available to any married couple or, from 2005–06, civil partnership where at least one spouse or partner was born before 6 April 1935.
The relief is given as a reduction in income tax liability restricted to the lower of 10% of the amount of the allowance or the claimant's total income tax liability.

3 The higher age allowances are available if the claimant's adjusted net income does not exceed the statutory income limit (subject to relief given as a reduction in tax liability as in note 2 above).
Where the adjusted net income exceeds the statutory limit, the maximum allowance is reduced by one-half of the excess (less any reduction made in the personal age allowance as in note 1 above) but it cannot be reduced to less than the basic couple's allowance.

National insurance contributions – self-employed

		2014–15	2013–14
Class 2	Flat rate per week	**£2.75**	£2.70
	Small earnings exception	**5,885**	£5,725
Class 4	Band	**7,956–41,865**	7,755–41,450
	Rate	**33,909@ 9%**	33,695@ 9%
	Amount payable to upper limit	**3,051.81**	3,032.55
	Charge on profits above the limit	**2%**	2%

Table of income tax reliefs (cont.)

2012–13	2011–12	2010–11	2009–10	2008–09
£	£	£	£	£
8,105	7,475	6,475	6,475	6,035
100,000	100,000	100,000	N/A	N/A
116,210	114,950	112,950	N/A	N/A
25,400	24,000	22,900	22,900	21,800
10,500	9,940	9,490	9,490	9,030
30,190	28,930	28,930	28,930	27,790
10,660	10,090	9,640	9,640	9,180
30,510	29,230	29,230	29,230	28,090
2,960	2,800	2,670	2,670	2,540
25,400	24,000	22,900	22,900	21,800
N/A	N/A	N/A	N/A	6,535
N/A	N/A	N/A	N/A	29,790
N/A	N/A	N/A	N/A	35,780
7,705	7,295	6,965	6,965	6,625
34,890	32,990	31,490	31,490	29,790
39,680	37,920	37,520	37,520	35,960
40,000	38,220	37,820	37,820	36,260
2,100	1,980	1,890	1,890	1,800

4 For marriages entered into before 5 December 2005, married couple's allowance is given to the husband (subject to right of transfer to the wife), the amount of the allowance being determined by the level of the husband's income. For marriages and civil partnerships entered into on or after that date, the allowance is given to whichever of the two partners has the higher total income for the tax year in question, the amount of the allowance being determined by the level of that partner's income (subject to the right to transfer half or all of the basic allowance or excess allowances to the partner). Couples married before 5 December 2005 may make a joint election to be brought within the above rules for couples marrying on or after that date. The election must be made before the start of the first tax year for which it is to have effect. It will continue to have effect for all subsequent tax years and is irrevocable.

5 From 2010–11, the basic personal allowance for income tax is gradually reduced to nil for individuals with adjusted net incomes in excess of £100,000. The reduction is £1 for every £2 of income over the limit. From 2013–14 the differing levels of personal allowances apply based on specified dates of birth. For 2012–13 and earlier years they applied to those under age 65, those age 65–74 and those age over 75. For 2015–16 there will be one level of basic personal allowance for individuals born after 5 April 1938 of £10,500. For individuals born before 6 April 1938 it will remain at £10,660. In 2015–16 a spouse or civil partner who is not liable to income tax above the basic rate will be able to transfer up to £1,050 of their personal allowance to their spouse or civil partner, provided the transferee is also not liable to income tax above the basic rate. Married couples or civil partnerships entitled to claim the married couple's allowance will not be entitled to make a transfer.

6 The allowance is available for persons who are registered blind but not for persons registered partially-sighted.

National insurance contributions – self-employed (cont.)

2012–13	2011–12	2010–11	2009–10	2008–09
£2.65	£2.50	£2.40	£2.40	£2.30
5,595	5,315	5,075	5,075	4,825
7,605–42,475	7,225–42,475	5,715–43,875	5,715–43,875	5,435–40,040
34,870@ 9%	35,250@ 9%	38,160@ 8%	38,160@ 8%	34,605@ 8%
3,138.30	3,172.50	3,052.80	3,052.80	2,768.40
2%	2%	1%	1%	1%

Cars, vans and related benefits

Cars

From 6 April 2002: The income tax charge is based on a percentage of the car's price graduated according to the level of the car's carbon dioxide measured in grams per kilometre (g/km). (ITEPA 2003 ss 114–148, 169; FA 2014 ss 23–25.)

CO_2 emissions (g/km)						*% of list price*	
2008–09–2009–10	***2010–11***	***2011–12***	***2012–13***	***2013–14***	***2014–15***	*Petrol*	*Diesel*[1]
N/A	75[1]	75[1]	75[1]	75[1]	**75**[1]	5%	8%
120[1]	120[1]	120[1]	99[1]	94[1]	**N/A**	10%	13%
N/A	N/A	N/A	100	95	**94**[1]	11%	14%
N/A	N/A	N/A	105	100	**95**	12%	15%
N/A	N/A	N/A	110	105	**100**	13%	16%
N/A	N/A	N/A	115	110	**105**	14%	17%
135	130	125	120	115	**110**	15%	18%
140	135	130	125	120	**115**	16%	19%
145	140	135	130	125	**120**	17%	20%
150	145	140	135	130	**125**	18%	21%
155	150	145	140	135	**130**	19%	22%
160	155	150	145	140	**135**	20%	23%
165	160	155	150	145	**140**	21%	24%
170	165	160	155	150	**145**	22%	25%
175	170	165	160	155	**150**	23%	26%
180	175	170	165	160	**155**	24%	27%
185	180	175	170	165	**160**	25%	28%
190	185	180	175	170	**165**	26%	29%
195	190	185	180	175	**170**	27%	30%
200	195	190	185	180	**175**	28%	31%
205	200	195	190	185	**180**	29%	32%
210	205	200	195	190	**185**	30%	33%
215	210	205	200	195	**190**	31%	34%
220	215	210	205	200	**195**	32%	35%
225	220	215	210	205	**200**	33%	35%
230	225	220	215	210	**205**	34%	35%
235	230	225	220	215	**210**	35%	35%

1 Where a car's CO_2 figure is not a multiple of 5, it is rounded down to the nearest 5. However, to qualify for the 10/13% rate a car's emissions figure must be exactly 120g/km or less for 2008–09 to 2011–12, 99g/km or less for 2012–13 and 94g/km or less for 2013–14. To qualify for the 11/14% rate in 2014–15 a car's emissions figure must be exactly 94g/km or less. From 2010–11 the emissions must be exactly 75g/km or less to qualify for the 5/8% rate.

For 2008–09 to 2010–11: For cars registered on or after 1.1.98 which are constructed to be capable of being propelled by bioethanol or E85 fuel, the percentage chargeable was reduced by 2%.

For 2010–11 to 2014–15: No benefit applies to cars which are incapable of producing carbon dioxide when driven.

For 2015–16: The relevant threshold will remain at 95g/km but the percentage applying at that threshold (the threshold percentage) will be increased from 12/15% to 14/17%. The maximum percentage will be increased to 37%. The 5/8% rate will apply for emissions of 50g/km or less (including for cars which are incapable of producing carbon dioxide when driven), a 9/12% rate will apply for emissions between 51–75g/km, and a 13/16% rate will apply for emissions between 76–94g/km.

Cars registered after 28 February 2001

For cars registered on or after 1.3.01, the definitive CO_2 emissions figure is recorded on the vehicle registration document. For cars first registered between 1.1.98 and 28.2.01, the Vehicle Certification Agency supply relevant information on their website at carfueldata.direct.gov.uk/ and in their free, twice-yearly edition of the 'New Car Fuel Consumption & Emission Figures' booklet.

Cars registered on or after 1 January 1998 with no CO_2 emission figures

Cylinder capacity of car[3]	*Appropriate percentage*[1, 2]
1,400cc or less	15%
Over 1,400cc up to 2,000cc	25%
Over 2,000cc	35%
Before 6 April 2010: Electrically propelled vehicle	15%
From 6 April 2010 to 5 April 2015: Cars incapable of producing CO_2 when driven	0%

1 **Diesel cars:** A 3% supplement applies to diesel cars up to a maximum of 35%. The supplement does not apply before 5.4.06 to diesel cars meeting the Euro IV emissions standards. For 2006–07 to 2010–11 it does not apply to such cars registered before 1 January 2006.

2 **Discounts:** Special discounts applied to cars, with or without CO_2 emission figures, registered on or after 1.1.98: 6% for electrically propelled vehicles (before 2010–11 only), 3% for hybrid electric vehicles (before 2011–12 only, 2% before 2006–07) and 2% for gas or bi-fuel cars with CO_2 emission figures for gas (before 2011–12 only, 1% before 2006–07).

3 **No cylinder capacity:** For a car with no cylinder capacity 35% applies.

Cars registered before 1.1.98: Tax is charged on 15% of the list price for engines to 1,400cc, 22% for engines of 1,401 to 2,000cc and 32% for engines above 2,000cc. Cars without a cylinder capacity are taxed on 32% of the list price.

Automatic cars for disabled drivers: CO_2 figure reduced to equivalent for manual car (ITEPA 2003 s 138).

Car unavailable for part of year: Value of the benefit is reduced proportionately (ITEPA 2003 s 143).

National Insurance: Also used to calculate the national insurance contributions payable by employers on the benefit of cars they provide for the private use of their employees, see p 109.

The cash equivalent is reduced proportionately where the car is not available for the whole tax year. The amount (as so reduced) is reduced by any payments made by the employee for private use.

List price of car:

(1) Includes qualifying accessories, excluding accessories provided after car made available if its list price was less than £100. Accessories designed for use only by disabled people also excluded. From 6 April 2011 accessories do not include certain security enhancements provided to meet the threat to an employee's personal physical security arising from the nature of the employment. Where a car is manufactured so as to be capable of running on road fuel gas, its price is proportionately reduced by so much of that price as is reasonably attributable to it being manufactured in that way. Where a new car is converted to run on road fuel gas, the equipment is not regarded as an accessory. With effect from 6 April 2009 disabled drivers of automatic cars who hold a disabled person's badge can use the list price of an equivalent manual car.

(2) Reduced by capital contributions made by employee up to £5,000.

(3) For 2010–11 and earlier years the list price as adjusted was capped at £80,000.

(4) Classic cars (aged 15 years or more and with a market value of £15,000 or more at end of tax year): substitute market value at end of tax year if higher than adjusted list price. Reduction for capital contributions (and for earlier years the £80,000 cap) applies.

(ITEPA 2003 ss 120–132)

Vans and fuel for vans

(ITEPA 2003 ss 114–119, 154–164, 168, 169A, 170; FA 2014 s 25; SI 2013/3033)

Van benefit	
2014–15 onwards	
Vehicle weight up to 3,500kg	**£3,090**
2007–08 to 2013–14	
Vehicle weight up to 3,500kg	£3,000

No charge applies to employees who have to take their van home and private use is restricted other than for ordinary commuting (insignificant use is disregarded).

For 2010–11 to 2014–15: No benefit applies to vans which are incapable of producing CO_2 when driven.

Van fuel benefit	
2014–15	**£581**
2013–14	£564
2010–11 to 2012–13	£550
2007–08 to 2009–10	£500

The fuel charge applies where the van benefit charge applies and fuel is provided for private use.

Related benefits

Parking facilities: No taxable benefit for work place provision of car or van parking spaces, or parking for bicycles or motorcycles (ITEPA 2003 s 237).

Cycles and cyclist's safety equipment: No taxable benefit in respect of the provision to employees of bicycles or cycling safety equipment for travel to and from work (ITEPA 2003 s 244) nor for subsequent transfer to the employee at market value (ITEPA 2003 s 206).

On-call emergency vehicles: No tax or NIC charge where emergency service workers have private use of their emergency vehicle when on call (ITEPA 2003 s 248A).

Bus services: No taxable benefit in respect of the provision of works buses with a seating capacity of 9 or more provided to employees (or their children) to travel to & from work (ITEPA 2003 s 242).

Car and motorcycle hire: restricted allowances

(ITTOIA 2005 ss 48–50B; CTA 2009 ss 56–58B)

Hire period before April 2009, if a car with a retail price when new of more than £12,000 is acquired under a rental lease the maximum allowable deduction in computing trading profits is restricted to:

$$\frac{£12{,}000 + P}{2P} \times R$$

P = retail price of car when new. R = annual rental.

Hire period from April 2009 (subject to transitional provisions), the disallowance is a flat rate of 15%. This applies only to cars with CO_2 emissions exceeding 130g/km (160g/km before 1 April 2013 (corporation tax) or 6 April 2013 (income tax)).

Capital allowances see p 33.

Car fuel: company cars

(ITEPA 2003 ss 149–153; SI 2013/3033)

The same percentage figures on p 78 used to calculate the car benefit charge for the company car, which are directly linked to the car's CO_2 emissions, are used to calculate the benefit charge for fuel provided for private motoring. The relevant percentage figure is multiplied by £16,900 for 2008–09 and 2009–10, by £18,000 for 2010–11, by £18,800 for 2011–12, by £20,200 for 2012–13, by £21,100 for 2013–14, and by £21,700 for 2014–15.

The benefit is reduced to nil if the employee is required to, and does, make good all fuel provided for private use. There is no taxable benefit where the employer only provides fuel for business travel. The charge is proportionately reduced where the employee stops receiving free fuel part way through the tax year, but where free fuel is subsequently provided in the same tax year, the full year's charge is payable. The benefit is proportionately reduced where a car is not available or is incapable of being used for part of a year (being at least 30 days).

CO_2 emissions (g/km)	*Petrol*	*Diesel*
2014–15	**£**	**£**
75	1,085	1,736
94	2,387	3,038
95	2,604	3,255
100	2,821	3,472
105	3,038	3,689
110	3,255	3,906
115	3,472	4,123
120	3,689	4,340
125	3,906	4,557
130	4,123	4,774
135	4,340	4,991
140	4,557	5,208
145	4,774	5,425
150	4,991	5,642
155	5,208	5,859
160	5,425	6,076
165	5,642	6,293
170	5,859	6,510
175	6,076	6,727
180	6,293	6,944
185	6,510	7,161
190	6,727	7,378
195	6,944	7,595
200	7,161	7,595
205	7,378	7,595
210	7,595	7,595

CO_2 emissions (g/km)	*Petrol*	*Diesel*
2013–14	**£**	**£**
75	1,055	1,688
94	2,110	2,743
95	2,321	2,954
100	2,532	3,165
105	2,743	3,376
110	2,954	3,587
115	3,165	3,798
120	3,376	4,009
125	3,587	4,220
130	3,798	4,431
135	4,009	4,642
140	4,220	4,853
145	4,431	5,064
150	4,642	5,275
155	4,853	5,486
160	5,064	5,697
165	5,275	5,908
170	5,486	6,119
175	5,697	6,330
180	5,908	6,541
185	6,119	6,752
190	6,330	6,963
195	6,541	7,174
200	6,752	7,385
205	6,963	7,385
210	7,174	7,385
215	7,385	7,385

CO_2 emissions (g/km)	*Petrol*	*Diesel*
2012–13	**£**	**£**
75	1,010	1,616
99	2,020	2,626
100	2,222	2,828
105	2,424	3,030
110	2,626	3,232
115	2,828	3,434
120	3,030	3,636
125	3,232	3,838
130	3,434	4,040
135	3,636	4,242
140	3,838	4,444
145	4,040	4,646
150	4,242	4,848
155	4,444	5,050
160	4,646	5,252
165	4,848	5,454
170	5,050	5,656
175	5,252	5,858
180	5,454	6,060
185	5,656	6,262
190	5,858	6,464
195	6,060	6,666
200	6,262	6,868
205	6,464	7,070
210	6,666	7,070
215	6,868	7,070
220	7,070	7,070

CO_2 emissions (g/km)	*Petrol*	*Diesel*
2011–12	**£**	**£**
75	940	1,504
120	1,880	2,444
125	2,820	3,384
130	3,008	3,572
135	3,196	3,760
140	3,384	3,948
145	3,572	4,136
150	3,760	4,324
155	3,948	4,512
160	4,136	4,700
165	4,324	4,888
170	4,512	5,076
175	4,700	5,264
180	4,888	5,452
185	5,076	5,640
190	5,264	5,828
195	5,452	6,016
200	5,640	6,204
205	5,828	6,392
210	6,016	6,580
215	6,204	6,580
220	6,392	6,580
225	6,580	6,580

CO_2 emissions (g/km)	*Petrol*	*Diesel*
2010–11	**£**	**£**
75	900	1,440
120	1,800	2,340
130	2,700	3,240
135	2,880	3,420
140	3,060	3,600
145	3,240	3,780
150	3,420	3,960
155	3,600	4,140
160	3,780	4,320
165	3,960	4,500
170	4,140	4,680
175	4,320	4,860
180	4,500	5,040
185	4,680	5,220
190	4,860	5,400
195	5,040	5,580
200	5,220	5,760
205	5,400	5,940
210	5,580	6,120
215	5,760	6,300
220	5,940	6,300
225	6,120	6,300
230	6,300	6,300

CO_2 emissions (g/km)	*Petrol*	*Diesel*
2008–09–2009–10	**£**	**£**
120	1,690	2,197
135	2,535	3,042
140	2,704	3,211
145	2,873	3,380
150	3,042	3,549
155	3,211	3,718
160	3,380	3,887
165	3,549	4,056
170	3,718	4,225
175	3,887	4,394
180	4,056	4,563
185	4,225	4,732
190	4,394	4,901
195	4,563	5,070
200	4,732	5,239
205	4,901	5,408
210	5,070	5,577
215	5,239	5,746
220	5,408	5,915
225	5,577	5,915
230	5,746	5,915
235	5,915	5,915

Mileage allowances

Advisory fuel rates for company cars

Engine size	*Cost per mile*		
	Petrol	*Diesel*	*LPG*
From 1 June 2014			
1,400cc or less	**14p**	**–**	**9p**
1,600cc or less	**–**	**12p**	**–**
1,401–2,000cc	**16p**	**–**	**11p**
1,601–2,000cc	**–**	**14p**	**–**
Over 2,000cc	**24p**	**17p**	**16p**
1 March 2014–31 May 2014			
1,400cc or less	14p	–	9p
1,600cc or less	–	12p	–
1,401–2,000cc	16p	–	11p
1,601–2,000cc	–	14p	–
Over 2,000cc	24p	17p	17p
1 December 2013–28 February 2014			
1,400cc or less	14p	–	9p
1,600cc or less	–	12p	–
1,401–2,000cc	16p	–	11p
1,601–2,000cc	–	14p	–
Over 2,000cc	24p	17p	16p
1 September 2013–30 November 2013			
1,400cc or less	15p	–	10p
1,600cc or less	–	12p	–
1,401–2,000cc	18p	–	11p
1,601–2,000cc	–	15p	–
Over 2,000cc	26p	18p	16p

Engine size	*Cost per mile*		
	Petrol	*Diesel*	*LPG*
1 June 2013–31 August 2013			
1,400cc or less	15p	–	10p
1,600cc or less	–	12p	–
1,401–2,000cc	17p	–	12p
1,601–2,000cc	–	14p	–
Over 2,000cc	25p	18p	18p
1 March 2013–31 May 2013			
1,400cc or less	15p	–	10p
1,600cc or less	–	13p	–
1,401–2,000cc	18p	–	12p
1,601–2,000cc	–	15p	–
Over 2,000cc	26p	18p	18p
1 December 2012–28 February 2013			
1,400cc or less	15p	–	11p
1,600cc or less	–	12p	–
1,401–2,000cc	18p	–	13p
1,601–2,000cc	–	15p	–
Over 2,000cc	26p	18p	18p
1 September 2012–30 November 2012			
1,400cc or less	15p	–	10p
1,600cc or less	–	12p	–
1,401–2,000cc	18p	–	13p
1,601–2,000cc	–	15p	–
Over 2,000cc	26p	18p	17p
1 June 2012–31 August 2012			
1,400cc or less	15p	–	11p
1,600cc or less	–	12p	–
1,401–2,000cc	18p	–	13p
1,601–2,000cc	–	15p	–
Over 2,000cc	26p	18p	19p
1 March 2012–31 May 2012			
1,400cc or less	15p	–	10p
1,600cc or less	–	13p	–
1,401–2,000cc	18p	–	12p
1,601–2,000cc	–	15p	–
Over 2,000cc	26p	19p	18p
1 December 2011–29 February 2012			
1,400cc or less	15p	–	10p
1,600cc or less	–	12p	–
1,401–2,000cc	18p	–	12p
1,601–2,000cc	–	15p	–
Over 2,000cc	26p	18p	18p
1 September 2011–30 November 2011			
1,400cc or less	15p	–	11p
1,600cc or less	–	12p	–
1,401–2,000cc	18p	–	12p
1,601–2,000cc	–	15p	–
Over 2,000cc	26p	18p	18p
1 June 2011–31 August 2011			
1,400cc or less	15p	–	11p
1,600cc or less	–	12p	–
1,401–2,000cc	18p	–	13p
1,601–2,000cc	–	15p	–
Over 2,000cc	26p	18p	18p

Engine size	Cost per mile		
	Petrol	Diesel	LPG
1 March 2011–31 May 2011			
1,400cc or less	14p	13p	10p
1,401–2,000cc	16p	13p	12p
Over 2,000cc	23p	16p	17p
1 December 2010–28 February 2011			
1,400cc or less	13p	12p	9p
1,401–2,000cc	15p	12p	10p
Over 2,000cc	21p	15p	15p
1 June 2010–30 November 2010			
1,400cc or less	12p	11p	8p
1,401–2,000cc	15p	11p	10p
Over 2,000cc	21p	16p	14p
1 December 2009–31 May 2010			
1,400cc or less	11p	11p	7p
1,401–2,000cc	14p	11p	8p
Over 2,000cc	20p	14p	12p
1 July 2009–30 November 2009			
1,400cc or less	10p	10p	7p
1,401–2,000cc	12p	10p	8p
Over 2,000cc	18p	13p	12p
1 January 2009–30 June 2009			
1,400cc or less	10p	11p	7p
1,401–2,000cc	12p	11p	9p
Over 2,000cc	17p	14p	12p
1 July 2008–31 December 2008			
1,400cc or less	12p	13p	7p
1,401–2,000cc	15p	13p	9p
Over 2,000cc	21p	17p	13p
1 January 2008–30 June 2008			
1,400cc or less	11p	11p	7p
1,401–2,000cc	13p	11p	8p
Over 2,000cc	19p	14p	11p

1 Advisory fuel rates can be used to negotiate dispensations for mileage payments from 28.01.02 where:
(a) employers reimburse employees for business travel in their company cars; or
(b) employers require employees to repay the cost of fuel used for private travel.
(In the case of (b) the figures may be used for reimbursements of private travel from 6 April 2001.)

2 Payments at or below these rates are tax and NIC free. The table figures will be accepted for VAT purposes.

3 Other rates may be used if the employer can demonstrate that they are justified.

4 Rates are currently reviewed by HMRC quarterly.

Authorised mileage rates

	Rate per business mile	
Cars or vans	*First 10,000 miles*	*Over 10,000 miles*
2011–12 onwards[1]	**45p**	**25p**
2002–03 to 2010–11[1]	40p	25p

1 Where the employer pays less than the authorised rate the employee can claim tax relief for the difference (ITEPA 2003 ss 229–232, 235, 236).

	Rate per business mile
Car passengers Allowance for each fellow passenger carried	
2002–03 onwards	**5p**
Cycles	
2002–03 onwards[1]	**20p**
Motorcycles	
2002–03 onwards[1]	**24p**

1 Where the employer pays less than the authorised rate the employee can claim tax relief for the difference (ITEPA 2003 ss 229–232, 235, 236).

Charities and Community Amateur Sports Clubs (CASCs)

Gift Aid and Gift Aid Small Donations schemes

Under the **Gift Aid scheme** an individual donor can claim higher rate relief (and, if applicable, additional rate relief from 2010–11) on the grossed up amount of a monetary donation against income tax and capital gains tax. The charity or CASC claims basic rate relief on the grossed up amount of the donation. Donors must make a declaration that they are UK taxpayers to allow the charity to reclaim the repayment. One declaration can cover a series of donations to the same charity and the declaration can be made by writing, by electronic means or orally, although an oral declaration is not effective until a written confirmation is sent to the donor. New model written declaration forms were issued by HMRC on 24 February 2012, and only forms based on the new wording will be accepted from 1 January 2013. A declaration can be backdated for up to four years prior to the declaration. The basic rate tax deemed to have been deducted by the donor at source is clawed back if the donor's tax liability is insufficient to match it. Following the reduction of the basic rate to 20% for 2008–09 onwards, a transitional relief supplement of 2% of grossed up qualifying donations was payable to charities for 2008–09 to 2010–11. Donors may elect in their self-assessment tax returns for donations to be treated as made in the preceding tax year for higher rate (and if applicable, additional rate) relief purposes.

From April 2004 to April 2012, taxpayers could nominate a charity to receive all or part of any tax repayment due to them. The nomination was made on the taxpayer's self-assessment tax return for 2003–04 and later years, with an indication of whether Gift Aid should apply to the donation. However, this scheme has been withdrawn for repayments due on tax returns for 2011–12 onwards, and for repayments made for earlier years on or after 6 April 2012.

Relief for payments falling due after 5 April 2000 under charitable covenants is given under the Gift Aid scheme.

From April 2013 the **Gift Aid Small Donations scheme** allows charities and CASCs to claim a gift aid style payment on broadly £5,000 of small cash donations of up to £20 each in circumstances where it is often difficult to obtain a gift aid declaration, such as street collections. The donations must not have been the subject of a gift aid declaration and must not be deductible in calculating the individual's income.

(ITA 2007 ss 413–430; FA 2012 s 50; Small Charitable Donations Act 2012)

Gifts in kind

Relief is available for gifts by traders to charities, community amateur sports clubs or educational establishments of goods produced or sold or of plant or machinery used for the purposes of the trade (CAA 2001 s 63(2)–(4); ITTOIA 2005 ss 107–109; CTA 2009 ss 105–107; CTA 2010 ss 658–671).

Gifts of land, shares and securities etc

Relief is available where a person disposes of listed shares and securities, unit trust units, AIM shares, etc or of freehold or leasehold interests in land to a charity by way of a gift or sale at an undervalue. The amount deductible from total income is the market value of the shares etc on the date of disposal plus incidental disposal costs less any consideration or value of benefits received by the donor or a connected person. This is in addition to any capital gains tax relief (ITA 2007 ss 431–446).

Payroll giving

Under the payroll giving scheme, employees authorise their employer to deduct charitable donations from their pay and receive tax relief on their donation at their top rate of tax (FA 2000 s 38; ITEPA 2003 ss 713–715; SI 1986/2211 as amended).

Inheritance tax relief see p 106. **Capital gains tax** see p 39. **Gifts of pre-eminent objects** see p 97.

Employment benefits

The following benefits on pp 86 to 90 cover some common benefits not detailed separately elsewhere. References to 'lower-paid' employees are to those whose annual remuneration plus benefits is less than £8,500.

Accommodation, supplies, etc used in employment duties

(ITEPA 2003 s 316)

The provision of accommodation, supplies or services used by employees in performance of employment duties is not taxable provided:

(a) if the benefit is provided on premises occupied by the employer, any private use by the employee (or the employee's family or household) is not significant; or

(b) in any other case, the sole purpose of providing the benefit is to enable the employee to perform those duties, any private use is not significant and the benefit is not an excluded benefit (eg the provision of a motor vehicle, boat or aircraft).

Assets given to employees

(ITEPA 2003 ss 203, 204)

If new, tax is chargeable on the cost to the employer (market value in the case of a 'lower-paid' employee). If used, tax is chargeable on the greater of:

(a) market value at the time of transfer; and

(b) where the asset is first applied for the provision of a benefit after 5 April 1980 and a person has been chargeable to tax on its use, market value when first so applied less amounts charged to tax for use up to and including the year of transfer.

Buses to shops

(SI 2002/205)

The provision of buses for journeys of ten miles or less from the workplace to shops etc on a working day is not taxable.

Cheap loans

(ITEPA 2003 ss 174–190)

A taxable benefit arises on employer-related loans to directors or employees earning £8,500 or more a year, on the difference between the interest paid and interest payable at the 'official rate' below. There is no tax charge where:

(a) all the employer-related loans (or all loans not qualifying for tax relief) do not exceed £10,000 (£5,000 before 6 April 2014);
(b) all the interest payable is or would be eligible for tax relief; and
(c) the loans are ordinary commercial loans.

The provisions can apply to alternative finance arrangements entered into after 21 March 2006.

The 'official rate' is:

From 6 April 2014	**3.25%**
6 April 2010 to 5 April 2014	4.00%
1 March 2009 to 5 April 2010	4.75%
6 April 2007 to 28 February 2009	6.25%

The average rate for the tax year is:

2014–15	**3.25%**
2013–14	4.00%
2012–13	4.00%
2011–12	4.00%
2010–11	4.00%
2009–10	4.75%
2008–09	6.10%

The official rate is set in advance for the whole of the following tax year, subject to review if the typical mortgage rates were to fall sharply during a tax year.

Childcare provision

(ITEPA 2003 ss 318–318D; SI 2006/882)

No liability arises:

(a) where the premises (which are not wholly or mainly used as a private dwelling) are made available by the employer or, where the scheme is provided under arrangements with other persons, by one or more of those persons; or
(b) where (a) does not apply, on the first £55 per week of registered or approved childcare, or where the employee joins the scheme after 5 April 2011, the first £55 (basic rate taxpayers), £28 per week (higher rate taxpayers), £25 per week (additional rate taxpayers, £22 per week before 6 April 2013) of registered or approved childcare.

Christmas parties and annual functions

(ITEPA 2003 s 264; SI 2003/1361)

Not taxable if cost does not exceed £150 per head per tax year and open to staff generally. Otherwise, fully taxable. Expenditure may be split between more than one function. (Not taxable on 'lower-paid' employees.)

Credit tokens

(ITEPA 2003 ss 90–96A, 363)

Where money goods or services are provided to employees through credit tokens, the cost to the employer, less any employee contribution, is taxable on the employee, except if they were used to buy certain non-taxable benefits.

Cyclists' breakfasts

(SI 2002/205; SI 2012/1808)

Before 6 April 2013 breakfast provided for employees arriving at the workplace by bicycle in recognition of having cycled to work is not taxable. No limit on number of such breakfasts per year. This exemption is removed from 2013–14 onwards.

Disabled employees

(ITEPA 2003 ss 246, 247; SI 2002/1596)

The provision of, or payment for, transport for disabled employees for ordinary commuting is tax free. This also applies to the provision of equipment, services or facilities to disabled employees to help them carry out their duties of employment.

Emergency service vehicles

(ITEPA 2003 s 248A)

There is no tax charge on any benefit arising from use of an emergency vehicle by an employee of an emergency service where private use is prohibited.

Employees' liability insurance

(ITEPA 2003 s 346)

This is non-taxable.

Eye tests and corrective appliances

(ITEPA 2003 s 320A)

No liability arises where the provision of tests or special corrective appliances are required under health and safety legislation and are available as required to employees generally.

Homeworkers

(ITEPA 2003 s 316A)

Employer contributions to additional household costs not taxable where employee works at home. Supporting evidence required if contributions exceed £4 per week (£18 per month for monthly paid employees). Between 6 April 2008 and 5 April 2012 the limit was £3 per week.

Incidental overnight expenses

(ITEPA 2003 ss 240, 241)

Not taxable where employee stays away from home on business and payment from employer does not exceed:

(a) £5 per night in the UK; or
(b) £10 per night overseas.

Living accommodation

(ITEPA 2003 ss 97–113)

A taxable benefit (the '*basic charge*') arises on the annual rental value (or actual rent if greater) less any sums made good by the employee. There is an *additional charge* (if the basic charge is not calculated on the full open market rental value) where the cost of accommodation (including costs of any capital improvements less amounts made good by the employee) exceeds £75,000. The additional charge is the excess cost over £75,000 multiplied by the official rate for cheap loans (see above) in force at the start of the tax year less any rent paid by the employee in excess of the basic charge.

For leases of ten years or less entered into on or after 22 April 2009, a lease premium paid is to be treated as if it were rent and spread over the period of the lease accordingly.

The charges are apportioned in the case of multiple occupation or if the property is provided for only part of the year or part is used exclusively for business purposes.

Exemption: No taxable benefit arises where living accommodation is provided:

(a) for the proper performance of duties;
(b) by reason that it is customary to do so; or
(c) by reason of special threat to the employee's security.

The above exemptions apply to a full-time working director whose interest in the company does not exceed 5%, otherwise only exemption (c) applies to directors.

Living expenses

(ITEPA 2003 ss 313–315)

A taxable charge arises on the cost to the employer of the employee's living expenses. For the provision of assets such as furniture, see 'Use of employer's assets' below.

Where the exemption for living accommodation above applies, the tax charge relating to living expenses (including the provision of furniture and items normal for domestic occupation) is restricted to 10% of the employee's net earnings from the related employment less any sums made good by the employee.

Expenditure on alteration and structural repairs which are normally the landlord's responsibility do not give rise to a taxable benefit.

Long service awards

(ITEPA 2003 s 323; SI 2003/1361)

Not taxable provided the employee has at least 20 years' service and cost to the employer does not exceed £50 for each year of service. No similar award may be made within ten years of such an award.

Meals

(ITEPA 2003 s 317)

Subsidised or free meals provided for staff generally at the workplace are not taxable. For 2011–12 onwards, however, this relief does not apply if the provision of meals is made under salary sacrifice or flexible remuneration arrangements.

Medical check-ups, insurance and treatment

(ITEPA 2003 ss 320B, 325; HMRC Employment Income Manual EIM21765)

Check-ups:

2009–10 onwards: One screening and one check-up each year not taxable.

2007–08 and 2008–09: By concession, HMRC continued the previous concessionary practice not to collect tax and NICs which might arise from the previous regulations.

Insurance: Premiums paid on behalf of employees (other than 'lower-paid' employees) are taxable unless for treatment outside the UK whilst the employee is performing duties abroad.

Recommended medical treatment: From a date to be appointed (expected to be Autumn 2014) any benefit in kind or payment of earnings, up to an annual cap of £500 per employee, will not be taxable where an employer meets the cost of certain recommended medical treatment in connection with an employee's return to work after a period of absence due to ill-health or injury.

Personal expenses

(ITEPA 2003 ss 70–72, 336–341)

Unless covered by specific exemptions, payments to an employee by reason of his employment in respect of expenses or allowances are taxable. Deduction is allowed for expenses the employee is obliged to incur which are:

(a) qualifying travelling expenses (broadly those necessarily incurred other than for ordinary commuting or private travel); or

(b) other amounts incurred wholly, exclusively and necessarily in the performance of employment duties.

Relocation expenses

(ITEPA 2003 ss 271–289)

Qualifying removal expenses and benefits up to £8,000 per move in connection with job-related residential moves are not taxable. Included are expenses of disposal, acquisition, abortive acquisition, transport of belongings, travelling and subsistence, bridging loans and duplicate expenses (replacement domestic items).

Scholarships

(ITEPA 2003 ss 211–215)

An employee is taxable on the cost of any scholarship from a trust fund which does not satisfy a 25% distribution test or which is paid because of the employee's employment.

Subscriptions and fees

(ITEPA 2003 ss 343–345)

Not taxable where paid to professional bodies and the employee has a contractual or professional requirement to be a member of the body.

Third party gifts

(ITEPA 2003 ss 270, 324; SI 2003/1361)

Gifts during the tax year of goods and non-cash vouchers up to £250 not taxable where provided by a party unconnected with the employer and not for services provided in connection with employment.

Use of employer's assets

(ITEPA 2003 ss 203–206, 242, 244, 319, 320; FA 2005 s 17; FA 2006 ss 60, 61, HMRC Brief 02/2012)

Tax is chargeable on the annual rental value of land and, for other assets, at 20% of the market value when they are first lent or the rental charge to the employer if higher. No taxable benefit arises on:

(a) the loan of a mobile phone for private use. From 6 April 2006 this is restricted to one mobile phone per employee and no longer extends to the employee's family or household but phones first loaned before 6 April 2006 are not affected by the change. HMRC's view from January 2012 is that exemption applies to smartphones with retrospective effect;

(b) the use of works buses (see p 79);

(c) cycles and cycle safety equipment (see p 79);

(d) to 5 April 2006, the loan of computer equipment for private use, provided use is not restricted to directors or senior staff and value of benefit does not exceed £2,500 (computers made available for private use before 6 April 2006 are not affected by the change).

No benefit arises on the subsequent purchase by an employee at market value of computer or cycling equipment previously on loan.

Vouchers

(ITEPA 2003 ss 73–89, 95, 96, 268–270, 362; FA 2012 Sch 39)

Vouchers are taxable as follows.

(a)	Cash vouchers	On amount for which voucher can be exchanged.
(b)	Non-cash vouchers	On cost to employer less any contribution from employee (except where used to obtain certain non-taxable benefits).
(c)	Luncheon vouchers	Before 6 April 2013 on excess over 15p per working day[1].
(d)	Transport vouchers	On cost to employer less any contribution from employee.

1 The 15p exemption on luncheon vouchers is repealed from 2013–14 onwards.

Employment exemption

Employee-ownership trusts

(ITEPA 2003 ss 312A–312I)

From 1 October 2014 an exemption from income tax applies to qualifying bonus payments of up to £3,600 per tax year made to employees, and qualifying former employees, by a company which is owned directly or indirectly by an employee-ownership trust which meets certain qualifying conditions.

For CGT relief relating to such companies see p 39.

Employment income

PAYE and national insurance thresholds

	2009–10	*2010–11*	*2011–12*	*2012–13*	*2013–14*	*2014–15*
	£	£	£	£	£	£
Weekly NI	110	110	136/139	144/146	148/149	**153**
Weekly PAYE	125	125	144	156	182	**192**
Monthly NI	476	476	589/602	624/634	641/646	**663**
Monthly PAYE	540	540	623	675	787	**833**

For full list of national insurance rates see p 109.

PAYE settlement agreements

(SI 2003/2682 Part 6)

These are voluntary agreements between the employer and HMRC under which the employer agrees to meet the tax payable on certain expenses and benefits in kind that are given to his employees. Once an agreement has been signed for a tax year, there is no need to:

- enter the items covered on form P9D or P11D;
- operate PAYE on them, or
- calculate a liability for included items which are liable for Class 1 or Class 1A NICs.

The employer pays Class 1B NICs on the items included in PAYE settlement agreements and on the total amount of tax payable. To be effective for a tax year, an agreement must be signed before 6 July following the end of the year and tax must be paid by 19 October following (or 22 October where paid electronically). They are most suited for payments and benefits provided on an irregular basis, or where benefits are for a group of employees and apportionment is difficult.

Personal service companies

(ITEPA 2003 ss 48–61)

These provisions are commonly known under the name 'IR35' and apply where personal services are provided to a client through an intermediary – normally the worker's personal service company. The effect of the legislation is to treat the worker as an employee of the client for working out the 'deemed employment payment'. The computation involves taking into account all payments and benefits, including those paid direct to the worker for a tax year other than by the intermediary for his services. Certain, restricted, allowable expenses, are deducted from 'earnings'. Finally, any payments or benefits received by the worker from the intermediary are deducted. Tax (under PAYE) and NIC is calculated and the amounts due are payable by the worker and his company. From 2013–14 the provisions are extended to office holders.

Managed service companies

(ITEPA 2003 ss 61A-61J)

Where an individual provides his services through a managed service company (as defined) all payments made to him by the company are deemed to be employment income and PAYE and NIC have to be applied.

National minimum wage

Hourly rate

Age of worker	*apprentice rate*[3]	*Under 18*[1]	*18–20*[2]	*21 or more*
From 1.10.14	**£2.73**	**£3.79**	**£5.13**	**£6.50**
1.10.13–30.9.14	£2.68	£3.72	£5.03	£6.31
1.10.12–30.9.13	£2.65	£3.68	£4.98	£6.19
1.10.11–30.9.12	£2.60	£3.68	£4.98	£6.08
1.10.10–30.9.11	£2.50	£3.64	£4.92	£5.93
1.10.09–30.9.10	n/a	£3.57	£4.83	£5.80
1.10.08–30.9.09	n/a	£3.53	£4.77	£5.73

1 Applies to all workers under 18 who are no longer of compulsory school age.

2 Applied to workers aged 18–21 before 1 October 2010. This rate also applied before that date to workers aged 22 or more, starting a new job with a new employer, doing accredited training.

3 From 1 October 2010 the apprentice rate applies to apprentices aged under 19 and other apprentices in their first year of apprenticeship.

Basis of assessment

(ITEPA 2003 ss 14–41E)

	Services performed			
	Wholly in UK	*Partly in UK*	*Partly abroad*	*Wholly abroad*
Persons domiciled in UK				
Non-resident[2]	All	That part	None	None
Resident[2]	All	All[1]	All[1]	All[1]
Persons domiciled outside the UK				
UK employer				
Non-resident	All	That part	None	None
Meets requirement for 3-year period of non-residence[3]	All	That part	Remittances	Remittances
Resident	All	All[1]	All[1]	All[1]
Foreign employer				
Non-resident	All	That part	None	None
Meets requirement for 3-year period of non-residence	All	That part	Remittances	Remittances
Resident[4]	All	That part	Remittances	Remittances

1 Exemption for seafarers if at least half of qualifying period of over 364 days worked abroad (including 183 consecutive days). Deduction extended in April 2011 with retrospective effect to seafarers who are resident for tax purposes in a European Economic Area or European Union State, other than the United Kingdom. (ITEPA 2003 ss 378–385, HMRC Brief 10/2012).

2 A statutory residence test was introduced from 6 April 2013 and ordinary residence was abolished from that date, subject to transitional provisions in certain cases for individuals who were resident but not ordinarily resident in the UK at the end of the tax year 2012–13. Before 6 April 2013 resident but not ordinarily resident taxpayers were taxed broadly on all UK earnings and remittances for duties performed abroad.

3 An employee meets the requirement for a 3-year period of non-residence for a tax year X if he has been non-resident for three consecutive tax years and year X is any of the three years immediately following that spell of non-residence.

4 From 2014–15 an anti-avoidance measure will tax UK resident non-domiciles on an arising basis in respect of certain overseas employment income where separate employment contracts have been artificially arranged to separate the UK and overseas employment to obtain a tax advantage.

Termination payments

(ITEPA 2003 ss 401–416)

The following lump sum payments are exempt from tax:

(a) Payments in connection with the cessation of employment on the death, injury or disability of the employee.

(b) Payments under tax-exempt pension schemes by way of compensation for loss of employment (or of earnings due to ill-health) or which can properly be regarded as a benefit earned by past service.

(c) Certain payments of terminal grants to members of the armed forces.

(d) Certain benefits under superannuation schemes for civil servants in Commonwealth overseas territories.

(e) Payments in respect of foreign service where the period of foreign service comprises:

(i) 75% of the whole period of service; or

(ii) the whole of the last 10 years of service; or
(iii) where the period of service exceeded 20 years, one-half of that period, including any 10 of the last 20 years.

Otherwise, a proportion of the payment is exempt, as follows:

$$\frac{\text{length of foreign service}}{\text{length of total service}} \times \text{amount otherwise chargeable}$$

(f) The first £30,000 of genuine ex gratia payments (where there is no 'arrangement' by the employer to make the payment).
(g) Statutory redundancy payments (included in computing £30,000 limit in (*f*) above).

Fixed rate expenses

For most classes of industry fixed rate allowances for the upkeep of tools and special clothing have been agreed between HMRC and the trade unions concerned. Alternatively, the individual employee may claim as a deduction his or her actual expenses (ITEPA 2003 s 367). (HMRC Employment Income Manual EIM32712.)

Industry	*Occupation*	*Deduction from 2008–09*
Agriculture	All workers[1]	100
Airlines	See note 5 below	
Aluminium	(*a*) Continual casting operators, process operators, de-dimplers, driers, drill punchers, dross unloaders, firemen[2], furnace operators and their helpers, leaders, mouldmen, pourers, remelt department labourers, roll flatteners	140
	(*b*) Cable hands, case makers, labourers, mates, truck drivers and measurers, storekeepers	80
	(*c*) Apprentices	60
	(*d*) All other workers[1]	120
Banks and building societies	Uniformed doormen and messengers	60
Brass and copper	Braziers, coppersmiths, finishers, fitters, moulders, turners and all other workers	120
Building	(*a*) Joiners and carpenters	140
	(*b*) Cement works, roofing felt and asphalt labourers	80
	(*c*) Labourers and navvies	60
	(*d*) All other workers	120
Building materials	(*a*) Stone masons	120
	(*b*) Tilemakers and labourers	60
	(*c*) All other workers	80
Clothing	(*a*) Lacemakers, hosiery bleachers, dyers, scourers and knitters, knitwear bleachers and dyers	60
	(*b*) All other workers	60
Constructional engineering[3]	(*a*) Blacksmiths and their strikers, burners, caulkers, chippers, drillers, erectors, fitters, holders up, markers off, platers, riggers, riveters, rivet heaters, scaffolders, sheeters, template workers, turners, welders	140
	(*b*) Banksmen, labourers, shop-helpers, slewers, straighteners	80
	(*c*) Apprentices and storekeepers	60
	(*d*) All other workers	100
Electrical and electricity supply	(*a*) Those workers incurring laundry costs only	60
	(*b*) All other workers	120
Engineering (trades ancillary to)	(*a*) Pattern makers	140
	(*b*) Labourers, supervisory and unskilled workers	80
	(*c*) Apprentices and storekeepers	60
	(*d*) Motor mechanics in garage repair shops	120
	(*e*) All other workers	120
Fire service	Uniformed firefighters and fire officers	80
Food	All workers	60
Forces personnel	See note 7 below	
Forestry	All workers	100
Glass	All workers	80
Healthcare staff in the NHS, private hospitals and nursing homes	(*a*) Ambulance staff on active service	140
	(*b*) Nurses and midwives, chiropodists, dental nurses, occupational, speech and other therapists, phlebotomists and radiographers	100
	(*c*) Plaster room orderlies, hospital porters, ward clerks, sterile supply workers, hospital domestics, hospital catering staff	100
	(*d*) Laboratory staff, pharmacists, pharmacy assistants	60
	(*e*) Uniformed ancillary staff: maintenance workers, grounds staff, drivers, parking attendants and security guards, receptionists and other uniformed staff	60
Heating	(*a*) Pipe fitters and plumbers	120
	(*b*) Coverers, laggers, domestic glaziers, heating engineers and their mates	120
	(*c*) All gas workers, all other workers	100
Iron mining	(*a*) Fillers, miners and underground workers	120
	(*b*) All other workers	100
Iron and steel	(*a*) Day labourers, general labourers, stockmen, time keepers, warehouse staff and weighmen	80
	(*b*) Apprentices	60
	(*c*) All other workers	140
Leather	(*a*) Curriers (wet workers), fellmongering workers, tanning operatives (wet)	80
	(*b*) All other workers	60
Particular engineering[4]	(*a*) Pattern makers	140
	(*b*) Chainmakers, cleaners, galvanisers, tinners and wire drawers in the wire drawing industry, tool-makers in the lock making industry	120
	(*c*) Apprentices and storekeepers	60
	(*d*) All other workers	80

Industry	*Occupation*	*Deduction from 2008–09*
Police force	Uniformed police officers (ranks up to and including Chief Inspector) Community Support officers and other police service employees — see note 6 below	140
Precious metals	All workers	100
Printing	(*a*) Letterpress section — electrical engineers (rotary presses), electrotypers, ink and roller makers, machine minders (rotary), maintenance engineers (rotary presses) and stereotypers	140
	(*b*) Bench hands (periodical and bookbinding section), compositors (letterpress section), readers (letterpress section), telecommunications and electronic section wire room operators, warehousemen (paper box making section)	60
	(*c*) All other workers	100
Prisons	Uniformed prison officers	80
Public service	(i) Dock and inland waterways	
	(*a*) Dockers, dredger drivers, hopper steerers	80
	(*b*) All other workers	60
	(ii) Public transport	
	(*a*) Garage hands (including cleaners)	80
	(*b*) Conductors and drivers	60
Quarrying	All workers	100
Railways	(See the appropriate category for craftsmen, eg engineers, vehicles etc.) All other workers	100
Seamen	Carpenters	
	(*a*) Passenger liners	165
	(*b*) Cargo vessels, tankers, coasters and ferries	140
Shipyards	(*a*) Blacksmiths and their strikers, boilermakers, burners, carpenters, caulkers, drillers, furnacemen (platers), holders up, fitters, platers, plumbers, riveters, sheet iron workers, shipwrights, tubers, welders	140
	(*b*) Labourers	80
	(*c*) Apprentices and storekeepers	60
	(*d*) All other workers	100
Textiles and textile printing	(*a*) Carders, carding engineers, overlookers and technicians in spinning mills	120
	(*b*) All other workers	80
Vehicles	(*a*) Builders, railway vehicle repairers, and railway wagon lifters	140
	(*b*) Railway vehicle painters and letterers, builders' and repairers' assistants	80
	(*c*) All other workers	60
Wood & furniture	(*a*) Carpenters, cabinet makers, joiners, wood carvers and woodcutting machinists	140
	(*b*) Artificial limb makers (other than in wood), organ builders and packing case makers	120
	(*c*) Coopers not providing own tools, labourers, polishers and upholsterers	60
	(*d*) All other workers	100

1 'All workers' and 'all other workers' refer only to manual workers who have to bear the cost of upkeep of tools and special clothing. They do not extend to other employees such as office staff.

2 'Firemen' means persons engaged to light and maintain furnaces.

3 'Constructional engineering' means engineering undertaken on a construction site, including buildings, shipyards, bridges, roads and other similar operations.

4 'Particular engineering' means engineering undertaken on a commercial basis in a factory or workshop for the purposes of producing components such as wire, springs, nails and locks.

5 A basic flat rate expenses allowance of £850 applies to all uniformed commercial pilots, co-pilots and other flight deck crew working in the UK (but not stewards/stewardesses). A further £100 allowance is allowed for the cost of travel to certain regular specified activities.

6 From 2008–09 the allowance for police officers applies to community support officers. Other police service employees who must clean their own uniform can claim a deduction of £60.

7 As announced in February 2014, a new flat-rate expenses allowance applies in relation to the laundering of uniforms for naval ratings and other ranks, backdated to 6 April 2008. Negotiations are continuing on a similar allowance for officers. The annual amount is £80 for the Royal Navy and £100 for the Army, RAF and Royal Marines.

Investment reliefs

Community investment tax relief

(ITA 2007 ss 333–382; CTA 2010 ss 218–269)

Investments made by an individual or company in an accredited community development finance institution (CDFI) are eligible for tax relief up to 25%. The investment may be a loan or a subscription for shares or securities. Tax relief may be claimed for the tax year or accounting period in which the investment is made and each of the four subsequent years. Relief for each year is broadly 5% of the invested amount, but from April 2013 any unused balance of the 5% annual relief can be carried forward, although not beyond the 5-year investment period, and only as long as some part of the investment remains within the CDFI. In addition, to comply with European State aid rules, from 1 April 2013 there is a limit on the amounts of relief a company can obtain in any 3-year period — the amount of CITR relief and any de minimis aid from other sources must not exceed €200,000.

Enterprise investment scheme

(ITA 2007 ss 156–257)

The EIS applies to investments in qualifying unquoted companies trading in the UK. Eligible shares must be held for at least three years from the issue date or commencement of trade if later. The following reliefs apply subject to this and other conditions.

Relief on investment

Maximum investment:	**From 2012–13**	**£1,000,000**
	2008–09 to 2011–12	£500,000
Minimum investment:	**From 2012–13**	**No minimum**
	1993–94 to 2011–12	£500
Maximum carry-back to preceding year	**From 2009–10**	**No restriction (subject to annual maximum)**
(Up to ½ amount invested between 6 April and 5 October)	2006–07 to 2008–09	£50,000
Rate of relief	**From 2011–12**	**30%**[1]
	1993–94 to 2010–11	20%[1]

1 Given as a deduction against income tax liability.

Other reliefs (TCGA 1992 ss 150A–150C, Sch 5B)

(a) A gain on a disposal of shares on which EIS relief has been given and not withdrawn is exempt from capital gains tax.

(b) Deferral relief is available for gains on assets where the disposal proceeds are reinvested in eligible shares in a qualifying company within one year before and three years after the disposal.

(c) A loss on a disposal of shares on which EIS relief has been given may be relieved against income tax or capital gains tax.

Seed enterprise investment scheme

(ITA 2007 ss 257A–257HG; FA 2014 ss 54, 55)

From 6 April 2012 SEIS applies to investments in companies with fewer than 25 employees and assets up to £200,000 carrying on or preparing to carry on new business. Eligible shares must be held for at least three years from the issue date. The following reliefs apply subject to this and other conditions.

Relief on investment

Maximum investment:	**From 2012–13**	**£100,000**
Maximum carry-back to preceding year	**From 2013–14**	**No restriction (subject to annual maximum)**[2]
Rate of relief	**From 2012–13**	**50%**[1]

1 Given as a deduction against income tax liability.
2 Carry back cannot therefore apply until 2013–14.

Other reliefs (TCGA 1992 ss 150E, 150G, Sch 5BB)

(a) A gain on a disposal of shares on which SEIS relief has been given and not withdrawn is exempt from capital gains tax.

(b) Reinvestment relief is available for certain gains on assets where the disposal proceeds are reinvested in SEIS and SEIS relief is claimed (see p 40).

Social investment tax relief

(FA 2014 Sch 11; ITA 2007 ss 257J–257TE)

Between 6 April 2014 and 5 April 2019 income tax relief is available to both resident and non-UK resident individuals who subscribe for qualifying shares or make qualifying debt investments in a social enterprise which meets the requirements, and who have a UK tax liability against which to set the relief. The investment must be held for a period of three years. The following reliefs apply subject to conditions.

Relief on investment

Maximum investment:	**From 2014–15**	**£1,000,000**
Maximum carry-back to preceding year	**From 2015–16**	**No restriction (subject to annual maximum)[2]**
Rate of relief	**From 2014–15**	**30%[1]**

1 Given as a deduction against income tax liability.
2 Carry back cannot therefore apply until 2015–16.

Other reliefs

(a) A gain on a disposal of shares on which SITR income tax relief has been given and not withdrawn is exempt from capital gains tax where shares held for at least 3 years.

(b) Deferral relief is available for gains arising on assets in the period 6 April 2014 to 5 April 2019 where the disposal proceeds are reinvested in shares or debt investments which also qualify for the SITR income tax relief (see p 40).

Venture capital trusts

(ITA 2007 ss 258–332)

An individual who subscribes for ordinary shares in a VCT obtains income tax reliefs at the rates in the table below subject to conditions. The shares must be held for at least five years.

Relief on investment

Maximum annual investment:	**From 2004–05**	**£200,000**
Rate of relief:	**From 2006–07**	**30%**

Other reliefs

(a) Dividends on shares within investment limit exempt from income tax (unless the investor's main purpose is tax avoidance) (ITTOIA 2005 s 709).

(b) Capital gains reliefs (see p 40).

Urban Regeneration Companies

Relief is available from 1 April 2003 for expenditure incurred by businesses in making contributions to designated Urban Regeneration Companies (ITTOIA 2005 ss 82, 86; CTA 2009 ss 82, 86).

Individual savings accounts ('ISAs')

(TA 1988 s 333; ITTOIA 2005 ss 694–701; SI 1998/1870; SI 2001/908; SI 2014/654; SI 2014/1450)

Savers can subscribe to an ISA up to the following limits per tax year.

	2008–09 to 2009–10[2]	2010–11	2011–12	2012–13	2013–14	**6.4.14–30.6.14**	**1.7.14–5.4.15**
Overall annual subscription limit	£7,200	£10,200	£10,680	£11,280	£11,520	**£11,880**	**£15,000[1]**
Cash limit	£3,600	£5,100	£5,340	£5,640	£5,760	**£5,940**	**£15,000[1]**

1 From 1 July 2014 ISAs are reformed into a simpler product, the 'New ISA' (NISA). All existing ISAs become NISAs and the overall annual subscription limit for these accounts will be increased to £15,000 for 2014–15. ISA savers are able to subscribe this full amount to a cash account.
2 For taxpayers aged 50 or over in 2009–10 the limits for 2010–11 apply for 2009–10 also, with effect from 6 October 2009.

The subscription limit applies to each spouse or civil partner. Shares acquired under an approved share incentive plan, profit sharing scheme or SAYE option scheme may be transferred to an ISA within 90 days without tax consequences. From 2008–09 PEPs are transferred into ISA accounts.

Reliefs

(a) Investments under the scheme are free from income tax and capital gains tax. When an investment is transferred to an investor he is deemed to have made a disposal and reacquisition at market value and any notional gain is exempt from capital gains tax.

(b) Withdrawals may be made at any time without loss of tax relief.

Junior individual savings accounts (Junior ISAs)

(ITTOIA 2005 s 695A; SI 2011/1780; SI 2014/654; SI 2014/1450)

A Junior ISA scheme was introduced from November 2011, available to all UK resident children under 18 who do not have a Child Trust Fund account. Children are able to have one cash and one stocks and shares Junior ISA at any time.

	2011–12 to 2012–13	2013–14	**6.4.14–30.6.14**	**1.7.14–5.4.15**
Overall annual subscription limit	£3,600	£3,720	**£3,840**	**£4,000**

National Savings Bank interest

(ITTOIA 2005 s 691; FA 2011 Sch 26)

Before 19 July 2011 the first £70 of any interest received from a National Savings Ordinary Account was tax free.

Miscellaneous reliefs

Employee shareholder shares

(ITEPA 2003 ss 226A–226D; SI 2013/1755)

The first £2,000 of the value of shares acquired through the adoption of the 'employee shareholder' employment status is not subject to income tax or national insurance. Applies from 1 September 2013. For the capital gains tax rules see p 39.

Foster carers and shared lives carers (Qualifying care)

(ITTOIA 2005 ss 803–828)

Generally, local authority payments to foster carers are not taxable to the extent they do no more than meet the actual costs of caring. In other cases, and for shared lives carers from 6 April 2010:

- where gross receipts do not exceed the 'individual limit' and shared lives care is not being provided to more than three people, the carer is treated as having a nil profit and nil loss for the tax year concerned;
- where gross receipts exceed the 'individual limit' and shared lives care is not being provided to more than three people, the carer can choose to either be taxed on the excess or compute profit or loss using the normal business rules.

The 'individual limit' is made up of a fixed amount of £10,000 per residence for a full tax year plus an amount per adult or child for each week or part week that the individual provides qualifying care. The weekly amounts are £200 for a child under 11 years and £250 for a child of 11 or over and an adult.

For 2010–11 only, shared lives carers could choose to apply the simplified arrangements for adult placement carers.

Gift of pre-eminent objects

(FA 2012 Sch 14)

Individuals who gift pre-eminent objects to the nation will receive a reduction in their UK tax liability of 30% of the value of the object they are donating. The tax reduction can be against income or capital gains tax and can be spread forward across a period of up to five years starting with the tax year in which the object is offered. The legislation has effect in relation to liabilities for tax years and accounting periods beginning on or after 1 April 2012. The gift must be accepted as pre-eminent by the Arts Council under the Cultural Gifts Scheme.

Landlord's energy-saving allowance

(ITTOIA 2005 ss 312–314; CTA 2009 ss 251–253; SI 2007/831; SI 2007/3278; SI 2008/1520)

From 6 April 2004 to 5 April 2015 individual landlords who let residential property and pay income tax may claim a deduction from the property business profits for expenditure in the dwelling-houses let to install:

- loft insulation or cavity wall insulation; or
- (from 7 April 2005) solid wall insulation; or
- (from 6 April 2006) draught-proofing and insulation for hot water systems; or
- (from 6 April 2007) floor insulation.

Expenditure is restricted to £1,500 per building until 5 April 2007 and to £1,500 per dwelling-house from 6 April 2007.

The relief is extended to corporate landlords of residential property for expenditure on or after 8 July 2008.

Life assurance premium relief

(TA 1988 s 266, Sch 14 para 7; FA 2012 Sch 39)

For premiums due and payable **before 6 April 2015**, or payable before that date and actually paid before 6 July 2015, relief for premiums paid on qualifying life assurance policies for contracts made before 14 March 1984 is available by deduction of 12.5% from admissible premiums.

Maintenance payments

(ITTOIA 2005 ss 727, 729; ITA 2007 ss 453–456)

Where either party to the marriage or civil partnership was born before 6 April 1935 tax relief may be claimed by the payer in respect of the lower of:

- the amount of the payments in the year concerned and
- the minimum amount of the married couple's allowance for the year concerned (see p 76).

The relief is restricted to 10% of the relevant amount. The payment must be made to the former/separated spouse or civil partner. It is made gross and is not taxable in the hands of the recipient.

Rent-a-room relief

(ITTOIA 2005 ss 784–802)

Gross annual receipts from letting furnished accommodation in the only or main home are exempt from tax up to a maximum of £4,250 (provided no other taxable income is derived from a trade, letting or arrangement from which the rent-a-room receipts are derived).

If the gross receipts exceed £4,250, the taxpayer can pay tax on the net receipts after deduction of expenses. Alternatively, the taxpayer can elect to pay tax on the amount by which the gross receipts exceed £4,250, without relief for the actual expenses.

An individual's maximum is halved to £2,125 if during the 'relevant period' for the year (normally the tax year) some other person received income from letting accommodation in that property.

An election can be made to disapply the relief for a particular tax year (for example, if the individual would otherwise make an allowable loss).

Simplified fixed rate deductions

(ITTOIA 2005 ss 94B–94I)

From 2013–14 individuals carrying on a trade, profession or vocation as self-employed sole traders or in partnership with other individuals can choose certain simplified expenses when calculating their profits for income tax purposes. Conditions apply.

Vehicle expenditure

Kind of vehicle	Rate per business mile
Car or goods vehicle	45p for the first 10,000 miles
	25p after that
Motor cycle	24p

Use of home for business purposes

Hours worked per month	Amount per month
25 or more	£10
51 or more	£18
101 or more	£26

Premises used both as a home and for business

Note: Amount below is the non-business use amount to be deducted from the total expenses claimed. The flat rate includes all household goods and services, food and non-alcoholic drinks and utilities. It does not include mortgage interest, rent of the premises, council tax or rates. A reasonable apportionment of these expenses should be made based on the extent of the private occupation of the premises — HMRC Brief 14/2013.

Number of occupants	Amount per month
1	£350
2	£500
3 or more	£650

Capped income tax reliefs

(ITA 2007 s 24A)

From 2013–14 a limit on previously uncapped income tax reliefs is imposed. The limit is set at the greater of £50,000 or 25% of the individual's adjusted total income for the tax year. The specified reliefs which, taken together, will be limited to the extent that they can be relieved by individuals against general income are:

Trade loss relief against general income (ITA 2007 s 64)
Early trade losses relief (ITA 2007 s 72)
Post-cessation trade relief (ITA 2007 s 96)
Property loss relief against general income (ITA 2007 s 120)
Post-cessation property relief (ITA 2007 s 125)
Employment loss relief against general income (ITA 2007 s 128)
Former employees deduction for liabilities (ITEPA 2003 s 555)
Share loss relief on non-Enterprise Investment Scheme / Seed Enterprise Investment Scheme shares (ITA 2007 Pt 4 Ch 6)

Losses on deeply discounted securities (ITTOIA 2005 ss 446, 454)
Qualifying loan interest (ITA 2007 Pt 8 Ch 1)

Pension provision from 6 April 2006

(FA 2004 ss 149–284, Schs 28–36; FA 2014 Schs 5–7)

From 6 April 2006, a new pension scheme tax regime fully replaced pre-existing rules for occupational pension schemes, personal (and stakeholder) pension schemes and retirement annuity schemes.

Tax relief on contributions

Individual contributions: Contributions to registered schemes are not limited by reference to a fraction of earnings and there is no earnings cap. There is no provision for the carry-back or carry-forward of contributions to tax years other than the year of payment.

An individual may make unlimited contributions and tax relief is available on contributions up to the higher of:

- the full amount of relevant earnings; or
- £3,600 provided the scheme operates tax relief at source.

Employer contributions: Employer contributions to registered schemes are deductible for tax purposes, with statutory provision for spreading abnormally large contributions over a period of up to four years. The contributions are not treated as taxable income of the employee, although from 6 April 2013 this relief does not extend to payments for the benefit of family members.

Special annual allowance charge: A special annual allowance charge applied for 2009–10 and 2010–11 for individuals with income of £130,000 or over. Tax relief above basic rate was recovered from pension savings above an individual's special annual allowance by the application of the special annual allowance charge. An individual's special annual allowance was the higher of their regular pension savings and £20,000 (or in certain circumstances, where contributions had been less regular than quarterly, £30,000).

Annual allowance

Each individual has an annual allowance as set out in the table below. If the annual increase in an individual's rights under all registered schemes exceeds the annual allowance, the excess is chargeable at the individual's marginal rate (40% for 2010–11 and earlier years). The individual is liable for the tax, unless, for 2011–12 onwards, he makes an election for the scheme to pay the charge if it exceeds £2,000. In such cases a consequential adjustment is made to the individual's entitlement to benefits.

Annual allowance	2009–10	2010–11	2011–12	2012–13	2013–14	**2014–15**
	£245,000	£255,000	£50,000[1]	£50,000[1]	£50,000[1]	**£40,000**[1]

1 From 2011–12 unused allowance can be carried forward three years. For these purposes the annual allowance for 2008–09 to 2010–11 is assumed to be £50,000.

Taxable benefits

'Tax-free' lump sum: The maximum 'tax-free' lump sum that can be paid to a member under a registered scheme is broadly the lower of:

- 25% of the value of the pension rights; and
- 25% of the member's lifetime allowance.

Lifetime allowance: Each individual has a lifetime allowance for contributions as set out in the table below. The excess over the lifetime allowance of the benefits crystallising (usually when a pension begins to be paid) is taxable at the following rates:

- 55% if taken as a lump sum;
- 25% in other cases.

Any tax due may be deducted from the individual's benefits.

Lifetime allowance	2009–10	2010–11	2011–12	2012–13	2013–14	**2014–15**
	£1,750,000	£1,800,000	£1,800,000	£1,500,000	£1,500,000	**£1,250,000**

Transitional. There are transitional provisions for the protection of lump sum and other pension rights accrued before 6 April 2006. Fixed protection is also available to protect pension rights from 6 April 2012 and from 6 April 2014 when the lifetime allowance is decreased. From 6 April 2014 'individual protection 2014' is also being introduced.

Age restrictions

Minimum pension age: The minimum pension age is 55 (50 before 6 April 2010). A pension cannot be paid before the minimum age except on grounds of ill health. Those with existing contractual rights to draw a pension earlier will have those rights protected and there is special protection for members of pre-6 April 2006 approved schemes with early retirement ages. A reduced lifetime allowance will apply in the case of early retirement before minimum pension age except in the case of certain professions such as the police and the armed forces (SI 2005/3451).

Maximum benefit age: Before 2011–12 benefits had to be taken by the age of 77 at the latest (age 75 before 22 June 2010). A member of a money purchase scheme could take a pension from the age of 77 (previously 75) by way of income withdrawal (known as an 'alternatively secured pension') instead of taking a scheme pension or purchasing a lifetime annuity. The maximum alternatively secured pension was 70% of a comparable annuity. These requirements are withdrawn for 2011–12 onwards.

Share schemes

Share incentive plans ('SIPs')

(TCGA 1992 ss 236A, 238A, Schs 7C, 7D Pt 1; ITEPA 2003 ss 488–515, Sch 2; FA 2014 ss 49–50, Sch 8)

Free share plan

2014–15 onwards	*annual maximum*	**£3,600**
2000–01 to 2013–14	*annual maximum*	£3,000

Partnership share plan

2014–15 onwards	*annual maximum*	**£1,800 or 10% of annual salary if lower**
2003–04 to 2013–14	*annual maximum*	£1,500 or 10% of annual salary if lower

Matching shares

2000–01 onwards	*Maximum number of shares given by employer to employee for each partnership share bought*	2

Shares are free of tax and NICs if held in the plan for five years. Dividends are tax free if reinvested in shares (restricted to a maximum of £1,500 per employee per tax year before 6 April 2013). Shares withdrawn from the plan at any time are exempt from capital gains tax and are treated as acquired by the employee at their market value at that time.

If shares are withdrawn within between three and five years (with exceptions such as on death, injury, disability, retirement, redundancy, or, from 17 July 2013, certain cash takeovers), liability to income tax and NICs arises on the lower of their value on entering and on leaving the plan. If shares are withdrawn within three years (with similar exceptions), liability is on their value on leaving the plan.

Employer self-certification replaces HMRC approval from 6 April 2014.

Enterprise management incentives

(TCGA 1992 s 238A, Sch 7D Pt 4; ITEPA 2003 ss 527–541, Sch 5; FA 2014 Sch 8)

Certain independent trading companies with gross assets not exceeding £30 million may grant share options then worth up to £250,000 (£120,000 for options granted before 16 June 2012, £100,000 for options granted before 6 April 2008) to an eligible employee. The total value of shares in respect of which unexercised qualifying options exist must not exceed £3 million. An additional restriction, limiting the scheme to companies with fewer than 250 full-time equivalent employees, applies to options granted on or after 21 July 2008.

Where the conditions of the scheme are complied with:

(a) There is no charge to tax or NICs when the option is granted provided the option to acquire the shares is not at less than their market values at that date, and there is no charge on exercise providing the option is exercised within ten years.

(b) Capital gains tax will be payable when the shares are sold, though for disposals on or after 6 April 2013, shares acquired through exercising EMI options on or after 6 April 2012 are eligible for capital gains tax entrepreneurs' relief if certain conditions are met.

Save as you earn (SAYE) share option schemes

(TCGA 1992 s 238A, Sch 7D Pt 2; ITEPA 2003 ss 516–519, Sch 3; FA 2014 Sch 8)

The scheme is linked to a savings arrangement, on which bonuses are exempt from tax, to provide funds for the acquisition of shares when the option is exercised at the end of a three or five-year contract. A five-year contract may offer the option of repayment on the seventh anniversary, although the 7-year savings period is withdrawn with effect from 23 July 2013. Employees who are already saving under existing SAYE contracts before 23 July 2013 are not affected by this change.

Monthly contributions to SAYE scheme

	up to 5 April 2014	**From 6 April 2014**
Minimum	£5–10[1]	**£5–£10**[1]
Maximum	£250	**£500**

[1] The company may choose a minimum savings contribution between £5 and £10.

See the HMRC website (www.hmrc.gov.uk/shareschemes/saye-change-bonus.htm) for the bonus rates.

Where the conditions of the scheme are complied with, no income tax charge arises on the employee in respect of:

(a) the grant of an option to acquire shares at a discount of up to 20% of the share price at time of the grant;
(b) the exercise of the option (options must not be exercised before the bonus date subject to exceptions such as on injury, disability, redundancy, retirement, death or, from 17 July 2013, certain cash takeovers); or
(c) any increase in the value of the shares.

Capital gains tax is chargeable on disposal of the shares: the CGT base cost is the consideration given by the employee for both the shares and the option.

Employer self-certification replaces HMRC approval from 6 April 2014.

Company share option plans ('CSOPs')

(TCGA 1992 s 238A, Sch 7D Pt 3; ITEPA 2003 ss 521–526, Sch 4; FA 2014 Sch 8)

Limit on value of shares under option held by employee at any one time

From 29 April 1996	£30,000

Scheme shares must be fully paid up, not redeemable and, for options granted before 17 July 2013, not subject to special restrictions. Only full-time directors or qualifying employees may participate in the scheme.

Where the conditions of the scheme are complied with, no tax charge arises on the employee in respect of:
(a) the grant of an option to acquire shares[1];
(b) the exercise of the option[2]; or
(c) any increase in the value of the shares.

Capital gains tax is chargeable on disposal of the shares: the CGT base cost is the consideration given by the employee for both the shares and the option.

Employer self-certification replaces HMRC approval from 6 April 2014.

1 At the time the option is granted the price at which shares can be acquired must not be less than the market value of shares of the same class at that time.

2 The option must be exercised between three and ten years after the grant (or may be exercised less than three years after the grant where the individual ceases to be an employee due to injury, disability, redundancy or retirement, or, from 17 July 2013, where there are certain cash takeovers of constituent companies). For options granted before 9 April 2003, the options must be exercised between three and ten years after the grant (without exception) and not less than three years after a previous exempt exercise of another option under the same or another approved company share option scheme.

Tax credits

(TCA 2002)

From 6 April 2003, child tax credit and working tax credit replaced children's tax credit, working families' tax credit and disabled person's tax credit in addition to the child-related elements of certain social security benefits. Administered and paid by HMRC, they are non-taxable. Claims must be made after the commencement of the tax year and can be backdated for a maximum of one month (three months before 6 April 2012). Universal credit will replace tax credits. New claimants in some areas started to claim universal credit from October 2013. Existing claimants will be gradually phased onto universal credit, and this is expected to be completed by December 2017 (see p 129).

Child tax credit and working tax credit

	2013–14 Annual amount	*2014–15* Annual amount
Child tax credit	£	£
Family element[1]	545	**545**
Child element (for each child or young person)	2,720	**2,750**
Addition for disabled child or young person	3,015	**3,100**
Enhancement for severe disabled child or young person	1,220	**1,255**
Working tax credit	£	£
Basic element	1,920	**1,940**
Lone parent and couple element	1,970	**1,990**
30-hour element	790	**800**
Disability element	2,855	**2,935**
Severe disability element	1,220	**1,255**
Childcare element – up to 70% (80% for 2006–07 to 2010–11) of eligible costs	**Weekly**	**Weekly**
– maximum eligible cost for one child	175	**175**
– maximum eligible cost for two or more children	300	**300**

1 Only one family element per family. Before 2011–12, baby element payable in addition in the first year of the child's life.

Income thresholds and withdrawal rates	***2013–14***	***2014–15***
Income threshold for those entitled to CTC and WTC	£6,420	**£6,420**
Withdrawal rate	41%	**41%**
Income threshold for those entitled to CTC only	£15,910	**£16,010**
Income rise disregard	£5,000	**£5,000**
Income fall disregard	£2,500	**£2,500**

Calculation of award. Tax credits are awarded on an annual basis. They are initially based on the income of the claimant or joint claimants for the preceding tax year and then adjusted based on actual income in the tax year in which the credit is claimed. Income broadly includes all taxable income excluding the first £300 of income from pensions, savings, property or foreign assets. If current year's income is greater than the previous year's income by less than £5,000 (£10,000 for 2012–13 and 2011–12, £25,000 before 2011–12), the award is not adjusted. If current year's income is greater than the previous year's income by £5,000 or more (£10,000 for 2012–13 and 2011–12, £25,000 before 2011–12), the award is adjusted to reflect current year's income less £5,000. An income fall disregard of £2,500 is introduced from 6 April 2012. This means that from 2012–13, where previous year's income exceeds the current year's income by not more than £2,500, the previous year's income will be used, but where the previous year's income exceeds the current year's income by more than £2,500, the current year's income plus £2,500 will be used. In any other case current year's income is used. Where circumstances change during a tax year and different rates apply, the award is recalculated on a proportional, daily basis. Such changes must be notified to HMRC within one month if tax credit entitlement will be reduced as a result.

Eligibility. CTC is payable to UK resident single parents and couples responsible for a child or young person. WTC is payable to UK residents who are at least 16 years old and, in the case of single persons, who work at least 16 hours a week. In the case of a couple, from 6 April 2012, they must jointly work at least 24 hours a week and one must work at least 16 hours a week, or where only one of the couple works that person must work for at least 24 hours a week. Additionally, the claimant (or one of them if a couple) must either:

- be at least 25 years old and work at least 30 hours a week; or
- have a dependent child or children; or
- before 6 April 2012, be over 50 and qualify for the 50+ element; or
- have a mental or physical disability which puts them at a disadvantage in getting a job and have previously been in receipt of some form of disability benefit; or
- from 6 April 2011, be over 60 and work at least 16 hours a week, regardless of whether they have dependent children.

Renewal claim. Claims for tax credit must be renewed by 31 July.

Inheritance tax

Rates of tax

(IHTA 1984 s 7, Schs 1, 1A; HMRC Inheritance Tax Manual IHTM14593)

From 15 March 1988 onwards

	Rate
Cumulative gross transfer rate:	
for gross transfers on death over the cumulative chargeable transfer limit	**40%**
reduced rate on death	**36%**[1]
for gross lifetime transfers over the cumulative chargeable transfer limit	**20%**
Grossing-up net transfer rate for each £1 over the chargeable transfer limit:	
for net transfers on death not bearing own tax	**2/3**
for net lifetime transfers	**1/4**

1 For deaths occurring on or after 6 April 2012 a reduced rate of 36% applies where at least 10% of the net estate is left to charity or registered community amateur sports clubs.

Nil rate bands

Period	*Limit*	*Period*	*Limit*
	£		£
2014–15	**325,000**[1]		
2013–14	325,000	2000–01	234,000
2012–13	325,000	1999–2000	231,000
2011–12	325,000	1998–99	223,000
2010–11	325,000	1997–98	215,000
2009–10	325,000	1996–97	200,000
2008–09	312,000	1995–96	154,000
2007–08	300,000	10.3.92–5.4.95	150,000
2006–07	285,000	6.4.91–9.3.92	140,000
2005–06	275,000	1990–91	128,000
2004–05	263,000	1989–90	118,000
2003–04	255,000	15.3.88–5.4.89	110,000
2002–03	250,000	17.3.87–14.3.88	90,000
2001–02	242,000	18.3.86–16.3.87	71,000

1 Any nil-rate band which is unused on a person's death can be transferred to their surviving spouse or civil partner for the purposes of the charge to tax on the death of the survivor on or after 9 October 2007.
2 The nil rate band is frozen at £325,000 until 2017–18.

Capital transfer tax nil rate bands

Period	***Limit***	***Period***	***Limit***
	£		**£**
6.4.85–17.3.86	67,000	26.3.80–8.3.82	50,000
13.3.84–5.4.85	64,000	27.10.77–25.3.80	25,000
15.3.83–12.3.84	60,000	13.3.75–26.10.77	15,000
9.3.82–14.3.83	55,000		

Estate duty nil rate bands (England, Scotland and Wales)

Period	***Limit***	***Period***	***Limit***
	£		**£**
22.3.72–12.3.75	15,000	9.4.62–3.4.63	4,000
31.3.71–21.3.72	12,500	30.7.54–8.4.62	3,000
16.4.69–30.3.71	10,000	10.4.46–29.7.54	2,000
4.4.63–15.4.69	5,000	16.8.14–9.4.46	100

Delivery of accounts: due dates

(IHTA 1984 s 216)

Type of transfer	*Due date*
Chargeable lifetime transfers	Later of: (*a*) 12 months after the end of the month in which the transfer took place; and (*b*) three months after the date on which the person delivering the account became liable
PETs which become chargeable	12 months after the end of the month in which the transferor died
Gifts with reservation chargeable on death	12 months after the end of the month in which the death occurred
Transfers on death	Later of: (*a*) 12 months after the end of the month in which the death occurred; and (*b*) three months after the date on which the personal representatives first act or the person liable first has reason to believe that he is liable to deliver an account
National heritage property	Six months after the end of the month in which the chargeable event occurred

Delivery of accounts: excepted transfers and estates

(SI 2004/2543; SI 2008/606)

Date of transfer or death	*6 April 2000–5 April 2002*	*6 April 2002–5 April 2003*	*6 April 2003–31 Aug 2006*	*From 1 Sept 2006*
Excepted transfers:	*Value below*	*Value below*	*Value below*	*Value below*
Total chargeable transfers since 6 April	£10,000	£10,000	£10,000	£10,000
Total chargeable transfers during last ten years	£40,000	£40,000	£40,000	£40,000
Excepted estates:				
Total gross value[1]	£210,000	£220,000	(see (*a*) below)	(see (*a*) below)
Total gross value of property outside UK	£50,000	£75,000	£75,000	£100,000
Aggregate value of 'specified transfers'[2]	£75,000	£100,000	£100,000	£150,000
Settled property passing on death	–	£100,000	£100,000	£150,000

For chargeable transfers after 5 April 2007, no account need be delivered where:

(i) the transfer is of cash or quoted shares or securities and the value of the transfer and other chargeable transfers made in the preceding seven years does not exceed the IHT threshold; or

(ii) the value of the transfer and other chargeable transfers made in the preceding seven years does not exceed 80% of the IHT threshold and the value of the transfer does not exceed the net amount of the threshold available to the transferor at the time of the transfer.

For footnotes see the list below.

Excepted estates

For deaths occurring after 5 April 2004, no account need be delivered where the deceased died domiciled in the UK provided either conditions (a) or (b) below are met, and both conditions (c) and (d) below are met.

- (a) the aggregate of the gross value of the estate, and of any 'specified transfers'[2] or 'specified exempt transfers'[3] does not exceed the appropriate IHT threshold[4];
- (b) the aggregate of the gross value of the estate, and of any 'specified transfers'[2] or 'specified exempt transfers'[3] does not exceed £1,000,000; for deaths after 28 February 2011 at least part of the estate passes to the person's spouse, civil partner or to a charity; and after deducting from that aggregate figure any exempt spouse, civil partner and charity transfers and total estate liabilities[6], it does not exceed the appropriate IHT threshold[4];
- (c) the gross value of settled property or foreign assets do not exceed the limits in the above table; and
- (d) there were no chargeable lifetime transfers in the seven years before death other than specified transfers not exceeding the limits in the above table[5].

For deaths occurring after 31 August 2006 and before 6 April 2011, an estate will not be an excepted estate if the provisions for alternatively secured pension funds in IHTA 1984 ss 151A–151C (now repealed) apply by reason of the individual's death.

For deaths after 5 April 2002 and before 6 April 2004, no account need be delivered where the deceased died domiciled in the UK provided that:

- (i) the aggregate of the gross value of the estate, and of any 'specified transfers' does not exceed the limits in the above table; and
- (ii) the gross value of settled property or foreign assets do not exceed the limits in the above table; and
- (iii) there were no chargeable lifetime transfers in the seven years before death other than specified transfers not exceeding the limits in the above table.

Where the deceased was never domiciled in the UK, no account need be delivered for deaths after 5 April 2002 provided that:

- the value of the estate in the UK is wholly attributable to cash and quoted shares and securities not exceeding £150,000 (£100,000 before 1 September 2006); and
- for deaths occurring after 31 August 2006 and before 6 April 2011, the provisions for alternatively secured pension funds in IHTA 1984 ss 151A–151C (now repealed) do not apply by reason of the individual's death.

1 See table above — This limit applies to the aggregate gross value of the estate and of 'specified transfers' and 'specified exempt transfers'. For deaths after 28 February 2011 transfers treated as normal expenditure out of income made within 7 years before death and totalling more than £3,000 in any tax year will be treated as chargeable transfers for these purposes.

2 'Specified transfers' are chargeable transfers of cash, quoted shares and securities and, after 6 April 2002, interests in or over land and, after 5 April 2004, personal chattels or corporeal moveable property. For deaths after 28 February 2011 transfers treated as normal expenditure out of income made within 7 years before death and totalling more than £3,000 in any tax year will be treated as chargeable transfers for these purposes.

3 'Specified exempt transfers' are transfers in the seven years before death between spouses or civil partners, gifts to charity, political parties or housing associations, transfers to maintenance funds for historical buildings, etc or to employee trusts.

4 For deaths after 5 April 2010 the IHT threshold for these purposes is increased by 100% where—
- (a) the deceased is a surviving spouse or civil partner;
- (b) a claim has been made for the transfer of the unused nil-rate band of their deceased spouse or civil partner;
- (c) all of the first deceased spouse's or civil partner's nil-rate band was unused; and
- (d) the first deceased met certain other criteria similar to those listed above for excepted estates.

5 For deaths after 28 February 2011 transfers treated as normal expenditure out of income made within 7 years before death and totalling more than £3,000 in any tax year will be treated as chargeable transfers for these purposes.

6 For deaths on or after 1 April 2014 total estate liabilities do not include those which are not discharged on or after death out of the estate in money or money's worth, or those which are prevented by any other provision in IHTA 1984 from being taken into account, or those attributable to financing the acquisition of, or maintenance or enhancement of the value of, excluded property.

Excepted settlements

No account need be delivered of property comprised in an excepted settlement (i.e. one with no qualifying interest in possession) where a chargeable event occurs after 5 April 2007 and cash not exceeding £1,000 is the only property comprised in the settlement. Other conditions to be fulfilled are that, the settlor has not provided further property, the trustees are UK resident throughout the settlement's existence and there are no related settlements.

Reliefs

The following is a summary of the main reliefs and exemptions under the Inheritance Tax Act 1984 (Parts II and V). The legislation should be referred to for conditions and exceptions.

Agricultural property

Transfer with vacant possession (or right to obtain it within 12 months); transfer on or after 1 September 1995, of land let (or treated as let) on or after that date.	100% of agricultural value
Any other case.	50% of agricultural value

Note: The 100% relief is extended in limited circumstances by Concession F17.

Annual gifts £3,000

Business property

Unincorporated business.	100%		
Unquoted shares (including shares in AIM or USM companies) (held for 2 years or more).[1]	100%	Controlling holding in fully quoted companies.	50%
Unquoted securities which alone, or together with other such securities and unquoted shares, give the transferor control of the company (held for 2 years or more).[1]	100%	Land, buildings, machinery or plant used in business of company or partnership.	50%
Settled property used in life tenant's business.	100%		

[1] Tax charges arising and transfers occurring after 5 April 1996. 10 March 1992–5 April 1996 minority holding of shares or securities of up to 25% in unquoted or USM company qualified for 50% relief; larger holdings qualified for 100% relief.

Charities, gifts to		Exempt
From 1 April 2002, Community Amateur Sports Clubs are treated as charities.		
Marriage/civil partnership gifts		
Made by:	parent	£5,000
	remoter ancestor	£2,500
	party to marriage/civil partnership	£2,500
	other person	£1,000
National purposes		
Property given or bequeathed to bodies listed in IHTA 1984 Sch 3.		Exempt
Political parties, gifts to		Exempt
Potentially exempt transfers		

Exempt if made 7 or more years before the date of death. Except for gifts with reservation etc, they include:

(a) transfers by individuals to other individuals or certain trusts for the disabled;
(b) transfers after 21 March 2006 by individuals to a bereaved minor's trust on the coming to an end of an immediate post-death interest;
(c) transfers before 22 March 2006 by individuals to accumulation and maintenance trusts;
(d) transfers by individuals into interest in possession trusts in which, for transfers after 21 March 2006, the beneficiary has a disabled person's interest; and
(e) certain transfers on the termination or disposal of an individual's beneficial interest in possession in settled property (in restricted circumstances following FA 2006).

Quick succession relief	
Estate increased by chargeable transfer followed by death within 5 years.	
Death within 1st year.	100%
Each additional year: decreased by	20%
Small gifts to same person	£250
Spouses/civil partners with separate domicile (one not being in the UK)	
Total exemption.	£325,000[1]

[1] For transfers of value before 6 April 2013 the total exemption was £55,000. From 6 April 2013 the limit is increased to the level of the prevailing IHT nil-rate band (see p 103). For transfers of value made on or after 6 April 2013 individuals can elect to be treated as domiciled in the UK if, at any time on or after 6 April 2013 and during the period of 7 years ending with the date on which the election is made, they have a UK-domiciled spouse or civil partner. The election may be made in some cases where the UK-domiciled individual had died. Personal representatives may make an election on behalf of a deceased person in certain circumstances. Other conditions apply.

Tapering relief

The value of the estate on death is taxed as the top slice of cumulative transfers in the 7 years before death. Transfers on or within 7 years of death are taxed on their value at the date of the gift on the death rate scale, but using the scale in force at the date of death, subject to the following taper:

Years between gift and death	*Percentage of full charge at death rates*
0–3	100
3–4	80
4–5	60
5–6	40
6–7	20

Penalties see p 18.

National insurance contributions

(SI 2001/1004)

From 6 April 2014

Class 1 contributions[1]				
Earnings limits and threshold		Weekly £	Monthly £	Yearly £
Lower earnings limit		111	481	5,772
Secondary threshold		153	663	7,956
Primary threshold		153	663	7,956
Upper earnings limit		805	3,489	41,865
Upper accruals point		770	3,337	40,040
		Not contracted out	**Contracted out** *Salary-related schemes*[3]	
Employees' contributions				
Weekly earnings:	Over £153.01–770	12%	10.6%	
	£770.01–£805	12%	12%	
	Over £805	2%	2%	
	– rebate £111–£153		1.4%[2, 3]	
Employers' contributions[4]				
Weekly earnings:	£153.01–£770	13.8%	10.4%	
	Over £770	13.8%	13.8%	
	– rebate £111–£153		3.4%[2, 3]	
Women at reduced rate				
Employees' contributions				
Weekly earnings:	£153.01–£805	5.85%		
	Over £805	2%		
Employers' contributions	Normal employers' contributions apply as above			
Class 1A and Class 1B contributions				13.8%

1 Employees' rates are nil for children under 16 and those over state pensionable age but employers' contributions are still payable. Employees' NICs are not payable on earnings up to the primary threshold, employers' NICs are not payable on earnings up to the secondary threshold. The primary and secondary thresholds are the same in 2014–15.

2 The rebate is given on earnings between the lower earnings limit and the primary threshold for employees, and between the lower earnings limit and the secondary threshold for employers. The rebate for employees is given to employers to the extent that insufficient contributions have been paid by the employee for offset.

3 From 2012 the rebates for defined benefit schemes (salary-related schemes) are 3.4% for employers and 1.4% for employees. Contracting out on a defined contribution basis (money purchase schemes) is abolished from 6 April 2012. Contracting out via a personal pension plan is also not possible from 6 April 2012. Contracting out via defined benefit schemes will no longer be possible from 6 April 2016 when the single-tier state pension is planned to be introduced.

4 From 6 April 2014 an employment allowance of £2,000 per year applies for businesses, charities and CASCs to be offset against their employer Class 1 secondary NICs. The allowance is claimed as part of the normal payroll process through RTI. Only one company in a group may claim. There are some excluded employers such as domestic employers, public authorities and those which carry out functions wholly or mainly of a public nature.

5 From 6 April 2015 employers with employees under the age of 21 will no longer be required to pay Class 1 secondary NICs on earnings up to the upper earnings limit for those employees.

6 April 2013–5 April 2014

Class 1 contributions[1]				
Earnings limits and threshold		Weekly £	Monthly £	Yearly £
Lower earnings limit		109	473	5,668
Secondary threshold[3]		148	641	7,696
Primary threshold[3]		149	646	7,755
Upper earnings limit		797	3,454	41,450
Upper accruals point		770	3,337	40,040
		Not contracted out	**Contracted out** *Salary-related schemes*[5]	
Employees' contributions				
Weekly earnings:	Over £149.01–770	12%	10.6%	
	£770.01–£797	12%	12%	
	Over £797	2%	2%	
	– rebate £109–£149		1.4%[2, 5]	
Employers' contributions[4]				
Weekly earnings:	£148.01–£770	13.8%	10.4%	
	Over £770	13.8%	13.8%	
	– rebate £109–£148		3.4%[2, 5]	
Women at reduced rate				
Employees' contributions				
Weekly earnings:	£149.01–£797	5.85%		
	Over £797	2%		
Employers' contributions	Normal employers' contributions apply as above			
Class 1A and Class 1B contributions				13.8%

1 Employees' rates are nil for children under 16 and those over state pensionable age but employers' contributions are still payable. Employees' NICs are not payable on earnings up to the primary threshold, employers' NICs are not payable on earnings up to the secondary threshold.

2 The rebate is given on earnings between the lower earnings limit and the primary threshold for employees, and between the lower earnings limit and the secondary threshold for employers. The rebate for employees is given to employers to the extent that insufficient contributions have been paid by the employee for offset.

3 From 6 April 2011 the primary threshold applies for employees' contributions and the secondary threshold applies for employers' contributions.

4 An employer NIC 'holiday' applies to new businesses started in certain regions between 22 June 2010 and 5 September 2013. Between 6 September 2010 and 5 September 2013 the businesses may qualify for a deduction of up to £5,000 of their employer Class 1 contributions for each of the first ten employees hired in the first year of business.

5 From 2012 the rebates for defined benefit schemes (salary-related schemes) are 3.4% for employers and 1.4% for employees. Contracting out on a defined contribution basis (money purchase schemes) is abolished from 6 April 2012. Contracting out via a personal pension plan is also not possible from 6 April 2012. Contracting out via defined benefit schemes will no longer be possible from 6 April 2016 when the single-tier state pension is planned to be introduced.

6 April 2012–5 April 2013

Class 1 contributions[1]				
Earnings limits and threshold		Weekly £	Monthly £	Yearly £
Lower earnings limit		107	464	5,564
Secondary threshold[3]		144	624	7,488
Primary threshold[3]		146	634	7,605
Upper earnings limit		817	3,540	42,475
Upper accruals point		770	3,337	40,040
		Not contracted out	**Contracted out** *Salary-related schemes[5]*	
Employees' contributions				
Weekly earnings:	Over £146.01–770	12%	10.6%	
	£770.01–£817	12%	12%	
	Over £817	2%	2%	
	– rebate £107–£146		1.4%[2, 5]	
Employers' contributions[4]				
Weekly earnings:	£144.01–£770	13.8%	10.4%	
	Over £770	13.8%	13.8%	
	– rebate £107–£144		3.4%[2, 5]	
Women at reduced rate				
Employees' contributions				
Weekly earnings:	£146.01–£817	5.85%		
	Over £817	2%		
Employers' contributions	Normal employers' contributions apply as above			
Class 1A and Class 1B contributions				13.8%

1 Employees' rates are nil for children under 16 and those over state pensionable age but employers' contributions are still payable. Employees' NICs are not payable on earnings up to the primary threshold, employers' NICs are not payable on earnings up to the secondary threshold.

2 The rebate is given on earnings between the lower earnings limit and the primary threshold for employees, and between the lower earnings limit and the secondary threshold for employers. The rebate for employees is given to employers to the extent that insufficient contributions have been paid by the employee for offset.

3 From 6 April 2011 the primary threshold applies for employees' contributions and the secondary threshold applies for employers' contributions.

4 An employer NIC 'holiday' applies to new businesses started in certain regions between 22 June 2010 and 5 September 2013. Between 6 September 2010 and 5 September 2013 the businesses may qualify for a deduction of up to £5,000 of their employer Class 1 contributions for each of the first ten employees hired in the first year of business.

5 From 2012 the rebates for defined benefit schemes (salary-related schemes) are reduced to 3.4% for employers and 1.4% for employees. Contracting out on a defined contribution basis (money purchase schemes) is abolished from 6 April 2012. Contracting out via a personal pension plan is also not possible from 6 April 2012. Contracting out via defined benefit schemes will no longer be possible from 6 April 2016 when the single-tier state pension is planned to be introduced.

6 April 2011–5 April 2012

Class 1 contributions[1]				
Earnings limits and threshold		Weekly £	Monthly £	Yearly £
Lower earnings limit		102	442	5,304
Secondary threshold[3]		136	589	7,072
Primary threshold[3]		139	602	7,225
Upper earnings limit		817	3,540	42,475
Upper accruals point		770	3,337	40,040
		Not contracted out	**Contracted out**	
Employees' contributions				
Weekly earnings:	Over £139.01–770	12%	10.4%	
	£770.01–£817	12%	12%	
	Over £817	2%	2%	
	– rebate £102–£139		1.6%[2]	
Employers' contributions[4]			*Salary-related schemes*	*Money purchase schemes*
Weekly earnings:	£136.01–£770	13.8%	10.1%	12.4%
	Over £770	13.8%	13.8%	13.8%
	– rebate £102–£136		3.7%[2]	1.4%[2]
Women at reduced rate				
Employees' contributions				
Weekly earnings:	£139.01–£817	5.85%		
	Over £817	2%		
Employers' contributions	Normal employers' contributions apply as above			
Class 1A and Class 1B contributions				13.8%

1 Employees' rates are nil for children under 16 and those over state pensionable age but employers' contributions are still payable. Employees' NICs are not payable on earnings up to the primary threshold, employers' NICs are not payable on earnings up to the secondary threshold.

2 The rebate is given on earnings between the lower earnings limit and the primary threshold for employees, and between the lower earnings limit and the secondary threshold for employers. The rebate for employees is given to employers to the extent that insufficient contributions have been paid by the employee for offset.

3 From 6 April 2011 the primary threshold applies for employees' contributions and the secondary threshold applies for employers' contributions.

4 An employer NIC 'holiday' applies to new businesses started in certain regions between 22 June 2010 and 5 September 2013. Between 6 September 2010 and 5 September 2013 the businesses may qualify for a deduction of up to £5,000 of their employer Class 1 contributions for each of the first ten employees hired in the first year of business.

6 April 2010–5 April 2011

Class 1 contributions[1]				
Earnings limits and threshold		Weekly £	Monthly £	Yearly £
Lower earnings limit		97	421	5,044
Earnings threshold		110	476	5,715
Upper earnings limit		844	3,656	43,875
Upper accruals point		770	3,337	40,040
Not contracted out		**Employees' contributions**		**Employers' contributions**
Weekly earnings:	£110.01–£844	11%		12.8%
	Over £844	1%		12.8%
Contracted out			*Salary-related schemes*	*Money purchase schemes*
Weekly earnings:	£110.01–£770	9.4%	9.1%	11.4%
	£770–£844	11%	12.8%	12.8%
	Over £844	1%	12.8%	12.8%
	– rebate £97–£110	1.6%[2]	3.7%	1.4%
Women at reduced rate				
Weekly earnings:	£110.01–£844	4.85%	*as above*	
	Over £844	1%	*as above*	
Class 1A and Class 1B contributions				12.8%

1 Employees' rates are nil for children under 16 and those over state pensionable age but employers' contributions are still payable. NICs are not payable on earnings up to the earnings threshold.

2 The rebate is given on earnings between the lower earnings limit and the earnings threshold. The rebate for employees is given to employers to the extent that insufficient contributions have been paid by the employee for offset.

6 April 2009–5 April 2010

Class 1 contributions[1]				
Earnings limits and threshold		Weekly £	Monthly £	Yearly £
Lower earnings limit		95	412	4,940
Earnings threshold		110	476	5,715
Upper earnings limit		844	3,656	43,875
Upper accruals point		770	3,337	40,040
Not contracted out		**Employees' contributions**		**Employers' contributions**
Weekly earnings:	£110.01–£844	11%		12.8%
	Over £844	1%		12.8%
Contracted out			*Salary-related schemes*	*Money purchase schemes*
Weekly earnings:	£110.01–£770	9.4%	9.1%	11.4%
	£770–£844	11%	12.8%	12.8%
	Over £844	1%	12.8%	12.8%
	– rebate £95–£110	1.6%[2]	3.7%	1.4%
Women at reduced rate				
Weekly earnings:	£110.01–£844	4.85%	*as above*	
	Over £844	1%	*as above*	
Class 1A and Class 1B contributions				12.8%

1 Employees' rates are nil for children under 16, men over 65 and women over 60 but employers' contributions are still payable. NICs are not payable on earnings up to the earnings threshold.

2 The rebate is given on earnings between the lower earnings limit and the earnings threshold. The rebate for employees is given to employers to the extent that insufficient contributions have been paid by the employee for offset.

Class 2, 3 and 4 contributions

	2014–15	**2013–14**	**2012–13**
Class 2 (self-employed)[1]			
Flat rate—per week	**£2.75**	£2.70	£2.65
Share fishermen—per week	**£3.40**	£3.35	£3.30
Volunteer development workers—per week	**£5.55**	£5.45	£5.35
Small earning exception—per year	**£5,885**	£5,725	£5,595
Class 3 (voluntary contributions)			
Flat rate—per week	**£13.90**	£13.55	£13.25
Class 4 (self-employed)[1]			
Lower annual profits limit	**£7,956**	£7,755	£7,605
Upper annual profits limit	**£41,865**	£41,450	£42,475
Rate between lower and upper limits	**9%**	9%	9%
Rate on profits above upper limit	**2%**	2%	2%
Maximum contributions			
Class 1 or Class 1/Class 2[2]	**£4,146.72**	£4,121.28	£4,267.56
– plus rate on earnings above upper limit	**2%**	2%	2%
Class 4 limiting amount[3]	**£3,197.56**	£3,175.65	£3,278.75
– plus rate on profits above upper limit	**2%**	2%	2%

1 Not payable if pensionable age is reached by the beginning of the tax year.

2 Where an earner has more than one employment (including self-employment), liability for Class 1 or Class 1 and Class 2 contributions cannot exceed a maximum amount equal to 53 employees' Class 1 contributions at the maximum standard rate, plus 2% (1% before 2011–12) on earnings over the individual's upper earnings limit (which varies depending on individual circumstances).

3 Where Class 4 contributions are payable in addition to Class 1 and/or Class 2 contributions, liability for Class 4 contributions cannot exceed such an amount as, when added to the Class 1/Class 2 contributions payable (after applying the maximum if appropriate), equals the limiting amount. The limiting amount is the maximum Class 4 contributions payable (including 2% (1% before 2011–12) on earnings over the upper profit limit) plus 53 Class 2 contributions. If a contributor expects to exceed this amount he may apply for deferment of Class 4 contributions for the year in question. Deferment has no effect on the 2% (1% before 2011–12) payable on earnings over the upper profit limit, which is still payable.

	2011–12	**2010–11**	**2009–10**
Class 2 (self-employed)[1]			
Flat rate—per week	£2.50	£2.40	£2.40
Share fishermen—per week	£3.15	£3.05	£3.05
Volunteer development workers—per week	£5.10	£4.85	£4.75
Small earning exception—per year	£5,315	£5,075	£5,075
Class 3 (voluntary contributions)			
Flat rate—per week	£12.60	£12.05	£12.05
Class 4 (self-employed)[1]			
Lower annual profits limit	£7,225	£5,715	£5,715
Upper annual profits limit	£42,475	£43,875	£43,875
Rate between lower and upper limits	9%	8%	8%
Rate on profits above upper limit	2%	1%	1%
Maximum contributions			
Class 1 or Class 1/Class 2[2]	£4,312.08	£4,279.22	£4,279.22
– plus rate on earnings above upper limit	2%	1%	1%
Class 4 limiting amount[3]	£3,305.00	£3,180.00	£3,180.00
– plus rate on profits above upper limit	2%	1%	1%

1 Not payable if pensionable age is reached by the beginning of the tax year.

2 Where an earner has more than one employment (including self-employment), liability for Class 1 or Class 1 and Class 2 contributions cannot exceed a maximum amount equal to 53 employees' Class 1 contributions at the maximum standard rate, plus 1% on earnings over the individual's upper earnings limit (which varies depending on individual circumstances).

3 Where Class 4 contributions are payable in addition to Class 1 and/or Class 2 contributions, liability for Class 4 contributions cannot exceed such an amount as, when added to the Class 1/Class 2 contributions payable (after applying the maximum if appropriate), equals the limiting amount. The limiting amount is the maximum Class 4 contributions payable (including 1% on earnings over the upper profit limit) plus 53 Class 2 contributions. If a contributor expects to exceed this amount he may apply for deferment of Class 4 contributions for the year in question. Deferment has no effect on the 1% payable on earnings over the upper profit limit, which is still payable.

Employers' contributions: benefits in kind

Class 1A national insurance contributions are payable by employers on most taxable benefits in kind, excluding benefits:

(1) which are covered by a dispensation;
(2) included in a PAYE settlement agreement;
(3) provided to employees not earning more than £8,500 pa (including benefits in kind and expenses payments);
(4) otherwise not required to be included on a P11D;
(5) on which Class 1 national insurance contributions were due.

Class 1B contributions are payable by employers by reference to the value of any items included in a PAYE settlement agreement (PSA) which would otherwise be earnings for Class 1 or Class 1A, including the amount of tax paid. Income tax and Class 1B contributions on a PSA are payable by 19 October after the end of the tax year to which the PSA relates (or 22 October if paid electronically).

Common benefits subject to Class 1 and Class 1A NICs (CWG5 2014)

Benefit		*NICs Class*	*PAYE or P11D*
Assets transferred to employees but not readily convertible assets		1A	P11D
Assets placed at employee's disposal for mixed business and private use		1A	P11D
Car fuel supplied for private motoring in company car		1A	P11D
Car/van fuel supplied for private motoring in privately owned car/van	– supplied using company credit card, garage account, agency card or employer's own fuel pump	1A	P11D
	– any other circumstances	1	P11D
Cars available for private use		1A	P11D
Car parking facilities other than at or near place of work or as part of business travel		1A	P11D
Car parking fees paid for or reimbursed to employee other than at or near place of work or as part of business travel		1	P11D
Childcare where employer contracts with provider and either the value exceeds the permitted maximum or the qualifying conditions are not met		1A	P11D
Childcare where employee reimbursed or additional salary provided to meet cost		1	PAYE
Christmas boxes	– cash	1	PAYE
	– goods	1A	P11D
Clothing and uniforms			
– cash payment to employee for clothing that can be worn at any time		1	PAYE or P11D[1]
– clothing provided by employer that can be worn at any time		1A	P11D
Council tax, unless employee provided with living accommodation which is not a benefit		1	P11D
Credit and charge cards – personal expenses on employer's card		1	P11D
Entertaining staff — expenses/ allowances	– employer contract with provider	1A	P11D
	– employee contract with provider	1	PAYE or P11D[1]
Expenses not covered by dispensation — any profit element in payment		1	P11D[4]
Food, groceries, farm produce	– employer contract with provider	1A	P11D
	– employee contract with provider	1	PAYE or P11D[1]
Goods transferred to employee	– employer contract with provider	1A	P11D
	– employee contract with provider	1	PAYE or P11D[1]
Holidays	– employer contract with provider	1A	P11D
	– employee contract with provider, or holiday vouchers	1	PAYE or P11D[1]
Income tax paid but not deducted from employee, or paid on notional payments not borne by employee within 90 days of receipt of each notional payment		1	P11D
Insurance premiums for pensions etc on employee's death or retirement, employee contract with provider		1	PAYE or P11D[1]
Living accommodation (beneficial)		1A	P11D
Loans	– non-qualifying	1A	P11D
	– written off	1	P11D
Meals vouchers (other than 15p a day of value before 6 April 2013)		1	P11D
Meals provided other than at canteen or at business premises open to all staff on a reasonable scale where all employees may obtain free or subsidised meal		1A	P11D

Benefit		NICs Class	PAYE or P11D
Medical, dental insurance or treatment provided in the UK by employer	– employer contract with provider	1A	P11D
	– employee contract with provider	1	PAYE or P11D[1]
Mobile phone[5] — cost of private calls, employee contract with provider		1	PAYE or P11D[1]
Personal bills		1	PAYE or P11D[1]
Readily convertible assets[2]		1	PAYE
Relocation payments	– qualifying over £8,000	1A	P11D
	– non-qualifying benefits or qualifying expenses paid after relevant day	1A	P11D
	– non-qualifying expenses	1	P11D
Round sum allowances (not identified as business expense)		1	P11D
Scholarships awarded to students because of parent's employment or payment of school fees	– employer contract with provider	1A	P11D
	– employee contract with provider	1	PAYE or P11D[1]
Social functions unless ITEPA 2003 s 264 satisfied		1A	P11D
Sporting or recreational facilities unless ITEPA 2003 s 261 satisfied		1A	P11D
Subscriptions, professional and fees not allowable as tax deduction	– employer contract with provider	1A	P11D
	– employee contract with provider	1	PAYE or P11D[1]
Telephones	– employer contract with provider, unless private use is insignificant or employee reimburses cost of all private calls	1A	P11D
	– employee contract with provider, unless used exclusively for business. If mixed use, not applicable to business calls if supported by evidence	1	PAYE or P11D[1]
Training payments	– employer contract with provider, unless work-related or encouraged by employer	1A	P11D
	– employee contract with provider, unless work-related or encouraged by employer	1	PAYE or P11D[1]
Vans available for commuting and other private use		1A[3]	P11D
Van fuel provided for use in van available for commuting and other private use		1A[3]	P11D
Vouchers (other than exceptions for childcare, meals, etc)		1	P11D

1 Payments by employer to provider should be entered on P11D. Reimbursements to the employee are subject to PAYE.

2 See detailed information in HMRC booklet CWG2(2014) para 155.

3 No Class 1A due if van is available mainly for employee's business travel and commuting and other private use is insignificant.

4 Specific and distinct business expenses within the payments should be recorded in appropriate section of P11D.

5 No limit to number of mobile phones which employer can contract to provide NIC free solely for business with insignificant private use. Only one mobile per employee NIC free for private use where employer contracts. No mobile phone may be provided NICs free to a member of an employee's family or household.

Overseas

Average rates of exchange

Average for year ending	***31.03.12***	***31.12.12***	***31.03.13***	***31.12.13***	***31.03.14***
Abu Dhabi (Dirham)	5.8691	6.8312	6.7680	5.7432	5.8235
Afghanistan (Afghani)	69.855	76.7676	78.8182	84.4652	87.5724
Albania (Lek)	162.360	171.530	170.707	165.328	166.511
Algeria (Dinar)	117.306	123.093	124.194	124.489	126.063
Angola (Readj Kwanza)	150.405	150.805	151.064	147.998	150.756
Antigua (EC$)	4.3144	4.2716	4.2684	4.2221	4.2811
Argentina (Peso)	6.7074	7.1818	7.4308	8.5036	9.5808
Armenia (Dram)	602.532	635.239	641.398	638.992	649.094
Aruba (Florin)	2.8603	2.8319	2.8298	2.7991	2.8382
Australia (A$)	1.5274	1.5304	1.5556	1.6337	1.6987
Austria (Euro)	1.1582	1.2335	1.2284	1.1784	1.1854
Azerbaijan (New Manat)	1.2579	1.2416	1.2401	1.2255	1.2423
Bahamas ($ pegged to US$)	1.5958	1.5829	1.5809	1.5626	1.5844
Bahrain (Dinar)	0.6231	0.5965	0.5960	0.5895	0.5977
Bangladesh (Taka)	122.098	129.562	128.041	122.258	123.2875
Barbados (BD$)	3.1958	3.1641	3.1618	3.1275	3.1746
Belarus (Rouble)	10,098.71	13,228.89	13,366.75	13,870.64	14,485.59
Belgium (Euro)	1.1582	1.2335	1.2284	1.1784	1.1854
Belize (Dollar)	3.1536	3.0510	3.0760	3.1327	3.1713
Benin (CFA Franc)	758.896	809.513	804.849	773.001	777.459
Bermuda ($ pegged to US$)	1.5958	1.5829	1.5809	1.5626	1.5844
Bhutan (Ngultrum)	76.2045	84.5328	85.8984	91.2180	95.7333
Bolivia (Boliviano)	11.0614	10.9317	10.9236	10.8047	10.9557
Bosnia-Herzegovina (Marka)	2.2628	2.4137	2.3998	2.3048	2.3181
Botswana (Pula)	11.1162	12.2967	12.5326	13.0610	13.6235
Brazil (Real)	2.7055	3.0916	3.1778	3.3614	3.5517
Brunei ($)	1.9994	1.9781	1.9658	1.9535	1.9950
Bulgaria (Lev)	2.2628	2.4137	2.3998	2.3048	2.3181
Burkina Faso (CFA Franc)	758.896	809.513	804.849	773.001	777.459
Burundi (Franc)	2,065.46	2,278.45	2,356.29	2,445.40	2,463.06
Cambodia (Riel)	6,475.17	6,389.11	6,364.80	6,271.77	6,355.80
Cameroon Republic (CFA Franc)	758.896	809.513	804.849	773.001	777.459
Canada (Can$)	1.5824	1.5836	1.5828	1.6077	1.6671
Cape Verde Islands (Escudo)	125.241	135.764	134.739	128.739	129.296
Cayman Islands (CI$)	16.876	1.2973	1.2964	1.2823	1.3002
Central African (CFA Franc)	758.896	809.513	804.849	773.001	777.459
Chad (CFA Franc)	758.896	809.513	804.849	773.001	777.459
Chile (Peso)	771.868	770.078	763.587	771.172	812.638
China (Renminbi Yuan)	10.2339	9.9881	9.9435	9.6231	9.6978
Colombia (Peso)	2,918.79	2,846.81[1]	2,838.02[2]	2,912.13	3,041.42
Comoros (Franc)	569.174	607.135	603.637	579.920	583.267
Congo Brazzaville (CFA Franc)	758.896	809.513	804.849	773.001	777.459
Congo Dem Rep (Zaire) (Congolese Franc)	1,452.24	1,454.91	1,428.35	1,401.71	1,447.82
Costa Rica (Colon)	810.612	795.485	791.742	781.662	800.230
Cote d'Ivoire (CFA Franc)	758.896	809.513	804.849	773.001	777.459
Croatia (Kuna)	8.6416	9.2760	9.2260	8.9217	8.9975
Cuba (Peso)	1.5979	1.5821	1.5809	1.5638	1.5856
Cyprus (Euro from 1.1.08)	1.1582	1.2335	1.2284	1.1784	1.1854
Czech Republic (Koruna)	28.6081	31.0509	30.9864	30.5078	31.2884
Denmark (Krone)	8.6238	9.1811	9.1501	8.7881	8.8413
Djibouti (Franc)	279.289	277.747	277.583	273.375	277.325
Dominica (EC$)	4.3144	4.2716	4.2684	4.2221	4.2811
Dominican Republic (Peso)	61.1402	61.9436	62.6011	64.9861	66.8580

Average for year ending	***31.03.12***	***31.12.12***	***31.03.13***	***31.12.13***	***31.03.14***
Dubai (Dirham)	5.8691	6.8312	6.7680	5.7432	5.8235
Ecuador (US$)	1.5958	1.5829	1.5809	1.5626	1.5844
Egypt (£)	9.5564	9.5980	9.8259	10.6995	10.9982
El Salvador (Colon)	13.9777	13.8392	13.8288	13.6788	13.8699
Equatorial Guinea (CFA Franc)	758.896	809.513	804.849	773.001	777.459
Eritrea (Nakfa)	23.9685	23.7301	23.7125	22.1810	22.4140
Estonia (Euro from 1.1.11)	1.1582	1.2335	1.2284	1.1784	1.1854
Ethiopia (Birr)	27.3735	28.1442	28.4876	29.2164	29.9920
European Community (Euro)	1.1582	1.2335	1.2284	1.1784	1.1854
Fiji Islands (F$)	2.8385	2.8347	2.8359	3.2102	3.3030
Finland (Euro)	1.1582	1.2335	1.2284	1.1784	1.1854
France (Euro)	1.1582	1.2335	1.2284	1.1784	1.1854
French Polynesia (CFP franc)	138.059	147.2666	146.4181	140.6243	141.4353
Gabon (CFA franc)	758.896	809.513	804.849	773.001	777.459
Gambia (Dalasi)	46.1451	49.3463	50.6148	53.4761	56.0269
Georgia (Lari)	47.1474	49.3209	49.2494	33.8427	22.4128
Germany (Euro)	1.1582	1.2335	1.2284	1.1784	1.1854
Ghana (Cedi)	2.5342	2.9353	3.0045	3.2082	3.4766
Greece (Euro)	1.1582	1.2335	1.2284	1.1784	1.1854
Grenada/Wind. Isles (EC$)	4.3144	4.2716	4.2684	4.2221	4.2811
Guatemala (Quetzal)	12.4276	12.4027	12.4212	12.2983	12.4464
Guinea Bissau (CFA Franc)	758.896	809.513	804.849	773.001	777.459
Guinea Republic (Franc)	11,045.72	11,031.34	10,969.92	10,966.44	11,127.28
Guyana (G$)	323.392	318.160	317.966	315.199	320.772
Haiti (Gourde)	64.5382	65.8809	66.4983	66.8173	68.4096
Honduras (Lempira)	30.2414	30.5512	30.8585	31.4132	31.8420
Hong Kong (HK$)	12.4121	12.2791	12.2635	12.1254	12.2975
Hungary (Forint)	328.864	356.921	354.579	349.451	355.054
Iceland (Krona)	187.988	181.908	183.822	191.535	188.894
India (Rupee)	76.2045	84.5328	85.8984	91.2180	95.7333
Indonesia (Rupiah)	14,013.84	14,803.46	15,031.82	16,184.62	17,358.54
Iran (Rial)	17,459.89	19,282.64	19,423.22	19,284.29	22,404.02
Iraq (Dinar)	1,863.11	1,838.80	1,836.93	1,815.73	1,841.45
Ireland (Euro)	1.1582	1.2335	1.2284	1.1784	1.1854
Israel (Shekel)	5.7699	6.1080	6.0742	5.6538	5.6502
Italy (Euro)	1.1582	1.2335	1.2284	1.1784	1.1854
Jamaica (J$)	137.063	139.788	142.588	155.153	162.911
Japan (Yen)	126.099	126.150	130.739	151.646	158.325
Jordan (Dinar)	1.1323	1.1206	1.1198	1.1073	1.1222
Kazakhstan (Tenge)	234.888	235.948	236.741	237.796	247.493
Kenya (Shilling)	142.959	133.744	134.698	134.673	136.329
Korea North (Won)	2.0773	2.0566	2.0551	2.0327	2.0611
Korea South (Won)	1,769.75	1,785.19	1,762.88	1,710.25	1,729.59
Kuwait (Dinar)	0.4410	0.6270	0.6176	0.4625	0.4691
Kyrgyz Republic (Som)	47.1474	49.3209	49.2494	56.7006	66.1143
Laos (New Kip)	12,758.14	12,601.88	12,565.26	12,237.39	12,452.84
Latvia (Lat)	0.8158	0.8605	0.8567	0.8273	0.9085
Lebanon (£)	2,407.45	2,380.24	2,378.45	2,357.41	2,390.31
Lesotho (Loti)	11.8049	13.0064	13.4189	14.9534	15.9737
Liberia ($ pegged to US$)	1.5958	1.5829	1.5809	1.5626	1.5844
Libya (Dinar)	1.9392	1.9778	1.9852	1.9686	1.9867
Lithuania (Litas)	3.9947	4.2611	4.2366	4.0689	4.0924
Luxembourg (Euro)	1.1582	1.2335	1.2284	1.1784	1.1854
Macao (Pataca)	12.8021	12.6402	12.6290	12.4931	12.6694
Macedonia (Denar)	71.1307	76.0097	75.8822	72.9158	73.0378
Madagascar (Malagasy Ariary)	3,282.52	3,479.53	3,489.24	3,467.39	3,546.86
Malawi (Kwacha)	255.309	395.980	468.933	567.309	604.846
Malaysia (Ringgit)	4.8819	4.8899	4.8883	4.9132	5.0669
Maldive Islands (Rufiyaa)	24.0370	24.3159	24.2995	24.0319	24.3661
Mali Republic (CFA Franc)	758.896	809.513	804.849	773.001	777.459

Average for year ending	***31.03.12***	***31.12.12***	***31.03.13***	***31.12.13***	***31.03.14***
Malta (Euro from 1.1.08)	1.1582	1.2335	1.2284	1.1784	1.1854
Mauritania (Ouguiya)	452.906	469.062	471.309	464.935	468.378
Mauritius (Rupee)	45.6847	47.7135	48.2077	48.0838	48.5412
Mexico (Peso)	20.1604	20.8757	20.6977	19.9464	20.4394
Moldova (Leu)	18.6449	19.1690	19.2562	19.6102	20.3848
Mongolia (Tugrik)	2,054.57	2,149.37	2,162.61	2,366.38	2,534.99
Montserrat (EC$)	4.3144	4.2716	4.2684	4.2221	4.2811
Morocco (Dirham)	12.7649	13.6812	13.6141	13.1518	13.2497
Mozambique (Metical)	44.6301	44.7312	45.8406	46.9425	47.9679
Myanmar (Burma) (Kyat)	10.2425	998.851	1,301.357	1,446.223	1,516.657
Nepal (Rupee)	121.368	135.203	137.470	145.634	152.856
Netherlands (Euro)	1.1582	1.2335	1.2284	1.1784	1.1854
New Caledonia (CFP Franc)	138.059	147.267	146.418	140.624	141.435
New Zealand (NZ$)	1.9819	1.9598	1.9466	1.9058	1.9323
Nicaragua (Gold Cordoba)	36.2063	37.2393	37.6463	38.5842	39.6278
Niger Republic (CFA Franc)	758.896	809.513	804.849	773.001	777.459
Nigeria (Naira)	250.633	251.436	250.418	248.796	254.237
Norway (Krone)	8.9649	9.2332	9.1375	9.1654	9.4858
Oman (Rial Omani)	0.6152	0.6091	0.6087	0.6021	0.6105
Pakistan (Rupee)	139.666	147.702	150.346	158.274	163.388
Panama (Balboa)	1.5979	1.5821	1.5809	1.5638	1.5856
Papua New Guinea (Kina)	3.5751	3.2606	3.2662	3.6015	3.8450
Paraguay (Guarani)	6,668.88	7,021.56	6,870.79	6,724.01	6,995.28
Peru (New Sol)	4.3665	4.1775	4.1301	4.2104	4.3677
Philippines (Peso)	68.7961	66.9121	65.9118	66.2357	68.7553
Poland (Zloty)	4.8349	5.1694	5.1138	4.9393	4.9811
Portugal (Euro)	1.1582	1.2335	1.2284	1.1784	1.1854
Qatar (Riyal)	5.8186	5.7604	5.7559	5.6934	5.7732
Romania (Leu)	4.9379	5.5127	5.4851	5.2051	5.2703
Russia (Rouble-Market)	47.1474	49.3209	49.2494	48.7858	51.2322
Rwanda (R Franc)	961.237	971.316	981.322	1,013.289	1,046.674
Saotome & Principe (Dobra)	28,351.28	29,877.96	29,487.03	27,972.63	28,147.85
Saudi Arabia (Riyal)	5.9846	5.9361	5.9297	5.8627	5.9451
Senegal (CFA Franc)	758.896	809.513	804.849	773.001	777.459
Serbia (Dinar)	118.896	139.699	139.837	133.136	135.015
Seychelles (Rupee)	20.3733	21.7087	21.1950	18.9889	19.0048
Sierra Leone (Leone)	6,990.35	6,872.89	6,846.49	6,758.09	6,861.48
Singapore (S$)	2.0009	1.9808	1.9655	1.9533	1.9941
Slovakia Euro from 1.1.09	1.1582	1.2335	1.2284	1.1784	1.1854
Slovenia (Euro)	1.1582	1.2335	1.2284	1.1784	1.1854
Solomon Islands (SI$)	11.8226	11.2242	11.2090	11.1778	11.3953
Somali Republic (Shilling)	2,511.69	2,491.09	2,479.86	2,146.78	1,970.63
South Africa (Rand)	11.8522	13.0070	13.4133	15.0113	15.9779
Spain (Euro)	1.1582	1.2335	1.2284	1.1784	1.1854
Sri Lanka (Rupee)	178.794	202.164	205.027	201.652	206.124
St Christopher & Nevis (EC$)	4.3144	4.2716	4.2684	4.2221	4.2811
St Lucia (EC$)	4.3144	4.2716	4.2684	4.2221	4.2811
St Vincent (EC$)	4.3144	4.2716	4.2684	4.2221	4.2811
Sudan Republic (£)	4.2857	5.5950	6.2465	7.0986	7.7303
Surinam (Dollar)	5.2731	5.2209	5.2170	5.1604	5.2325
Swaziland (Lilangeni)	11.8049	13.0064	13.4189	14.9539	15.9743
Sweden (Krona)	10.4489	10.7413	10.5955	10.1769	10.3348
Switzerland (Franc)	1.4073	1.4870	1.4857	1.4497	1.4579
Syria (Pound)	80.3194	100.278	105.433	156.194	188.354
Taiwan (New T$)	47.0278	46.8585	46.6620	46.3469	47.3300
Tajikistan (Somoni)	47.1474	49.3209	49.2494	35.3392	25.1865
Tanzania (Shilling)	2,565.88	2,509.60	2,515.53	2,528.80	2,566.59
Thailand (Baht)	48.7955	49.2233	48.7142	47.9401	49.6769
Togo Republic (CFA Franc)	758.896	809.513	804.849	773.001	777.459
Tonga Islands (Pa'Anga)	1.5274	1.5304	1.5556	1.6337	1.6987
Trinidad and Tobago (TT$)	10.2329	10.1373	10.1305	10.0309	10.1690
Tunisia (Dinar)	2.2764	2.4768	2.4902	2.5345	2.5930

Average for year ending	***31.03.12***	***31.12.12***	***31.03.13***	***31.12.13***	***31.03.14***
Turkey (Lira)	2.7522	2.8500	2.8409	2.9592	3.1755
Turkmenistan (New Manat)	4.5436	4.5008	4.4988	4.4501	4.5126
Uganda (New Shilling)	4,055.64	3,956.55	4,059.66	4,055.19	4,041.72
Ukraine (Hryvnia)	12.7843	12.7927	12.8132	12.7394	13.1779
United Arab Emirates (Dirham)	5.8691	6.8312	6.7680	5.7432	5.8235
Uruguay (Peso Uruguayo)	30.6354	32.1042	31.8732	31.8131	33.4297
USA (US$)	1.5958	1.5829	1.5809	1.5626	1.5844
Uzbekistan (Sum)	2,792.52	2,986.95	3,056.43	3,257.23	3,390.21
Vanuatu (Vatu)	148.545	149.246	149.114	150.247	154.664
Venezuela (Bolivar Fuerte)	6.8624	6.7942	7.0805	9.2977	9.9760
Vietnam (Dong)	33,256.91	33,021.29	32,986.35	32,865.62	33,421.13
Wallis & Futuna Islands (CFP Franc)	138.059	147.267	146.418	140.624	141.435
Western Samoa (Tala)	3.6667	3.6316	3.6238	3.6078	3.6877
Yemen (Republic of) (Rial)	345.455	341.023	339.742	336.215	340.972
Zambia (Kwacha)	7,907.84	8,132.81	6,262.30	8.4061	8.6750
Zimbabwe (Dollar)	604.136	598.385	597.904	591.439	600.036

[1] HMRC previously gave this figure as 60,320.53 but have subsequently updated it on their website.
[2] HMRC previously gave this figure as 56,996.12 but have subsequently updated it on their website.

Rates of exchange on year-end dates

	31.03.12	***31.12.12***	***31.03.13***	***31.12.13***	***31.03.14***
Australia (A$)	1.5423	1.5657	1.4626	1.8513	1.7988
Canada (Can$)	1.5969	1.6185	1.5489	1.7598	1.8401
Denmark (Krone)	8.9259	9.1989	8.8392	8.9671	9.031
European Community (Euro)	1.1998	1.233	1.1857	1.202	1.2096
Hong Kong (HK$)	12.405	12.5991	11.826	12.8422	12.9322
Japan (Yen)	131.487	140.549	142.058	174.08	171.691
Norway (Krone)	9.1137	9.0463	8.8618	10.0483	9.9813
South Africa (Rand)	12.262	13.7914	13.9881	17.3472	17.535
Sweden (Krona)	10.6016	10.5746	9.9125	10.6374	10.8091
Switzerland (Franc)	1.4442	1.4879	1.4439	1.473	1.4727
USA (US$)	1.5978	1.6255	1.5233	1.6563	1.6672

Note: The material on pp 117–120 is reproduced from information provided by HMRC and is Crown copyright. The 31.12.13 figures and the 31.3.14 figures are correct as at 8 July 2014.

Double taxation agreements (including protocols and regulations)

Agreements in force covering taxes on income and capital gains

Country	*SI/SR & O*
Albania	**2013/3145**
Antigua & Barbuda	**1947/2865**
	1968/1096
Argentina	**1997/1777**
Armenia[1]	**2011/2722**
Austria	**1970/1947**
	1979/117
	1994/768
	2010/2688
Australia	**2003/3199**
Azerbaijan	**1995/762**
Bahrain	**2012/3075**
Bangladesh	**1980/708**
Barbados	**2012/3076**
Belarus[1]	**1986/224**
Belgium	**1987/2053**
	2010/2979
Belize	**1947/2866**
	1968/573
	1973/2097
Bolivia	**1995/2707**
Bosnia Herzegovina[2]	**1981/1815**
Botswana	**2006/1925**
British Virgin Islands	**2009/3013**
Brunei	**1950/1977**
	1968/306
	1973/2098
	2013/3146
Bulgaria	**1987/2054**
Canada	**1980/709**
	1980/1528
	1980/1996
	1985/1996
	2003/2619
Cayman Islands	**2010/2973**
Chile	**2003/3200**
China[4]	**2011/2724**
	2013/3142
Croatia[2]	**1981/1815**
Cyprus	**1975/425**
	1980/1529
Czech Republic[3]	**1991/2876**
Denmark	**1980/1960**
	1991/2877
	1996/3165
Egypt	**1980/1091**
Estonia	**1994/3207**
Ethiopia	**2011/2725**
Falkland Islands	**1997/2985**
Faroes	**2007/3469**
Fiji	**1976/1342**
Finland	**1970/153**
	1973/1327
	1980/710
	1985/1997
	1991/2878
	1996/3166
France	**2009/226**

Country	*SI/SR & O*
Gambia	**1980/1963**
Georgia	**2004/3325**
	2010/2972
Germany	1967/25
	1971/874
	2010/2975[5]
Ghana	**1993/1800**
Greece	**1954/142**
Grenada	**1949/361**
	1968/1867
Guernsey	**1952/1215**
	1994/3209
	2009/3011
Guyana	**1992/3207**
Hong Kong	**2010/2974**
Hungary	**2011/2726**[6]
Iceland	**1991/2879**
India	**1993/1801**
	2013/3147
Indonesia	**1994/769**
Irish Republic	**1976/2151**
	1976/2152
	1995/764
	1998/3151
Isle of Man	**1955/1205**
	1991/2880
	1994/3208
	2009/228
Israel	**1963/616**
	1971/391
Italy	**1990/2590**
Ivory Coast	**1987/169**
Jamaica	**1973/1329**
Japan	**2006/1924**
Jersey	**1952/1216**
	1994/3210
	2009/3012
Jordan	**2001/3924**
Kazakhstan	**1994/3211**
	1998/2567
Kenya	**1977/1299**
Kiribati (and Tuvalu)	**1950/750**
	1968/309
	1974/1271
Korea (South)	**1996/3168**
Kuwait	**1999/2036**
Kyrgyzstan[1]	
Latvia	**1996/3167**
Lesotho	**1997/2986**
Liechtenstein	**2012/3077**
Libya	**2010/243**
Lithuania[1]	**2001/3925**
	2002/2847
Luxembourg	**1968/1100**
	1980/567
	1984/364
	2010/237
Macedonia[2]	**2007/2127**
Malawi	**1956/619**

Country	SI/SR & O
	1964/1401
	1968/1101
	1979/302
Malaysia	**1997/2987**
	2010/2971
Malta	**1995/763**
Mauritius	**1981/1121**
	1987/467
	2003/2620
	2011/2442
Mexico	**1994/3212**
	2010/2686
Moldova[1]	**2008/1795**
Mongolia	**1996/2598**
Montenegro[2]	**1981/1815**
Montserrat	**1947/2869**
	1968/576
	2011/1083
Morocco	**1991/2881**
Myanmar (Burma)	**1952/751**
Namibia	**1962/2352**
	1962/2788
	1967/1489
	1967/1490
Netherlands	**2009/227**
	2013/3143
New Zealand	**1984/365**
	2004/1274
	2008/1793
Nigeria	**1987/2057**
Norway	**2013/3144**
Oman	**1998/2568**
	2010/2687
Pakistan	**1987/2058**
Panama	**2013/3149**
Papua New Guinea	**1991/2882**
Philippines	**1978/184**
Poland	**2006/3323**
Portugal	**1969/599**
Qatar	**2010/241**
	2011/1684
Romania	**1977/57**
Russian Federation	**1994/3213**
St Kitts and Nevis	**1947/2872**
Saudi Arabia	**2008/1770**
Serbia[2]	**1981/1815**
Sierra Leone	**1947/2873**
	1968/1104
Singapore	**1997/2988**
	2010/2685
	2012/3078
Slovak Republic[3]	**1991/2876**
Slovenia[2]	**2008/1796**
Solomon Islands	**1950/748**
	1968/574
	1974/1270
South Africa	**2002/3138**
	2011/2441
Spain	**2013/3152**
Sri Lanka	**1980/713**
Sudan	**1977/1719**
Swaziland	**1969/380**
Sweden	**1984/366**
Switzerland	**1978/1408**
	1982/714
	1994/3215
	2007/3465
	2010/2689
	2012/3079
Taiwan	**2002/3137**
Tajikistan[1]	***1986/224***
Thailand	**1981/1546**
Trinidad and Tobago	**1983/1903**
Tunisia	**1984/133**
Turkey	**1988/932**
Turkmenistan[1]	**1986/224**
Tuvalu (and Kiribati)	**1950/750**
	1968/309
	1974/1271
Uganda	**1993/1802**
Ukraine	**1993/1803**
USA	**2002/2848**
Uzbekistan	**1994/770**
Venezuela	**1996/2599**
Vietnam	**1994/3216**
Zambia	**1972/1721**
	1981/1816
Zimbabwe	**1982/1842**

1 Following dissolution of the USSR, new agreements are in force with Azerbaijan, Estonia, Georgia, Kazakhstan, Latvia, Lithuania, Moldova, the Russian Federation, Ukraine and Uzbekistan. *SI 1986 No 224* (former USSR agreement) has been treated as continuing to apply to Belarus, Tajikistan and Turkmenistan (for Belarus until coming into force of *SI 1995 No 2706*). However Tajikistan considers that the UK/USSR convention has never had effect in Tajikistan. The UK will not therefore apply the terms of the convention in the case of residents of Tajikistan for profits arising on or after 1 April 2014 (corporation tax) and for income and gains arising on or after 6 April 2014 (income and capital gains tax). The convention was similarly so treated by the UK until 31 March 2002 for Armenia, Georgia, Kyrgyzstan, Moldova and Lithuania (none of which considered itself bound by that convention) but as ceasing so to apply after that date (but new treaties now in force with Armenia, Lithuania, Moldova and Georgia). (SP 4/01.)

2 *SI 1981 No 1815* (former Yugoslavia agreement) treated as remaining in force between the UK and, respectively, Bosnia-Herzegovina, Croatia and Serbia and Montenegro. (SP 3/04.) Negotiations for new double taxation convention taking place with Croatia, Serbia and Montenegro (Revenue Press Release, 29 September 2004).

3 *SI 1991 No 2876* (former Czechoslovakia agreement) treated as remaining in force between the UK and, respectively, Czech Republic and Slovak Republic. (SP 5/93.)

4 Hong Kong Special Administrative Region has its own agreement.

5 Treaty replaces 1967/25 with effect from 1 January 2011 or 6 April 2011 depending on type of income. However, where a resident of Germany was, before 30 December 2010, in receipt of a UK pension (including State Pension) or annuity relievable under Article X of prior treaty 1967/25, the individual may elect for the terms of the prior treaty to continue to apply to the pension or annuity.

6 New treaty effective in UK from 1 January 2012 for property income dividends, interest, royalties (and annuities not subject to PAYE), 6 April 2012 for pensions and annuities within PAYE. Prior treaty was 1978/1056.

Tax information exchange agreements in force

Country	*SI*	*Country*	*SI*
Anguilla	**2010/2677**	Grenada	**2011/1687**
Antigua and Barbuda	**2011/1075**	Guernsey	**2009/3011**
Aruba	**2011/2435**	Isle of Man	**2009/228**
Bahamas	**2010/2684**	Jersey	**2009/3012**
Belize	**2011/1685**	Liberia	**2011/2434**
Bermuda	**2008/1789**	Liechtenstein	**2010/2678**
British Virgin Islands	**2009/3013**	San Marino	**2011/1688**
Curaçao, Sint Maarten and BES Islands (formerly the Netherlands Antilles)	**2011/2433**	St Christopher and Nevis	**2011/1077**
Dominica	**2011/1686**	St Lucia	**2011/1076**
Gibraltar	**2010/2680**	St Vincent and Grenadines	**2011/1078**
		Turks and Caicos Islands	**2010/2679**

Tax information exchange agreements signed but not in force

Marshall Islands	Jersey Exchange of Letters[1]	British Virgin Islands Exchange of Letters[1]
Brazil	Guernsey Exchange of Letters[1]	Turks and Caicos Islands Exchange of Letters[1]
Uruguay	Gibraltar Exchange of Letters[1]	

1 These will amend the existing tax information exchange agreements.

Tax information exchange agreements in force — EU savings directives

Country	*SI*	*Country*	*SI*
Aruba	**2005/1458**	Isle of Man	**2005/1263**
British Virgin Islands	**2005/1457**	Jersey	**2005/1261**
Gibraltar	**2006/1453**	Montserrat	**2005/1459**
Guernsey	**2005/1262**	former Netherlands Antilles (now known as Curaçao, Sint Maarten and BES Islands)	**2005/1460**

International agreements in force to improve tax compliance

Isle of Man, Guernsey, Jersey, Gibraltar	**2014/520**
USA	**2013/1962**

Agreements in force covering shipping and air transport profits

Country	***SI/SR & O***	***Country***	***SI/SR & O***
Algeria (air)	**1984/362**	Iran (air)	**1960/2419**
Armenia (USSR air)*	**1974/1269**	Kyrgyzstan (USSR air)*	**1974/1269**
Belarus (USSR air)*	**1974/1269**	Lebanon	**1964/278**
Brazil	**1968/572**	Moldova (USSR air)*	**1974/1269**
Cameroon (air)	**1982/1841**	Saudi Arabia (air)	**1994/767**
China (air)	**1981/1119**	Tajikistan (USSR air)*	**1974/1269**
Congo Democratic Republic	**1977/1298**	Turkmenistan (USSR air)*	**1974/1269**
Ethiopia (air)	**1977/1297**		
Georgia (USSR air)*	**1974/1269**		
Hong Kong (air)	**1998/2566**		
(shipping)	**2000/3248**		

* HMRC have confirmed that this Arrangement will be treated in the same way as the Convention covering income and capital gains (SI 1986/224). See note 1 p 122.

Agreements in force covering estates, inheritances and gifts

France*	**1963/1319**	Pakistan*	**1957/1522**
India*	**1956/998**	South Africa	**1979/576**
Ireland	**1978/1107**	Sweden	**1981/840**
Italy*	**1968/304**		1989/986
Netherlands	**1980/706**	Switzerland	**1994/3214**
	1996/730	USA	**1979/1454**

* Agreements pre-date UK inheritance tax/capital transfer tax.

Overseas income – basis of assessment

(ITTOIA 2005 Pt 8; ITEPA 2003 ss 573–576A; ITA 2007 ss 809A–809Z10)

	Professions, trades, etc	Pensions	Other income
Non-residents	Exempt	Exempt	Exempt
Residents			
(1) **Foreign domicile**[2]	Remittance	Remittance	Remittance
(2) **UK domicile**	Arising	90%[1] arising	Arising

[1] Pensions paid by the governments of the Federal Republic of Germany or of Austria to victims of Nazi persecution are exempt.

[2] Where from 6 April 2008, an individual not domiciled (or, before 6 April 2013, not ordinarily resident) in the UK who has overseas income (or, for non-domiciles only, gains) in excess of £2,000 claims the remittance basis, he will not qualify for personal allowances or the capital gains tax annual exemption. The claim for remittance basis must be made annually. If the individual is not UK domiciled (or before 6 April 2013, not ordinarily resident) in a year and has been resident in the UK for at least seven out of the last nine tax years and has overseas income or gains in excess of £2,000, there is an additional charge of £30,000. This charge is increased to £50,000 from 6 April 2012 for non-domiciles who have been UK resident for at least twelve tax years in the previous fourteen.

[3] A statutory residence test is introduced from 6 April 2013 and ordinary residence is abolished from that date, subject to transitional provisions in certain cases for individuals who were resident but not ordinarily resident in the UK at the end of the tax year 2012–13. Before 6 April 2013 UK-domiciled taxpayers who were not ordinarily resident were taxed on the remittance basis.

Employment income liability of non-resident employees see p 91.

Tax-free (FOTRA) securities

(FA 1996 s 154; FA 1998 s 161; ITTOIA 2005 ss 713, 714; CTA 2009 s 1279)

Interest on all government stock is exempt from tax where the beneficial owner is not resident in the UK. Except in the case of 3½% War Loan 1952 or after, the exemption does not apply where the securities are held for the purposes of a trade or business carried on in the UK.

Social security benefits

Taxable state benefits

	Weekly 7.4.14	Total 2014–15 (52 weeks)	Weekly 8.4.13	Total 2013–14 (52 weeks)
	£	£	£	£
Bereavement benefits[1]				
Bereavement allowance: standard rate	**111.20**	**5,782**	108.30	5,631
Widowed parent's allowance	**111.20**	**5,782**	108.30	5,631
Carer's allowance	**61.35**	**3,190**	59.75	3,107
– Adult dependency increase[7]	**36.10**	**1,877**	35.15	1,827
Employment and support allowance[6]				
–under 25	**57.35**	**–**	56.80	–
–25 or over	**72.40**	**–**	71.70	–
Incapacity benefit[6]				
Long-term (after 52 weeks)	**104.10**	**5,413**	101.35	5,270
– Adult dependency increase	**60.45**	**3,143**	58.85	3,060
– Age increase: higher rate	**11.00**	**572**	10.70	556
lower rate	**6.15**	**319**	6.00	312
Short term				
– Under pension age: higher rate	**92.95**	**–**	90.50	–
– Adult dependency increase	**47.10**	**–**	45.85	–
– Over pension age: higher rate	**104.10**	**–**	101.35	–
– Adult dependency increase	**58.20**	**–**	56.65	–
Industrial death benefit[2]				
Widow's pension: higher rate	**113.10**	**5,881**	110.15	5,727
lower rate	**33.93**	**1,764**	33.05	1,718
Widower's pension	**113.10**	**5,881**	110.15	5,727
Invalidity allowance[3]				
Higher rate	**21.25**	**1,105**	20.70	1,076
Middle rate	**13.70**	**712**	13.30	691
Lower rate	**6.85**	**356**	6.65	345
Jobseeker's allowance[4]				
Single: under 25	**57.35**	**–**	56.80	–
25 or over	**72.40**	**–**	71.70	–
Couple: both under 18	**57.35**	**–**	56.80	–
both under 18 higher rate	**86.65**	**–**	85.80	–
one under 18, one under 25	**57.35**	**–**	56.80	–
one under 18, one 25 or over	**72.40**	**–**	71.70	–
both 18 or over	**113.70**	**–**	112.55	–
State pension				
Single person (Category A or B)	**113.10**	**5,881**	110.15	5,727
Single person (Category B lower) based on spouse's or civil partner's insurance	**67.80**	**3,525**	66.00	3,432
Adult dependency increase[7]	**64.90**	**3,374**	63.20	3,286
Non-contributory pension				
– single (Category C (higher) or Category D)	**67.80**	**3,525**	66.00	3,432
– single (Category C (lower))	**40.50**	**2,106**	39.45	2,051
Age addition (over 80) (each)	**0.25**	**13**	0.25	13
Statutory adoption pay				
Rate[5]	**138.18**	**–**	136.78	–
Earnings threshold	**111.00**	**–**	109.00	–
Statutory maternity pay				
Rate[5]	**138.18**	**–**	136.78	–
Earnings threshold	**111.00**	**–**	109.00	–
Statutory paternity pay				
Rate[5]	**138.18**	**–**	136.78	–
Earnings threshold	**111.00**	**–**	109.00	–

	Weekly 7.4.14	*Total 2014–15 (52 weeks)*	*Weekly 8.4.13*	*Total 2013–14 (52 weeks)*
	£	**£**	**£**	**£**
Statutory sick pay				
Rate	**87.55**	**–**	86.70	–
Earnings threshold	**111.00**	**–**	109.00	–

1 Paid to widows, widowers and the civil partner of the deceased for up to 52 weeks.

2 For deaths before 11 April 1988 only.

3 When paid with retirement pensions. See note below on non-taxable benefits on p 129.

4 Where the allowance exceeds the amount shown above, the excess is not taxable.

5 The allowance is 90% of average weekly earnings if less than the above amount. In the first six weeks the rate of SMP is 90% of average weekly earnings even if higher than the standard rate.

6 Employment and support allowance replaces incapacity benefits for new claimants on or after 27 October 2008. Only contributory employment and support allowance is taxable. Income related allowance is not taxable.

7 Not available to new retirees or new carer's allowance claimants from 6 April 2010. To be withdrawn completely on 5 April 2020.

8 **A cap is placed on the total amount of benefit** that most people aged 16 to 64 can receive. Most local councils introduced this between 15 July and 30 September 2013. Bromley, Croydon, Enfield and Haringey Councils introduced it on 15 April 2013. The cap applies to the total amount that the people in a household receive from certain benefits. The cap is £500 a week for couples (with or without children living with them), £500 a week for single parents whose children live with them, and £350 a week for single adults who don't have children, or whose children don't live with them. See www.gov.uk/benefit-cap.

9 **Universal credit** is being phased in gradually from 29 April 2013 and replaces some of the benefits above. Initially it applies to new claimants in Greater Manchester and Cheshire but is being introduced to the rest of the UK from October 2013 and will be completed by 2017. For current rates see table of non-taxable benefits on p 129. See www.gov.uk/universal-credit.

Non-taxable state benefits

Weekly rates from		***7.4.14***	***8.4.13***
		£	**£**
Attendance allowance			
Higher rate (day and night)		**81.30**	79.15
Lower rate (day or night)		**54.45**	53.00
Child benefit[3]			
Eldest child		**20.50**	20.30
Each subsequent child		**13.55**	13.40
Child dependency addition			
Paid with state pension; widowed mother's/parent's allowance; short-term incapacity benefit - higher rate or over state pension age; long-term incapacity benefit; carer's allowance; severe disablement allowance; industrial death benefit (higher rate);		**11.35**	11.35
Disability living allowance[2]			
Care component	higher rate	**81.30**	79.15
	middle rate	**54.45**	53.00
	lower rate	**21.55**	21.00
Mobility component	higher rate	**56.75**	55.25
	lower rate	**21.55**	21.00
Personal independence payment[2]			
Daily living component	enhanced rate	**81.30**	79.15
	standard rate	**54.45**	53.00
Mobility component	enhanced rate	**56.75**	55.25
	standard rate	**21.55**	21.00
Guardian's allowance		**16.35**	15.90
Incapacity benefit (short-term)[1]			
Under pension age – lower rate (first 28 weeks)		**78.50**	76.45
– Adult dependency increase		**47.10**	45.85
Over pension age – lower rate (first 28 weeks)		**99.90**	97.25
– Adult dependency increase		**58.20**	56.65
Maternity allowance (where SMP not available)			
Standard rate		**138.18**	136.78
MA threshold		**30.00**	30.00
Severe disablement allowance			
Basic rate		**73.75**	71.80
Age-related addition	higher rate	**11.00**	10.70
	middle rate	**6.15**	6.00
	lower rate	**6.15**	6.00
– Adult dependency increase		**36.30**	35.35
Amount payable per assessment period[5] in:		***2014–15***	***2013–14***
Universal credit[5]			
Standard allowance			
Single:	under 25	**249.28**	246.81
	25 or over	**314.67**	311.55
Couples:	both under 25	**391.29**	387.42
	either 25 or over	**493.95**	489.06

1 Incapacity benefit replaced invalidity allowance from April 1995. The benefits are taxable except those paid in the first 28 weeks of incapacity and those paid to persons already receiving invalidity benefit on 13 April 1995 so long as they remain incapable of work.

2 Personal Independence Payment (PIP) started to replace Disability Living Allowance (DLA) for new claims by eligible people aged 16 to 64 from 8 April 2013. PIP will be introduced in stages over a number of years for existing DLA claimants.

3 See note on p 75 regarding the income tax charge arising to certain child benefit claimants from 7 January 2013.

4 **A cap is placed on the total amount of benefit** that most people aged 16 to 64 can receive. Most local councils introduced this between 15 July and 30 September 2013. Bromley, Croydon, Enfield and Haringey Councils introduced it on 15 April 2013. The cap applies to the total amount that the people in a household receive from certain benefits. The cap is £500 a week for couples (with or without children living with them), £500 a week for single parents whose children live with them, and £350 a week for single adults who don't have children, or whose children don't live with them. See www.gov.uk/benefit-cap.

5 **Universal credit** is being phased in gradually from 29 April 2013 and will replace some of the benefits listed in the above tables. Initially it applies to new claimants in Greater Manchester and Cheshire but is being introduced to the rest of the UK from October 2013 and will be completed by 2017. An assessment period is a calendar month from effective date of claim.

Other non-taxable benefits include:

Bereavement payment (lump sum £2,000)
Back to Work bonus

Child tax credit (see Tax Credits, p 101)
Christmas bonus (with retirement pension)
Cold weather payments
Housing benefit (income related)
Income support (income related)
Industrial injuries disablement pension

Pension credit
Pneumoconiosis, byssinosis and miscellaneous disease benefits
Social fund payments
Vaccine damage (lump sum)
War pensions
Winter fuel payment
Working tax credit (see Tax Credits, p 101)

Stamp taxes

Stamp duty land tax

(FA 2003 Schs 2A–9)

Stamp duty land tax applies to contracts entered into (or varied) after 10 July 2003 and completed after 30 November 2003 and to leases granted after that date (FA 2003 ss 55, 56, Sch 5). With effect from 22 July 2004, it also applies to the transfer of an interest in land into, or out of, a partnership and to the acquisition of an interest in a partnership where the partnership property includes an interest in land. With effect from 19 July 2006, it applies to transfers of partnership interests only where the sole or main activity of the partnership is investing or dealing in interests in land. The power to raise stamp duty land tax will devolve to the Scottish Parliament from 1 April 2015.

Effective date	3.9.08–31.12.09	1.1.10–5.4.11	6.4.11–21.3.12	22.3.12–19.3.14	**From 20.3.14**	**Rate**
Land transactions		*Consideration*[1]				
Residential property[4]	Up to £175,000	Up to £125,000	Up to £125,000	Up to £125,000	**Up to £125,000**	**Nil**
	£175,001–£250,000	£125,001–£250,000[2]	£125,001–£250,000[2]	£125,001–£250,000	**£125,001–£250,000**	**1%**
	£250,001–£500,000	£250,001–£500,000	£250,001–£500,000	£250,001–£500,000	**£250,001–£500,000**	**3%**
	£500,001 or more	£500,001 or more	£500,001–£1,000,000	£500,001–£1,000,000	**£500,001–£1,000,000**	**4%**
	–	–	£1,000,001 or more	£1,000,001–£2,000,000	**£1,000,001–£2,000,000**	**5%**
	–	–	–	£2,000,001 or more	**£2,000,001 or more**	**7%**
Non-natural persons[5]	–	–	–	£2,000,001 or more	**£500,001 or more**	**15%**[5]
Non-residential or mixed property	Up to £150,000	Up to £150,000	Up to £150,000	Up to £150,000	**Up to £150,000**	**Nil**
	£150,001–£250,000	£150,001–£250,000	£150,001–£250,000	£150,001–£250,000	**£150,001–£250,000**	**1%**
	£250,001–£500,000	£250,001–£500,000	£250,001–£500,000	£250,001–£500,000	**£250,001–£500,000**	**3%**
	£500,001 or more	£500,001 or more	£500,001 or more	£500,001 or more	**£500,001 or more**	**4%**
Lease rentals		*On net present value of rent over term of lease (applying a discount rate of 3.5%)*[3]				
Residential property	Up to £175,000	Up to £125,000	Up to £125,000	Up to £125,000	**Up to £125,000**	**Nil**
	£175,001 or more	£125,001 or more	£125,001 or more	£125,001 or more	**£125,001 or more**	**1%**
Non-residential or mixed property	Up to £150,000	Up to £150,000	Up to £150,000	Up to £150,000	**Up to £150,000**	**Nil**
	£150,001 or more	£150,001 or more	£150,001 or more	£150,001 or more	**£150,001 or more**	**1%**
Premiums The same tax is payable for a premium granted as for a land transaction. Special rules apply to a premium in respect of non-residential property where the rent exceeds £1,000 a year. For transactions before 12 March 2008, the rules applied to all property where the rent exceeded £600 a year.						

1 Rates apply to the full consideration, not only to that in excess of the previous band.

2 For residential property, purchases by first-time buyers between 25 March 2010 and 24 March 2012 inclusive attracted a nil rate of SDLT for purchase consideration up to £250,000.

3 Rates apply to the amount of npv in the slice, not the whole value.

4 With effect from 19 July 2011, where a purchaser (or a connected person) of residential property acquires more than one dwelling from the same vendor (or a connected person) and makes a claim, the rate of SDLT will be calculated based on the mean consideration for each property, subject to a minimum rate of 1%.

5 From 21 March 2012 a 15% rate applies to certain non-natural persons (ie companies, partnerships with at least one company member, and collective investment schemes) acquiring a residential property where consideration exceeds a specified threshold, which is £2,000,000 from 21 March 2012 to 19 March 2014, and £500,000 from 20 March 2014. Relief is available for genuine property businesses so that the charge is at the lower percentage in certain cases. See p 65 for the annual tax on enveloped dwellings and capital gains tax charge which also apply to such properties.

Exemptions and reliefs

No SDLT (or, where relevant, stamp duty) is chargeable on:

(1) transfers to charities for use for charitable purposes.
(2) transfers to bodies established for national purposes.
(3) gifts inter vivos.
(4) certain transfers on divorce or dissolution of a civil partnership.
(5) transfers of property to beneficiaries under a will or an intestacy.
(6) land transfers within groups of companies.
(7) land transferred in exchange for shares on company reconstruction and acquisitions.
(8) certain transfers to or leases granted by registered providers of social housing. (Although the relief is repealed for the old stamp duty rules for instruments executed on or after 6 April 2013, it still applies to stamp duty land tax).
(9) sale and leaseback and lease and leaseback arrangements involving commercial and residential property.
(10) certain acquisitions of residential property by house building companies or property traders from personal representatives, or when people move into a new dwelling or a chain of transactions break down, or by employers involving employee relocations.
(11) for transactions with an effective date before 6 April 2013, transfers on sale of residential property for a consideration of up to £150,000 in disadvantaged parts of the UK. This also applied to leases broadly, on rent where the relevant rental value did not exceed £150,000 and to premiums not exceeding £150,000. No claims can be made after 5 May 2014.
(12) from 1 October 2007 until 30 September 2012 for new zero carbon homes (including flats) with a purchase price of up to £500,000, there was no SDLT charged. Where the purchase price was in excess of £500,000, the SDLT liability on the purchase price was reduced by £15,000.
(13) from 25 March 2010 until 24 March 2012 purchases of residential property by first-time buyers for consideration of more than £125,000 but not more than £250,000 (see p 131).
(14) demutualisation of building societies and insurance companies.
(15) incorporation of limited liability partnerships.
(16) transfers of land between public bodies under a statutory reorganisation.
(17) compulsory purchase of land facilitating redevelopment.
(18) land transactions in compliance with planning obligations enforceable against the vendor and made within five years of the obligation where the purchaser is one of certain public authorities.
(19) transfers by a local constituency association in consequence of a reorganisation of parliamentary constituencies.
(20) purchases or leases of certain diplomatic or consular premises or headquarters premises of certain international organisations.

Relief from SDLT may also apply on:

(a) right to buy transactions, shared ownership leases and rent to loan transactions.
(b) alternative property finance schemes.
(c) exercise of collective rights by leaseholders.
(d) crofting community right to buy.
(e) certain arrangements relating to land transactions involving public or educational bodies.
(f) acquisitions of interests in land by certain National Health Service bodies.

Stamp duty

(FA 1999 Sch 13)

For contracts entered into (or varied) after 10 July 2003 and completed after 30 November 2003 and for leases granted after that date, stamp duty is abolished for all transfers other than stocks and marketable securities, and interests in partnerships. From 22 July 2004 stamp duty is also abolished for certain partnership transactions involving an interest in land. From those dates, transfers of land are subject to stamp duty land tax (see p 131).

Shares, etc	
Shares put into depository receipts or put into duty free clearance systems	1.5%
Purchase of own shares by company	0.5%
Transfers of stock or marketable securities	0.5%
Takeovers, mergers, demergers, schemes of reconstruction and amalgamation (except where no real change of ownership)	0.5%

1 Stamp duty is rounded to the next multiple of £5.
2 For instruments executed after 11 March 2008 stamp duty is not chargeable where the amount or value of the consideration is less than £1,000.
3 From April 2014 transfers of interests in exchange traded funds will be exempt from stamp duty and stamp duty reserve tax.
4 From 28 April 2014 no stamp duty or stamp duty reserve tax is due on trades in 'recognised growth markets' such as the Alternative Investment Market and the ISDX Growth Market.

Fixed duties

Instruments affecting land transactions	£5

From 13 March 2008 fixed duties are generally abolished other than as above. The £5 rate applies to instruments effected from 1 October 1999.

Stamp Duty Reserve Tax (SDRT)

(FA 1986 Part IV)

Agreements to transfer chargeable securities for money or money's worth (eg renounceable letters of allotment)[1]	0.5%
Chargeable securities put into a clearance service[2] or converted into depositary receipts where the transfer is not an integral part of an issue of share capital[4]	1.5%
Dealings of units in unit trusts and shares in open-ended investment companies before 30 March 2014[3]	0.5%
Transfers of foreign currency bearer shares and agreements to transfer sterling or foreign currency convertible or equity-related loan stock issued by UK companies	0.5%

1 If the transaction is completed by a duly stamped instrument within six years from the date on which the charge is imposed, the SDRT will be cancelled or repaid.

2 Where the operator of a clearance service elects to collect and account for SDRT on the normal rate of 0.5% on dealing within the system the higher SDRT charge of 1.5% does not apply.

3 From 6 April 2001 transfers of units in a unit trust and surrenders of shares in open-ended investment companies are exempt when held within individual pension accounts. From 30 March 2014 the exemption applies to all transfers of units in a unit trust and all surrenders of shares in open-ended investment companies, although the charge will remain on non pro-rata in specie redemptions.

4 Following the cases of HSBC Holdings plc and the Bank of New York Mellon Corporation v HMRC and HSBC Holdings plc and Vidacos Nominees Limited v Commissioners for HMRC, SDRT of 1.5% is no longer applicable on issues of UK shares to depositary receipt issuers and clearance services. Claims for repayment of SDRT may be made.

5 From April 2014 transfers of interests in exchange traded funds will be exempt from stamp duty and stamp duty reserve tax.

6 From 28 April 2014 no stamp duty or stamp duty reserve tax is due on trades in 'recognised growth markets' such as the Alternative Investment Market and the ISDX Growth Market.

Interest on unpaid tax

Stamp duty land tax. *From 26 September 2005*: Interest runs from the end of 30 days after the effective date of transaction (normally completion), or the date of a disqualifying event, until the tax is paid. In the case of a deferred payment, interest runs from the date the payment is due until the tax is paid. A penalty carries interest from the date determined until the date of payment.

Stamp duty. *For instruments executed from 1 October 1999*: Interest runs from the end of 30 days after the date the instrument is executed until the tax is paid. Amounts less than £25 are not charged.

Stamp duty reserve tax. Interest is charged from 14 days after the transaction date for exchange transactions and otherwise from seven days after the end of the month of the transaction. Amounts less than £25 are not charged.

Rates: see p 4.

Repayment supplement

Stamp duty land tax. *From 26 September 2005*: Interest is added to repayments of overpaid stamp duty land tax and runs from the date tax was paid or an amount was lodged with HMRC, or the date a penalty was made, to the date the order for repayment is issued.

Stamp duty. *For instruments executed from 1 October 1999*: Interest is added to repayments of overpaid stamp duty and runs from 30 days after the date the instrument is executed or the date of payment if later. Amounts less than £25 are not paid.

Stamp duty reserve tax. Interest is paid from the date the tax was paid to the date the order for repayment is issued.

Rates: see p 6.

Penalties

Offence	*Penalty*
Stamp duty land tax and stamp duty reserve tax	
Inaccuracy in return or other document (FA 2007 Sch 24).	See **Penalties — modernised penalty regime** on p 12
Inaccuracy in return or other document as a result of third party providing incorrect (or withholding) information (FA 2007 Sch 24).	See **Penalties — modernised penalty regime** on p 12
Failure to notify HMRC of an error in an assessment (within 30 days) (FA 2007 Sch 24).	See **Penalties — modernised penalty regime** on p 12
Failure to comply with HMRC investigatory powers with effect from 1 April 2010 (FA 2008 Sch 36).	(*a*) Initial penalty of £300; (*b*) if failure/obstruction continues, a further penalty of up to £60 per day; (*c*) if failure/obstruction continues after penalty under (*a*) imposed, a tax-related amount determined by the Upper Tribunal.
Provision of inaccurate information or document when complying with an information notice with effect from 1 April 2010 (FA 2008 Sch 36).	Up to £3,000 per inaccuracy.
Stamp duty – for instruments executed from 1 October 1999	
Failure to present instrument for stamping within 30 days after execution (or the day in which it is first received in the UK if executed outside the UK) (Stamp Act 1891 s 15B; SI 1999/2537). (Extended to instruments executed from 24 July 2002 for transfers of UK land and buildings, wherever executed (FA 2002 s 114).)	If presented within one year after the end of the 30-day period: the lower of £300 or the amount of the unpaid duty. If presented more than one year after the end of the 30-day period: the greater of £300 or the amount of unpaid duty.
Stamp duty land tax – contracts completed after 30 November 2003	
Failure to deliver a land transaction return by the filing date (FA 2003 Sch 10 paras 3, 4).	£100 if return delivered within three months of filing date, otherwise £200. If not delivered within 12 months, penalty up to amount of tax chargeable.
Failure to comply with notice to deliver return within specified period (FA 2003 Sch 10 para 5).	Up to £60 for each day on which the failure continues after notification.
Failure to keep and preserve records under FA 2003 Sch 10 para 9 or Sch 11 para 4 (FA 2003 Sch 10 para 11, Sch 11 para 6).	Up to £3,000 unless the information is provided by other documentary evidence.
Failure (From 1 August 2005) to disclose certain SDLT proposals or arrangements (TMA 1970 s 98C; SI 2005/1868; SI 2005/1869; SI 2010/2743).	(*a*) Up to £600 per day during 'initial period' (but tribunal can determine a higher penalty up to £1 million); (*b*) further penalty up to £600 per day while failure continues. Both the initial penalty in (*a*) above and the secondary penalty in (*b*) above can be increased up to £5,000 per day that failure continues from 10 days after the order is made.
Failure (From 1 August 2005) to provide prescribed information relating to disclosure certain SDLT proposals or arrangements (TMA 1970 s 98C; SI 2005/1868; SI 2005/1869; SI 2010/2743).	(*a*) Initial penalty up to £5,000; (*b*) further penalty up to £600 per day while failure continues. This can be increased up to £5,000 per day after a tribunal has issued a disclosure order.
Failure (From 1 August 2005) to provide scheme reference number relating to certain SDLT proposals or arrangements (TMA 1970 s 98C; SI 2005/1868; SI 2005/1869; SI 2010/2743);	(*a*) Penalty of £100 in respect of each scheme to which the failure relates;
for second failure, occurring within three years from the date on which the first failure began;	(*b*) penalty of £500 in respect of each scheme to which the failure relates;
for subsequent failures, occurring within three years from the date on which the previous failure began.	(*c*) penalty of £1,000 in respect of each scheme to which the failure relates.
Repealed provisions	
Fraudulently or negligently delivering an incorrect return or failing to remedy an error without unreasonable delay (FA 2003 Sch 10 para 8).	*Up to the difference between the amount payable and the amount that would have been chargeable on the basis of the return delivered.* ***Repealed and replaced by penalty under FA 2007 Sch 24 above after 31 March 2010.***
Fraudulently or negligently giving a self-certificate for a chargeable transaction or failing to remedy an error in respect of such certificate without unreasonable delay (FA 2003 Sch 11 para 3).	*Up to the amount of tax chargeable.* ***Repealed for transactions after 11 March 2008.***

Offence	*Penalty*
Failure to comply with notice to produce documents etc under FA 2003 Sch 10 para 14 (FA 2003 Sch 10 para 16).	*(a) Initial penalty of £50;* *(b) further penalty for each day the failure continues up to £30 if penalty determined by HMRC, or £150 if determined by the court.* ***Repealed with effect from 1 April 2010 and replaced by penalties under FA 2008 Sch 36. Penalties still apply after 31 March 2010 to notices issued before 1 April 2010***.
Stamp duty reserve tax	
Failure to notify HMRC and pay tax (TMA 1970 s 93, SI 1986/1711 as applied in practice by HMRC; see under 'Penalties and appeals —stamp duty reserve tax' on HMRC website).	If notified within one year of the payment deadline: the lower of £100 or the amount of the unpaid duty. If notified more than one year after the payment deadline: £100 plus up to the amount of unpaid duty, subject to a reduction for mitigating factors.

Value added tax

Rates

(VATA 1994 s 2)

	From 4.1.11		1.1.10–3.1.11		1.12.08–31.12.09	
	Rate	*VAT fraction*	*Rate*	*VAT Fraction*	*Rate*	*VAT Fraction*
Standard rate	**20%**	**1/6**	17.5%	7/47	15.0%	3/23
Reduced rate (see p 142)	**5.0%**	**1/21**	5.0%	1/21	5.0%	1/21
Flat-rate scheme for farmers	**4.0%***		4.0%[1]		4.0%*	

1 Flat rate addition to sale price

Registration limits

UK taxable supplies

(VATA 1994 Sch 1 para 1, Sch 1A para 1; SI 2014/703)

A person who is UK-established (from 1 December 2012[3], previously both UK and non-UK established persons) and makes taxable supplies is liable to be registered:

(a) at the end of any month, or

(b) at any time, if:

	(a) turnover in the past year[1] *(b) turnover in the next 30 days*[2] *exceeds:*	*Unless, in the case of (a), turnover for next year not expected to exceed:*
1.4.14 onwards	**£81,000**	**£79,000**
1.4.13–31.3.14	£79,000	£77,000
1.4.12–31.3.13	£77,000	£75,000
1.4.11–31.3.12	£73,000	£71,000
1.4.10–31.3.11	£70,000	£68,000
1.5.09–31.3.10	£68,000	£66,000
1.4.08–30.4.09	£67,000	£65,000

1 The value of taxable supplies in the year then ending.

2 If there are reasonable grounds for believing the value of taxable supplies will exceed limit.

3 For supplies made on or after 1 December 2012 non-UK established businesses are required to register for VAT regardless of the value of taxable supplies made in the UK.

Supplies from other EC countries ('distance selling')

(VATA 1994 Sch 2)

A business person in another EC country not registered or liable to be registered in the UK is liable to be registered on any day if, in the period beginning with 1 January in that year, the value of supplies by that person to non-taxable persons in the UK exceeds:

1.1.93 onwards	**£70,000**

Acquisitions from other EC countries

(VATA 1994 Sch 3)

A person not registered or liable to be registered under the above rules is liable to be registered:

(a) at the end of any month if, in the period beginning with 1 January in that year, the value of taxable goods acquired by that person for business purposes (or for non-business purposes if a public body, charity, club, etc) from suppliers in other EC countries exceeds the following limits; or

(b) at any time, if there are reasonable grounds for believing the value of such acquisitions in the next 30 days will exceed the following limits:

1.4.14 onwards	**£81,000**
1.4.13–31.3.14	£79,000
1.4.12–31.3.13	£77,000
1.4.11–31.3.12	£73,000
1.4.10–31.3.11	£70,000
1.5.09–31.3.10	£68,000
1.4.08–30.4.09	£67,000

Deregistration limits

UK taxable supplies

(VATA 1994 Sch 1 para 4; SI 2014/703)

A registered taxable person who is UK-established (from 1 December 2012[1], previously both UK and non-UK established persons) ceases to be liable to be registered if, at any time, HMRC are satisfied that the value of taxable supplies in the year then beginning will not exceed:

1.4.14 onwards	**£79,000**
1.4.13–31.3.14	£77,000
1.4.12–31.3.13	£75,000
1.4.11–31.3.12	£71,000
1.4.10–31.3.11	£68,000
1.5.09–31.3.10	£66,000
1.4.08–30.4.09	£65,000
Unless the reason for not exceeding the limit during that year is that the person will cease making taxable supplies or suspend making taxable supplies for 30 days or more.	

1 For supplies made on or after 1 December 2012 non-UK established businesses are required to register for VAT regardless of the value of taxable supplies made in the UK.

Supplies from other EC countries ('distance selling')

(VATA 1994 Sch 2)

A person registered under these provisions ceases to be liable to be registered if, at any time:

(a) relevant supplies in year ended 31 December last before that time did not exceed following limit; and

(b) HMRC are satisfied that value of relevant supplies in year immediately following that year will not exceed following limit:

1.1.93 onwards	**£70,000**

Acquisitions from other EC countries

(VATA 1994 Sch 3)

A person registered under these provisions ceases to be liable to be registered if, at any time:

(a) relevant acquisitions in year ended 31 December last before that time did not exceed following limits; and

(b) HMRC are satisfied that value of relevant acquisitions in year immediately following that year will not exceed following limits:

1.4.14 onwards	**£81,000**
1.4.13–31.3.14	£79,000
1.4.12–31.3.13	£77,000
1.4.11–31.3.12	£73,000
1.4.10–31.3.11	£70,000
1.5.09–31.3.10	£68,000
1.4.08–30.4.09	£67,000

Annual accounting scheme

(SI 1995/2518 regs 49–55)

A business may, subject to conditions, complete one VAT return a year. Quarterly or monthly interim payments to be made.

	Can join if taxable supplies in next year not expected to exceed:	*Must leave at end of accounting year if taxable supplies exceeded:*
1.4.06 onwards	**£1,350,000**	**£1,600,000**
1.4.04–31.3.06	£660,000	£825,000

Cash accounting scheme

(SI 1995/2518 regs 56–65)

A business may, subject to conditions, account for and pay VAT on the basis of cash paid and received. It can join the scheme at any time as follows.

	Can join if taxable supplies in next year not expected to exceed:	*Must leave at end of VAT period if taxable supplies in previous year exceed:*	*Unless turnover for next year not expected to exceed:*
1.4.07 onwards	**£1,350,000**	**£1,600,000**	**£1,350,000**
1.4.04–31.3.07	£660,000	£825,000	£660,000

Flat-rate scheme for small businesses

(SI 1995/2518 regs 55A–55V)

A business which expects its taxable supplies in the next year to be no more than £150,000 and (before 1 April 2009) its total business income to be no more than £187,500 (including VAT) can opt to join a flat-rate scheme. The appropriate percentage below is applied to total turnover generated, including exempt income, to calculate net VAT due. Once in the scheme a business may continue to use it until its total business income exceeds £230,000, and if income does exceed this limit, the business can still remain in the scheme if the income in the following year is estimated not to exceed £191,500.

Category of business	*Appropriate %*		
	From 4.1.11	***1.1.10–3.1.11***	***1.12.08–31.12.09***
Accountancy or book-keeping	**14.5**	13	11.5
Advertising	**11**	10	8.5
Agricultural services	**11**	10	7
Any other activity not listed elsewhere	**12**	10.5	9
Architect	**14.5**	13	11
Boarding or care of animals	**12**	10.5	9.5
Business services that are not listed elsewhere	**12**	10.5	9.5
Catering services, including restaurants and takeaways	**12.5**	11	10.5
Civil and structural engineer or surveyor	**14.5**	13	11
Computer and IT consultancy or data processing	**14.5**	13	11.5
Computer repair services	**10.5**	9.5	10
Dealing in waste or scrap	**10.5**	9.5	8.5
Entertainment or journalism	**12.5**	11	9.5
Estate agency and property management services	**12**	10.5	9.5
Farming or agriculture that is not listed elsewhere	**6.5**	6	5.5
Film, radio, television or video production	**13**	11.5	9.5
Financial services	**13.5**	12	10.5
Forestry or fishing	**10.5**	9.5	8
General building or construction services	**9.5**	8.5	7.5
Hairdressing or other beauty treatment services	**13**	11.5	10.5
Hiring or renting goods	**9.5**	8.5	7.5
Hotel or accommodation	**10.5**	9.5	8.5
Investigation or security	**12**	10.5	9
Labour-only building or construction services[1]	**14.5**	13	11.5
Laundry or dry-cleaning services	**12**	10.5	9.5
Lawyer or legal services	**14.5**	13	12
Library, archive, museum or other cultural activity	**9.5**	8.5	7.5
Management consultancy	**14**	12.5	11
Manufacturing fabricated metal products	**10.5**	9.5	8.5
Manufacturing food	**9**	8	7
Manufacturing that is not listed elsewhere	**9.5**	8.5	7.5
Manufacturing yarn, textiles or clothing	**9**	8	7.5

Category of business	*Appropriate %*		
	From 4.1.11	***1.1.10–3.1.11***	***1.12.08–31.12.09***
Membership organisation	**8**	7	5.5
Mining or quarrying	**10**	9	8
Packaging	**9**	8	7.5
Photography	**11**	10	8.5
Post Offices	**5**	4.5	2
Printing	**8.5**	7.5	6.5
Publishing	**11**	10	8.5
Pubs	**6.5**	6	5.5
Real estate activity not listed elsewhere	**14**	12.5	11
Repairing personal or household goods	**10**	9	7.5
Repairing vehicles	**8.5**	7.5	6.5
Retailing food, confectionery, tobacco, newspapers or children's clothing	**4**	3.5	2
Retailing pharmaceuticals, medical goods, cosmetics or toiletries	**8**	7	6
Retailing that is not listed elsewhere	**7.5**	6.5	5.5
Retailing vehicles or fuel	**6.5**	6	5.5
Secretarial services	**13**	11.5	9.5
Social work	**11**	10	8
Sport or recreation	**8.5**	7.5	6
Transport or storage, couriers, freight, removals and taxis	**10**	9	8
Travel agency	**10.5**	9.5	8
Veterinary medicine	**11**	10	8
Wholesaling agricultural products	**8**	7	5.5
Wholesaling food	**7.5**	6.5	5
Wholesaling that is not listed elsewhere	**8.5**	7.5	6

[1] That is, services where value of materials supplied is less than 10% of turnover of such services; any other services are 'general building or construction services'.

Partial exemption

(SI 1995/2518 regs 106–107)

A registered person who makes taxable and exempt supplies is partly exempt and may not be able to deduct (or reclaim) all his input tax. Where, however, input tax attributable to exempt supplies in a prescribed accounting period or tax year is within the de minimis limits below, all such input tax is attributable to taxable supplies and recoverable (subject to the normal rules).

De minimis limits	£625 per month on average and 50% of all input tax for the period concerned

Capital goods scheme

(SI 1995/2518 regs 112–116)

Input tax adjustment following change in taxable use of capital goods

Item	*Value*	*Adjustment period*
Computer equipment	£50,000 or more	Five years
Ships, boats or other vessels[1]	£50,000 or more	Five years
Aircraft[1]	£50,000 or more	Five years
Land and buildings	£250,000 or more[2]	Ten years (for adjustment periods commenced before 1 January 2011, five years where interest had less than ten years to run on acquisition)

1 Applies for goods acquired on or after 1 January 2011.

2 Figure reduced to £1 where owner ('O') of item or a person to whom O has granted an interest in that item:
(a) uses that item to make a grant falling within VATA 1994 Sch 9 Group1 Item 1(ka) (self-storage facilities excluded from exemption);
(b) decides, no later than 31 March 2013, to treat the item as a capital item; and
(c) makes a written record to that effect, specifying the date of the decision.

Adjustment formula where adjustment period begins before 1 January 2011

$$\frac{\text{Total input tax on item}}{\text{Length of adjustment period}} \times \text{adjustment percentage}$$

Adjustment formula where adjustment period begins on or after 1 January 2011

$$\frac{\text{Total VAT on item}}{\text{Length of adjustment period}} \times \text{adjustment percentage}$$

The adjustment percentage is the percentage change in the extent to which the item is used (or treated as used) in making taxable supplies between the first interval in the adjustment period & a subsequent interval. (The first interval generally ends on the last day of the tax year in which the input tax was incurred.) For goods acquired on or after 1.1.11 total VAT includes any non-business VAT & the extent to which a capital item is used for business purposes must be determined when ascertaining taxable use for each subsequent interval.

Zero-rated supplies

A zero-rated supply is a taxable supply, but the rate of tax is nil (VATA 1994 Sch 8).

Group 1 – Food
Group 2 – Sewerage services and water
Group 3 – Books etc
Group 4 – Talking books for the blind and handicapped and wireless sets for the blind
Group 5 – Construction of buildings etc
Group 6 – Protected buildings
Group 7 – International services
Group 8 – Transport
Group 9 – Caravans and houseboats
Group 10 – Gold
Group 11 – Bank notes
Group 12 – Drugs, medicines, aids for the handicapped etc
Group 13 – Imports, exports etc
Group 15 – Charities etc
Group 16 – Clothing and footwear
Group 18 – European Research Infrastructure Consortia (from 1 January 2013)

Reduced rate supplies

(VATA 1994 Sch 7A)

Group 1 – Domestic fuel and power
Group 2 – Installation of energy-saving materials
Group 3 – Grant-funded installation of heating equipment or security goods or connection of a gas supply
Group 4 – Women's sanitary products
Group 5 – Children's car seats and bases
Group 6 – Residential conversions
Group 7 – Residential renovations and alterations
Group 8 – Contraceptive products (from 1 July 2006)
Group 9 – Welfare advice or information (from 1 July 2006)
Group 10 – Installation of mobility aids for the elderly (from 1 July 2007)
Group 11 – Smoking cessation products (from 1 July 2007)
Group 12 – Caravans (from 6 April 2013)
Group 13 – Cable-suspended transport systems (from 1 April 2013)

Exempt supplies

(VATA 1994 Sch 9)

Group 1 – Land

Group 2 – Insurance

Group 3 – Postal services

Group 4 – Betting, gaming, dutiable machine games and lotteries

Group 5 – Finance

Group 6 – Education

Group 7 – Health and welfare

Group 8 – Burial and cremation

Group 9 – Subscriptions to trade unions, professional and other public interest bodies

Group 10 – Sport, sports competitions and physical education

Group 11 – Works of art etc

Group 12 – Fund-raising events by charities and other qualifying bodies

Group 13 – Cultural services etc

Group 14 – Supplies of goods where input tax cannot be recovered

Group 15 – Investment gold

Group 16 – Supplies of services by groups involving cost sharing (from 17 July 2012)

EC Sales Lists

(SI 1995/2518 regs 2, 21–23)

All VAT-registered businesses in the UK must provide HMRC with details of goods and services supplied to a VAT-registered customer in another EU country.

The requirement for returns is as follows:

Supplies of		**Frequency**
Goods	Supplies of goods are in excess of £35,000 (£70,000 before 1 January 2012) in any of the current or last four quarters	Monthly
Goods	Supplies of goods are below £35,000 (£70,000 before 1 January 2012) per quarter in the current and previous four quarters	Quarterly on 31 March, 30 June, 30 September and 31 December
Services supplied to a business where the place of supply is where the customer belongs		Quarterly as above
Goods and services where a business is required to submit monthly lists for goods		Monthly for all supplies, or monthly for goods and quarterly for services
Goods or services supplied by a business completing annual VAT returns	Total annual taxable turnover does not exceed £145,000; annual value of supplies to other EU countries not more than £11,000 (and do not include *New Means of Transport*)	On application — annual on agreed due date
Goods only supplied	Total annual taxable turnover does not exceed the VAT registration threshold plus £25,500; annual value of supplies to other EU countries not more than £11,000 (and do not include *New Means of Transport*	On application — annual in simple format on agreed due date

The due date for returns is 21 days after the end of the period if submitted online and 14 days after the end of the period if submitted on paper.

Country	**Code**
Austria[10]	AT
Belgium	BE
Bulgaria	BG
Croatia[13]	HR
Cyprus[9]	CY
Czech Republic	CZ
Denmark[2]	DK
Estonia	EE
Finland[3]	FI
France[4]	FR
Germany[5]	DE
Greece[11]	EL
Hungary	HU
Ireland	IE
Italy[6]	IT
Latvia	LV
Lithuania	LT
Luxembourg	LU
Malta	MT
Netherlands[12]	NL
Poland	PL
Portugal[7]	PT
Romania	RO
Slovak Republic	SK
Slovenia	SI
Spain[8]	ES
Sweden	SE

1 Countries not listed in the table above are not part of the EU VAT area and so sales to those countries should not be included on the EC sales list. The following are not part of the EU VAT area; Andorra, The Channel Islands, Gibraltar, Mount Athos, San Marino, and Vatican City. The UK and the Isle of Man are part of the EU VAT area, but sales to these should not be included on the list.

2 Does not include the Faroe Islands and Greenland.

3 Does not include Aland Islands.
4 Includes Monaco; excludes Martinique, Guadeloupe, Reunion, St Pierre & Miquelon, and French Guiana.
5 Does not include Busingen and Isle of Heligoland.
6 Does not include communes of Livigno and Campione d'Italia and the Italian waters of Lake Lugano.
7 Includes the Azores and Madeira.
8 Includes the Balearic Islands but excludes Ceuta, Melilla, and the Canary Islands.
9 Includes British sovereign base areas of Akrotiri and Dhekelia, but excludes those areas in United Nations buffer zone and to the north of that where the Republic of Cyprus does not have effective control.
10 Includes Jungholz and Mittelberg.
11 Excludes Mount Athos.
12 Excludes Antilles (now Curaçao, Sint Maarten and BES Islands).
13 Croatia joined the EU on 1 July 2013. Supplies of goods, or services subject to the reverse charge, to a VAT registered customer in Croatia, must be included in the ESL.

Intrastat

(SI 1992/2790)

All VAT-registered businesses in the UK must complete boxes 8 and 9 on the VAT return showing the total value of goods supplied to and acquired from other EC member states respectively. Businesses with a total value of such supplies (dispatches) or acquisitions (arrivals) exceeding a threshold must make supplementary declarations containing further information each month. Thresholds are set for each calendar year and recent thresholds are shown below. If a person's dispatches or arrivals in the previous calendar year exceeded the current year's threshold, supplementary declarations must be made for the full current year. If the cumulative total of dispatches or arrivals in a year exceeds that calendar year's threshold, supplementary declarations must be made for the rest of the year, starting in the month in which the threshold is exceeded. Additional delivery terms information must be provided on the supplementary declaration only if the annual value of arrivals or dispatches exceeds the delivery terms threshold, and the information must be submitted from the start of the next calendar year. If the delivery terms threshold for arrivals is exceeded, but not that for dispatches, delivery terms must be provided for arrivals only, and vice versa. From April 2012 declarations must be submitted electronically and will be due 21 days after the end of the month in which there is EU trade to declare.

Year	**Supplies (dispatches) threshold per calendar year**	**Acquisitions (arrivals) threshold per calendar year**	**Delivery terms threshold per calendar year**
From 1.1.14	**£250,000**	**£1,200,000**	**£24,000,000**
1.1.10–31.12.13	£250,000	£600,000	£16,000,000
1.1.09–31.12.09	£270,000	£270,000	£16,000,000
1.1.08–31.12.08	£260,000	£260,000	£14,500,000

Some of the EU country codes and the areas included for intrastat purposes differ from those used for EC sales list purposes. The intrastat codes are as follows.

Country	*Code*
Austria	AT
Belgium	BE
Bulgaria	BG
Croatia[12]	HR
Cyprus[9]	CY
Czech Republic	CZ
Denmark[2]	DK
Estonia	EE
Finland[3]	FI
France[4]	FR
Germany[5]	DE
Greece[10]	GR
Hungary	HU
Ireland	IE
Italy[6]	IT
Latvia	LV
Lithuania	LT
Luxembourg	LU
Malta	MT
Netherlands	NL
Poland	PL
Portugal[7]	PT
Romania	RO
Slovak Republic	SK
Slovenia	SI
Spain[8]	ES
Sweden	SE
United Kingdom[11]	GB

1 Andorra and Liechtenstein are both outside the customs territory (and therefore the statistical territory) of the EU.
2 Does not include the Faroe Islands.
3 Includes Aland Islands.
4 Includes Monaco, but excludes all French Overseas departments and territories. Martinique, Guadeloupe, Reunion, Mayotte, and French Guiana are part of the statistical territory of France but because customs documentation is still required for exports to, or imports from, these territories HMRC continue to collect trade statistics from that documentation and it must not be declared on the intrastat.
5 Includes Isle of Heligoland but excludes Busingen.
6 Does not include communes of Livigno and Campione d'Italia, the Italian waters of Lake Lugano and the Vatican. Livigno is part of the statistical territory of Italy but because customs documentation is still required for exports to, or imports from, this territory HMRC continue to collect trade statistics from that documentation and it must not be declared on the intrastat.
7 Includes the Azores and Madeira.
8 Includes the Balearic Islands but excludes Ceuta, Melilla, and the Canary Islands. The Canary Islands are part of the statistical territory of Spain but because customs documentation is still required for exports to, or imports from, these territories HMRC continue to collect trade statistics from that documentation and it must not be declared on the intrastat.
9 Includes UK sovereign base areas but excludes Northern Cyprus.
10 Includes Mount Athos.
11 Includes the Isle of Man and the Channel Islands but excludes Gibraltar.
12 Croatia joined the EU on 1 July 2013. Dispatches and arrivals to/from Croatia should be included from this date.

VAT Mini One Stop Shop (VAT MOSS)

From 1 January 2015 the place of supply for business-to-consumer (B2C) supplies of broadcasting, telecommunications and e-services (digital services) will be determined by the location of the consumer. The changes will affect all businesses that supply digital services to consumers (ie private individuals), whether or not they are registered for UK VAT, because there are no registration limits for digital service supplies made to consumers outside the UK. Any business supplying digital services to a consumer in another member state therefore has to charge VAT on the supply in that member state and register for VAT in that member state. Supplies of digital services to businesses only (including the self-employed) are not affected by the changes.

To avoid having to register for VAT in every EU member state where digital services are supplied, a business may opt to use the VAT Mini One Stop Shop online service (VAT MOSS). This will be available from 1 January 2015, but registration can be made from October 2014. Using the VAT MOSS online service means a business can submit a single calendar quarterly VAT MOSS return and payment covering all its EU digital service supplies. If the business registers for the VAT MOSS online service in the UK, HMRC will send an electronic copy of the appropriate part of the VAT MOSS return, and the related VAT payment, to each relevant member state's tax authority.

Car fuel

(VATA 1994 ss 56, 57, Schs 4, 6; FA 2013 Sch 38)

Where an employer pays mileage allowances, he may use the advisory fuel rates on p 83 to calculate the input VAT to reclaim on the fuel element. Receipts must still be retained.

VAT-inclusive scale figures can be used to assess VAT due on fuel provided at no cost (from 11 December 2012, previously at below cost) for private journeys by registered traders or their employees, where the fuel has been provided from business resources. The figures represent the tax-inclusive value of the fuel supplied to each individual and relate to return periods beginning on the dates shown. If the trader or employer opts to use the scale figures he must use them for all supplies of fuel for private use made for no consideration in the prescribed accounting period. From 17 July 2013, the scale charge may also be used as an alternative to accounting for VAT on the required open market value where the fuel is supplied for a consideration below that value.

	12 months £	*3 months* £	*1 month* £
From 1 May 2014: CO_2 band			
120 or below	627	156	52
125	939	234	78
130	1,004	251	83
135	1,064	266	88
140	1,129	282	94
145	1,190	297	99
150	1,255	313	104
155	1,315	328	109
160	1,381	345	115
165	1,441	360	120
170	1,506	376	125
175	1,567	391	130
180	1,632	408	136
185	1,692	423	141
190	1,757	439	146
195	1,818	454	151
200	1,883	470	156
205	1,943	485	161
210	2,008	502	167
215	2,069	517	172
220	2,134	533	177
225 or above	2,194	548	182

	12 months £	*3 months* £	*1 month* £
1 May 2013–30 April 2014: CO_2 band			
120 or below	675	168	56
125	1,010	253	84
130	1,080	269	89
135	1,145	286	95
140	1,215	303	101
145	1,280	320	106
150	1,350	337	112
155	1,415	354	118
160	1,485	371	123
165	1,550	388	129
170	1,620	404	134
175	1,685	421	140
180	1,755	438	146
185	1,820	455	151
190	1,890	472	157
195	1,955	489	163
200	2,025	506	168
205	2,090	523	174
210	2,160	539	179
215	2,225	556	185
220	2,295	573	191
225 or above	2,360	590	196

	12 months £	*3 months* £	*1 month* £
1 May 2012–30 April 2013: CO_2 band			
120 or below	665	166	55
125	1,000	250	83
130	1,065	266	88
135	1,135	283	94
140	1,200	300	100
145	1,270	316	105
150	1,335	333	111
155	1,400	350	116
160	1,470	366	122
165	1,535	383	127
170	1,600	400	133
175	1,670	416	138
180	1,735	433	144
185	1,800	450	150
190	1,870	467	155
195	1,935	483	161
200	2,000	500	166
205	2,070	517	172
210	2,135	533	177
215	2,200	550	183
220	2,270	567	189
225 or above	2,335	583	194

	12 months £	3 months £	1 month £
1 May 2011–30 April 2012: CO_2 band			
120 or below	630	157	52
125	945	236	78
130	1,010	252	84
135	1,070	268	89
140	1,135	283	94
145	1,200	299	99
150	1,260	315	105
155	1,325	331	110
160	1,385	346	115
165	1,450	362	120
170	1,515	378	126
175	1,575	394	131
180	1,640	409	136
185	1,705	425	141
190	1,765	441	147
195	1,830	457	152
200	1,890	472	157
205	1,955	488	162
210	2,020	504	168
215	2,080	520	173
220	2,145	536	178
225 or above	2,205	551	183

	12 months £	3 months £	1 month £
1 May 2010–30 April 2011: CO_2 band			
120 or below	570	141	47
125	850	212	70
130	850	212	70
135	910	227	75
140	965	241	80
145	1,020	255	85
150	1,080	269	89
155	1,135	283	94
160	1,190	297	99
165	1,250	312	104
170	1,305	326	108
175	1,360	340	113
180	1,420	354	118
185	1,475	368	122
190	1,530	383	127
195	1,590	397	132
200	1,645	411	137
205	1,705	425	141
210	1,760	439	146
215	1,815	454	151
220	1,875	468	156
225	1,930	482	160
230 or above	1,985	496	165

Interest and penalties

Default interest

(VATA 1994 s 74)

Interest runs on the amount of any VAT assessed (or paid late by voluntary disclosure):

- from the reckonable date (normally the latest date on which a return is required for the period in question);
- until the date of payment (although in practice it runs to the date shown on the notice of assessment or notice of voluntary disclosure if paid within 30 days of that date).

The period of interest cannot commence more than three years before the date of assessment or payment.

The rates of interest are as follows:

Period	*Rate*
From 29 September 2009	**3%**
24 March 2009–28 September 2009	2.5%
27 January 2009–23 March 2009	3.5%
6 January 2009–26 January 2009	4.5%
6 December 2008–5 January 2009	5.5%
6 November 2008–5 December 2008	6.5%
6 January 2008–5 November 2008	7.5%
6 August 2007–5 January 2008	8.5%
6 September 2006–5 August 2007	7.5%
6 September 2005–5 September 2006	6.5%
6 September 2004–5 September 2005	7.5%
6 December 2003–5 September 2004	6.5%
6 August 2003–5 December 2003	5.5%*

Interest on VAT overpaid in cases of official error

(VATA 1994 s 78)

Where VAT has been overpaid or underclaimed due to an error by HMRC, then on a claim HMRC must pay interest:

- from the date they receive payment (or authorise a repayment) for the return period in question;
- until the date on which they authorise payment of the amount on which interest is due.

This provision does not require HMRC to pay interest on an amount on which repayment supplement is due.

The rates of interest are as follows:

Period	*Rate*
from 29 September 2009	**0.5%**
27 January 2009–28 September 2009	0%
6 January 2009–26 January 2009	1%
6 December 2008–5 January 2009	2%
6 November 2008–5 December 2008	3%
6 January 2008–5 November 2008	4%
6 August 2007–5 January 2008	5%
6 September 2006–5 August 2007	4%
6 September 2005–5 September 2006	3%
6 September 2004–5 September 2005	4%
6 December 2003–5 September 2004	3%
6 August 2003–5 December 2003	2%*
6 November 2001–5 August 2003	3%

* Due to an administrative error the rate of default and statutory interest was too high by one percentage point between 6 August 2003 and 5 September 2003. HMRC will not seek to recover amounts overpaid by HMRC and will seek to identify businesses overcharged (see Business Brief 17/05 as of 9 September 2005).

Repayment supplement – VAT

(VATA 1994 s 79)

Where a person is entitled to a repayment the payment due is increased by a supplement of the greater of:

(i) 5% of that amount; or
(ii) £50.

The supplement will only be paid if:

(a) the return or claim is received by HMRC not later than the last day on which it is required to be made;
(b) HMRC do not issue a written instruction making the refund within the relevant period; and

(c) the amount shown on the return or claim does not exceed the amount due by more than 5% of that amount or £250, whichever is the greater.

The 'relevant period' is 30 days beginning with the receipt of the return or claim or, if later, the day after the last day of the VAT period to which the return or claim relates.

Penalties and surcharges

Offence	*Penalty*
Inaccuracy in return or other document (FA 2007 Sch 24)[1].	See **Penalties — modernised penalty regime** on p 12.
Failure to notify obligation to register for VAT, change in supplies made by person exempted from registration, acquisition affecting exemption, acquisition of goods from another member state and unauthorised issue of an invoice (FA 2008 Sch 41).	See **Penalties — modernised penalty regime** on p 12.
Inaccuracy in return or other document as a result of third party providing incorrect (or withholding) information (FA 2007 Sch 24).	See **Penalties — modernised penalty regime** on p 12.
Failure to inform HMRC of an error in an assessment within 30 days of the date of the assessment (FA 2007 Sch 24).	See **Penalties — modernised penalty regime** on p 12.
Failure to comply with HMRC investigatory powers with effect from 1 April 2009 (FA 2008 Sch 36).	(*a*) Initial penalty of £300; (*b*) if failure/obstruction continues, a further penalty of up to £60 per day; (*c*) if failure/obstruction continues after penalty under (*a*) imposed, a tax-related amount determined by the Upper Tribunal.
Provision of inaccurate information or document when complying with an information notice (FA 2008 Sch 36).	Up to £3,000 per inaccuracy.
Failure to submit a return electronically if required to do so by SI 1995/2518 reg 25 for prescribed accounting periods starting on or after 1 April 2012. Before 1 April 2012, failure of a *specified person* to make a *specified return* using an electronic return system for prescribed accounting periods ending on or after 31 March 2011 (SI 1995/2518 reg 25A). 'Specified person' was broadly a person registered for VAT on or after 1 April 2010, or one registered before that date who at 31 December 2009 or any later date has an annual VAT exclusive turnover of £100,000 or more. Penalty will only apply to prescribed accounting periods ending on or after 31 March 2013 where the person is required to make an electronic return only as a result of the removal of the turnover test from 1 April 2012.	Annual VAT exclusive turnover of: £22,800,001 or more — £400 £5,600,001 to £22,800,000 — £300 £100,001 to £5,600,000 — £200 £100,000 or under — £100
Failure to submit return or pay VAT due within time limit (where a return is late but the VAT is paid on time or no VAT is due, a default is recorded but no surcharge arises) (VATA 1994 s 59)[2]. Failure to pay tax due under the payment on account scheme on time (VATA 1994 s 59A).	The greater of £30 and a specified percentage of outstanding VAT for period, depending on number of defaults in surcharge period: first default in period 2%, second default 5%, third default 10%, fourth and further defaults 15%. (Surcharge assessments are not issued for sums of less than £400 unless the rate of the surcharge is 10% or more.) **Due to be replaced by penalties under FA 2009 Schs 55 and 56 from a date to be appointed.**
Issuing incorrect certificate stating that certain supplies fall to be zero-rated or taxed at the reduced rate (VATA 1994 s 62).	Difference between tax actually charged and tax which should have been charged.
Material inaccuracy in EC sales statement (VATA 1994 s 65).	£100 for each material inaccuracy in two-year penalty period (which commences following notice of second material inaccuracy).
Failure to submit an EC sales statement (VATA 1994 s 66).	Greater of £50 or a daily penalty (maximum 100 days) £5 for the first, £10 for the second, £15 for the third or subsequent failure in the default period.
Breach of walking possession agreement (VATA 1994 s 68).	50% of VAT due or amount recoverable.
Failure to preserve records for prescribed period (VATA 1994 ss 69, 69B).	£500.
Failure to preserve records specified in HMRC direction (VATA 1994 ss 69, 69B).	£200 for each day of failure (maximum 30 days).
Breaches of regulatory provisions, including failure to notify cessation of liability or entitlement to be registered, failure to keep records and non-compliance with any regulations made under VATA 1994 (VATA 1994 s 69).	Greater of £50 and a daily penalty (maximum 100 days) of a specified amount depending on number of failures in preceding two years: £5* per day if no previous failures; £10* per day if one previous failure; £15* per day if two or more previous failures.
Where failure consists of not paying VAT or not making a return in the required time.	*1/6, 1/3 and 1/2 of 1% of the VAT due respectively, if greater.

Offence	Penalty
Breaches of regulatory provisions involving failure to pay VAT or submit return by due date (VATA 1994 s 69).	Greater of £50 and a daily penalty (for no more than 100 days) of a specified amount depending on number of failures in preceding two years: greater of £5 and 1/6 % of VAT due if no previous failures; greater of £10 and 1/3% of VAT due if one previous failure; greater of £15 and 1/2% of VAT due if two or more previous failures.
Failure to comply with the requirements of the investment gold scheme (VATA 1994 s 69A).	17.5% of the value of transactions concerned.
Import VAT (FA 2003 ss 24–41):	
– failures relating to non-compliance	maximum penalty of £2,500
– evasion.	maximum penalty equal to VAT sought to be evaded.
Failure to notify the use of a designated avoidance scheme (VATA 1994 Sch 11A paras 10, 11).	15% of the tax avoided (applies to businesses with supplies of £600,000 or more).
Failure to disclose certain schemes within 30 days of the due date or the first return affected (VATA 1994 Sch 11A paras 10, 11).	£5,000 (applies to businesses with supplies exceeding £10 million).
Repealed provisions	
Evasion of VAT: conduct involving dishonesty (VATA 1994 ss 60, 61[3]).	*Amount of tax evaded or sought to be evaded (subject to mitigation).* ***Repealed and replaced by penalty under FA 2007 Sch 24 for periods beginning on or after 1 April 2008 and ending on or after 1 April 2009 subject to the exceptions shown below***[1].
Misdeclaration or neglect (VATA 1994 s 63).	*15% of VAT which would have been lost if inaccuracy had not been discovered.* ***Repealed and replaced by penalty under FA 2007 Sch 24 for periods beginning on or after 1 April 2008 and ending on or after 1 April 2009***.
Repeated misdeclarations (VATA 1994 s 64).	*15% of VAT which would have been lost if second and subsequent inaccuracies within penalty period had not been discovered.* ***Repealed and replaced by penalty under FA 2007 Sch 24 for periods ending on or after 1 April 2008 and ending on or after 1 April 2009***.
Failure to notify liability for registration or a change in nature of supplies by person exempted from registration (VATA 1994 s 67).	*Greater of £50 and a specified percentage of the tax for which the person would have been liable, depending on the period of failure: nine months or less 5%; over nine and up to 18 months 10%; over 18 months 15%.* ***Repealed after 31 March 2010 and replaced by penalty under FA 2008 Sch 41***.
Failure to notify acquisition of excise duty goods or new means of transport (VATA 1994 s 67).	*Greater of £50 and: 5% of the tax for which the person would have been liable if period of failure is three months or less, 10% if over three and up to six months and 15% if over six months.* ***Repealed after 31 March 2010 and replaced by penalty under FA 2008 Sch 41***.
Unauthorised issue of invoices (VATA 1994 s 67).	*Greater of £50 and 15% of amount shown as or representing VAT.* ***Repealed after 31 March 2010 and replaced by penalty under FA 2008 Sch 41***.

1 In relation to VAT MOSS returns, a penalty under FA 2007 Sch 24 only applies when the recipient of the supply is in the UK. If an inaccuracy on a UK return relates to a supply to a recipient in another member state, there is no penalty under UK legislation, but a penalty may apply in that other member state in which the recipient is located. If an inaccuracy on (say) a French VAT return relates to a supply to a recipient in the UK, there could be a penalty under UK legislation.

2 In relation to VAT MOSS returns, a penalty for a late return or late payment could be charged by each member state in which the supplies are deemed to be made.

3 Penalties under VATA 1994 ss 60, 61 will continue to be charged for acts or omissions not relating to an inaccuracy in a document or failure to notify HMRC of an under-assessment (SI 2008/568 and SI 2009/571).

Index

A

Accounts, inheritance tax
due dates 104
excepted estates 105
Advisory fuel rates 83
Age allowance 76
Aggregates levy 67
Agricultural buildings allowances 29
Agricultural property relief 106
Air passenger duty 67
Alternative finance investment bonds 26
Annual accounting scheme, VAT 140
Annual exemption
capital gains tax 35
inheritance tax 106
Annual tax on enveloped dwellings 65
Approval applications 27
Authorised mileage rates 85
Average exchange rates 117

B

Bank base rates 1
Bank levy 70
Basic rate of income tax 75
Basis of assessment
employment income 91
overseas income 125
Benefits, employee 86–90
Benefits, social security 127–130
Blind person's allowance 76
Bus services 79, 87
Business property relief 106

C

Capital allowances
agricultural buildings 29
claims, time limits 21
conversions into flats over shops, etc 30
disadvantaged areas 34
dredging 29
elections, time limits 23
enterprise zones 30, 34
flat conversions 30
industrial buildings 29
know-how 30
mineral extraction 33
motor cars 33
patent rights 33

Capital allowances – *cont.*
plant and machinery 30–33
rates 29–34
renovation of business premises 34
research and development 33
scientific research 33
Capital gains tax
annual exemption 35
ATED properties 65
chattel exemption 35
claims, time limits 22
due date 2
elections, time limits 22
employee-ownership trusts 39
employee shareholder shares 39
enterprise investment scheme 39
entrepreneurs' relief 37
exemptions 35
high value UK residential property 36
hold-over relief for gifts 39
incorporation relief 40
indexation allowance 41–59
interest on overdue tax 4
leases 38
penalties 12–21
personal representatives 40
rates 36
reliefs 40
retail prices index 60–61
returns, penalties 12, 14
roll-over relief 40
seed enterprise investment scheme 40
share identification rules 37
social investment tax relief 40
trustees 35, 36, 41
venture capital scheme 40
Capital goods scheme, VAT 142
Capped income tax reliefs 98
Cars
advisory fuel rates 83
authorised mileage rates 85
benefit 78
capital allowances 33
capital gains exemption 39
fuel for private use
taxable benefit 80
VAT 147
hired: restricted allowances 80
mileage allowances 83
private use 78
Carbon price floor 70
Cash accounting scheme, VAT 140
Certificates of tax deposit 9

Charities
capital gains exemption 39
gift aid 86
gift aid small donations 86
gifts in kind 86
gifts to, inheritance tax relief 106
payroll giving scheme 86
Chattels, capital gains exemption 35
Cheap loans to employees 87
Child benefit income tax charge 75
Child tax credit 101
Claims, time limits
capital allowances 23
capital gains tax 22
corporation tax 23
income tax 22
Clearance applications 27
Clearing houses 25–26
Climate change levy 70
Community investment tax relief 95
Company share option plans 101
Compensation, capital gains exemption 39
Computer equipment 90
Construction industry scheme 75
Corporation tax
annual tax on enveloped dwellings 65
claims, time limits 23
corporate venturing scheme 64
disincorporation relief 64
due date 2
elections, time limits 23
gifts of pre-eminent objects 64
interest on overdue tax 4
interest on overpaid tax 7
marginal relief 63
patent box 64
penalties 12–21
rates 63
real estate investments trusts 64
reliefs 64
research and development expenditure 64
returns, penalties 12–16
Corporate venturing scheme 64
Cycles and cycle safety equipment 79

D

Default interest – VAT
VAT 150
Default surcharge 151
Deregistration limits, VAT 139
Disabled employees, equipment 88
Disadvantaged areas, capital allowances 34
Disincorporation relief 65
Dividends 75
Double taxation agreements
air transport profits 124
capital taxes 124
income and capital gains 121
shipping profits 124
tax compliance agreements 123
Double taxation agreements – *cont.*
tax information exchange agreements 123
Dredging allowances 29
Due dates of tax 2–3

E

Elections, time limits
capital allowances 23
capital gains tax 22
corporation tax 23
income tax 22
Employees
accommodation, supplies etc used in employment duties 84
assets given to employees 86, 115
bus services for 79
car benefits 78
cheap loans 87
childcare 87
Christmas parties, annual functions 87, 113
clothing and uniforms 115
computers provided for private use 90
credit cards and tokens 87, 115
cycles and cycle safety equipment 79
cyclists breakfasts 87
disabled, equipment etc 88
emergency vehicles 79, 88
employee's liability insurance 88
entertaining 115
eye tests 88
fixed-rate expenses 93
flat rate expenses 93
fuel benefits 80, 115
holidays 115
homeworkers 88
incidental overnight expenses 88
living accommodation 88
living expenses 88
loan benefits 87, 115
long service awards 89
meals 89, 115
medical check-ups 89
medical insurance, etc. 89, 114
medical treatment 89
mileage rates 85
mobile phones 89
national minimum wage 91
notional payments 115
parking facilities for 79, 115
payments in kind 115
personal expenses 89, 116
relocation benefits 89, 116
round sum allowances 116
scholarships and school fees 89, 116
share schemes 100
shareholder status 39, 97
tax paid for 115
telephone costs 116
third party gifts 89
use of employer's assets 89

Employees – *cont.*
van benefits 79
vouchers 90, 116
Employee shareholder status 39, 97
Employment benefits 86–90
Employment exemption 90
Employment income 90
basis of assesment 91
due dates of tax 2
fixed rate expenses 93
termination payments 91
Employee-ownership trusts 39, 90
Enterprise investment scheme
capital gains exemption 39
income tax relief 95
Enterprise management incentives 100
Enterprise zones 30, 34
Entrepreneurs' relief 36, 37
Environmental taxes and other levies 67–73
Excepted estates, inheritance tax 105
Excepted transfers 104
Exchange rates
average 117
year end 120
Exchanges
alternative finance investment bonds 26
recognised foreign exchanges 26
recognised futures exchanges 25
recognised investment exchanges 25
recognised stock exchanges 24
Exempt supplies, VAT 143

F

Filing dates 11
Fixed rate expenses 93
Flat conversions, capital allowances 30
Flat rate scheme for small businesses, VAT 140
Foreign exchange rates
average 117
year end 120
Foreign income
basis of assessment 125
employment income 91
Foster carers 97
FOTRA securities 125
Fuel duty 71
Fuel for private use
income tax 80
VAT 147–149
Futures exchanges 25

G

Gift aid 86
Gift aid small donations 86
Gifts in kind 86
Gifts of land, shares etc 86
Gifts of pre-eminent objects 39, 64, 97

H

Harmonised interest regime 4
High value UK residential property 36, 65, 131
Hired cars and motorcycles 80
Hold-over relief for gifts 39
Hotels, capital allowances 29

I

Income tax
capped reliefs 98
claims, time limits 21
due dates 2
elections, time limits 21
interest on overdue tax 4
lease premiums 38
penalties 12–21
personal allowances 76
rates 75
reliefs 76, 95
returns, penalties 12–21
Incorporation relief 40
Indexation allowance 41–59
Individual savings accounts (ISAs) 96
Industrial buildings allowances
enterprise zones 34
rates 29
Inheritance tax
agricultural property relief 104
annual exemption 106
business property relief 106
charitable gifts, exemption 106
due dates for accounts 104
due dates for tax 3
excepted transfers estates and settlements 103, 104
gifts, reliefs 106
interest on overdue tax 7
marriage/civil partnership gifts, exemption 106
national purposes, gifts exemption 106
nil rate bands 103
non-domiciled spouse/civil partner 107
penalties 12–21
political parties, gifts exemption 106
potentially exempt transfers 106
quick succession relief 107
rates 103
reliefs 106
small gifts exemption 107
tapering relief 107
Insurance premium tax 71
Insurance premiums, life 97
Interest rates
bank base rates 1
capital gains 2, 6
certificates of tax deposit 9
corporation tax 4, 7

Interest rates – *cont.*
default, VAT 150
income tax 2, 6
income tax on company payments 5
inheritance tax 7
national insurance contributions 3, 6
official, cheap loans 87
overpaid tax 6
stamp duties 4, 6
unpaid tax 3
VAT 150
Investment exchanges 25
Investment reliefs
community investment tax relief 95
enterprise investment scheme 95
individual savings accounts 96
junior ISAs 97
National Savings Bank interest 97
seed enterprise investment scheme 95
social investment tax relief 96
urban regeneration companies 96
venture capital trusts 96

J

Junior ISAs 97

K

Know-how, capital allowances 30

L

Landfill tax 72
Landlord's energy-saving allowance 97
Leases
depreciation table 38
premiums 38
stamp duties 131–135
Life assurance premium relief 97

M

Machinery and plant allowances 30–33
cars 33
rates 30
Maintenance payments 98
Managed services companies 91
Marginal relief, corporation tax 63
Marriage/civil partnership gifts, inheritance tax relief 106
Married couple's allowance 76
Mileage allowances 83
Minimum wage, national 91
Misdeclarations, VAT 152
Mobile phones 89
Motorcycles 80

N

National insurance contributions
Class 1 109, 115
Class 1A, 1B 109, 115
Class 3 114
Classes 2 and 4 3, 76, 114
employees under age 21 109
employers' contributions on benefits 115
employer NIC holiday 110
employment allowance 109
interest on overdue contributions 3
interest on overpaid contributions 6
rates 109
weekly and monthly thresholds 90
National minimum wage 91
National Savings Bank interest 97
Nazi persecution, pensions to victims 125
Non-domiciled individuals
employment income 91
overseas income 125
spouses/civil partners, inheritance tax 107
Non-residents
employment income 91
overseas income 125

O

Official rate of interest, employee loans 87
Offshore matters, penalties, territory categories 15
Overseas income, basis of assessment
employment income 91
overseas income 125

P

Parking facilities 79
Partial exemption, VAT 141
Patent rights, capital allowances 33
Patent box 64
Payment dates of tax 2–3
PAYE
penalties 12–21
settlement agreements 90
weekly and monthly thresholds 90
Payroll giving scheme 86
Penalties
corporation tax returns 12–21
inheritance tax 12–21
interest on 8, 21
mitigation of 21
offshore matter, territory categories 15
personal tax returns 12–21
special information returns 18
stamp taxes 132

Penalties – *cont.*
VAT 151
Pension provision
from 6 April 2006 99
personal pension schemes 99
Personal allowances 76
Personal pension schemes 99
Personal representatives 40
Personal service companies 88
Plant and machinery allowances
rates 30–33
Potentially exempt transfers 106
Premiums on leases
capital gains tax 38
income tax 38
stamp taxes 131

Q

Qualifying corporate bonds 39
Qualifying care relief 97
Quick succession relief 107

R

Rates of tax
annual tax on enveloped dwellings 65
capital gains tax 36
corporation tax 63
environmental taxes and other levies 67–71
income tax 75
inheritance tax 103
stamp taxes 131–133
VAT 137
Real Estate Investment Trusts 64
Recognised clearing houses 25–26
Recognised futures exchanges 25
Recognised investment exchanges 25
Recognised stock exchanges 24
Reduced rate supplies, VAT 142
Registration limits, VAT 137
Reliefs
capped income tax reliefs 98
capital gains 39
corporation tax 64
income tax 76, 95
inheritance tax 106
Remission of tax 9
Renovation of business premises 34
Rent, stamp duties 131, 132
Rent-a-room relief 98
Repayment supplement – general 7
Repayment supplement – stamp duty 133
Repayment supplement – VAT 150
Research and development 33, 64
Retail prices index 60–61
Retirement pensions 99
Return filing dates 11
Roll-over relief 40

S

Save as you earn (SAYE) share option schemes 100
Scientific research allowances 33
Seafarers' deduction 91
Securities, tax-free for non-residents 125
Security, PAYE, failure to provide 21
Seed enterprise investment scheme 40, 95
Share identification rules 37
Share incentive plans 100
Share schemes 100
Shared lives carers 97
Small gifts relief 107
Simplified fixed rate deductions 98
Social investment tax relief 40, 96
Social security benefits
cap on benefits 128, 130
non-taxable 129
taxable 127
Special relief 9
Stamp taxes
disadvantaged areas 132
exemptions 132
fixed 133
interest 4, 133
land transactions 131
leases 131, 132
penalties 134
premiums 131, 132
rates 131, 132
reliefs 132
rent 131, 132
repayment supplement 6, 133
stamp duty 132
stamp duty land tax 131
stamp duty reserve tax 133
stock transfers 132, 133
State benefits
cap on benefits 128, 130
non-taxable 129
taxable 127
Stock exchanges 24
Student loans 11
Subscriptions 28, 89
Supplement VAT 150

T

Tapering relief, inheritance tax 107
Tax credits 101
Tax information exchange agreements 123
Termination payments 91
Time limits, claims and elections 21
Toll roads, capital allowances 29
Trustees
capital gains annual exempt amount 35
expenses allowable for CGT 41
Trusts
capital gains tax rates 36
income tax rates 75

U

Universal credit 129
Urban regeneration companies 96

V

Van, employee benefit 79
VAT
annual accounting scheme 140
capital goods scheme 142
car fuel advisory rates 83, 147
car fuel for private use 147–149
cash accounting scheme 140
default interest 150
default surcharge 151
deregistration limits 139
EC sales lists 144
EU country codes 144
evasion 151
exempt supplies 143
failure to notify liability 151
flat-rate scheme for small businesses 140
interest on overpaid tax 150
intrastat 145

VAT – *cont.*
Mini One Stop Shop (MOSS) 146
partial exemption 141
penalties 151
rates 137
reduced rate supplies 142
registration limits 137
repayment supplement 150
zero-rated supplies 142
Vehicle excise duty 73
Venture capital trusts
capital gains exemptions 40
income tax reliefs 96

W

Withdrawal of self assessment 11
Working tax credit 101

Z

Zero-rated supplies, VAT 142